HUMAN DESTINY

HUMAN DESTINY

EXPLORING TODAY'S VALUE-SYSTEMS

JOHN A. HAMMES

Our Sunday Visitor, Inc.
Huntington, Indiana 46750

Cover designed by ERIC NESHEIM

ISBN 0-87973-752-2
Library of Congress Catalog Card Number 78-62241

Published, printed, and bound in U.S.A. by
Our Sunday Visitor, Inc.
Noll Plaza
Huntington, Indiana 46750

752

ACKNOWLEDGMENTS

The author and publisher gratefully express their appreciation to the following publishers and authors for permission to quote from their copyrighted material.

American Association for the Advancement of Science and Dr. H. H. Suter: for a letter to the editor by H. H. Suter, *Science* 168 (May 15, 1970), 777.

Association Press: for excerpts from the *Documents of Vatican II*, ed. W. M. Abbott. Copyright 1966.

Confraternity of Christian Doctrine: for excerpts from the *New American Bible*. Copyright 1970 by the Confraternity of Christian Doctrine. All rights reserved.

Doubleday & Company: for extracts from *The Jerusalem Bible*. Copyright 1966 by Darton, Longman & Todd, Ltd., and Doubleday & Company, Inc.

Wm. B. Eerdmans Publishing Company: for extracts from M. Hamilton, ed., *The New Genetics and the Future of Man* (1972).

InterVarsity Press: for extracts from O. Guinness's *The Dust of Death* (1973).

Journal of Psychology and Theology: for permission to reprint "Atheistic Humanistic and Christian Humanistic Perspectives on the Human Condition" (1975) and "Beyond Freedom and Dignity: Behavioral Fixated Delusion?" (1973), by John A. Hammes.

Dr. Paul Kurtz: for extracts from P. Kurtz, ed., *Moral Problems in Contemporary Society: Essays in Humanistic Ethics* (Prentice-Hall, 1969). Copyright 1969 by Paul Kurtz.

Plenum Publishing Corporation: for extracts from B. Hilton, et al., eds., *Ethical Issues in Human Genetics: Genetic Counseling and the Use of Genetic Knowledge* (1973).

Theological Studies: for an extract from R. T. Francoeur's article "We Can—We Must: Reflections on the Technological Imperative" (1972).

D. van Nostrand Company: for extracts from J. R. Royce's *The Encapsulated Man: An Interdisciplinary Essay on the Search for Meaning.* Copyright 1964 by D. van Nostrand Company.

Yale University Press: for extracts from P. Ramsey's *Fabricated Man: The Ethics of Genetic Control* (1970).

To John,

Paul,

Penny,

and Mary Jessica

PREFACE

All higher forms of life manifest inquisitiveness. On the human level, as young children begin to develop speech, one of their more frequently uttered words is "Why?" From this human capability of self-awareness and reflection eventually comes the quest for meaning. Why are we here? Where did we come from? Where are we going? What is the significance of suffering, evil, life, death? Contemporary society, like all societies of the past, is asking these questions. In this book, I attempt to provide answers.

In Part I, man's search for ultimate meaning and values is explored, first on a philosophical level and then on a religious level. Among the world's living religions, Christianity is presented as providing the fullest interpretation of ultimate meaning, in the personality and teachings of Jesus Christ. Part II deals with the application of Christian values to contemporary moral and ethical problems. My belief is that in the present age of confused pluralism, Christianity can illumine the path to truth.

I wish to express my appreciation to my students, whose inquiries into the values of human life motivated the writing of this book. My thanks go also to Ms. Gin Ivey, for her assistance in the first draft, as well as to Ms. Geraldine Moon, for her efficient and critical typing of the final work.

This book is dedicated to my children. May their quest for wisdom, knowledge, and ultimate meaning be fulfilled —in the possession of him who is the Way, the Truth, and the Life (John 14.16).   *J.A.H.*
Athens, Georgia

CONTENTS

PART I

THE VALUE QUEST

x

APPENDICES

PART I
THE VALUE QUEST

1

THE SEARCH FOR MEANING

"The alienated man is everyman and no man, drifting in a world that has little meaning for him and over which he exercises no power, a stranger to himself and to others."
—E. and M. Josephson, *Man Alone: Alienation in Modern Society.*

ALTHOUGH present human civilization is considered by contemporary man to be an improvement over those of the past, and even though he has achieved remarkable technological goals, it would appear that modern man is still plagued by the problem of making sense of the world and of himself. Broadly speaking, it is the problem of the *search* for meaning, and specifically the problem of *explaining* the meaning *of human existence.* The present chapter examines the interrelatedness of meaning and values, as well as contemporary meaningless and alienation.

Values and meaning are intrinsically related, in the sense that values have significance, importance, and meaning. Whatever is deemed to be of worth is seen as valuable and meaningful. We tend to internalize values and make them part of ourselves, with the result that the loss of treasured values is experienced as a personal loss. Suicide is often attributed to the person's inability to cope with the lack, or loss, of meaning in his life. Too, the suspicion or awareness that one's world-view, or system of philosophical values, may be inauthentic or invalid can be the occasion of anxiety, despair, and hopelessness. The experience of meaninglessness is related to another human experience—alienation. Let us examine further the concepts of alienation and meaninglessness, and their relevance to values.

Contemporary Alienation

To *alienate* means "to make strange," or "to make another's." The term *alienation* has come to mean primarily "a state of estrangement." Schacht and Kaufman trace this meaning from Hegel to Kierkegaard, Marx, and contemporary existentialism (Schacht, 1970). One can, of course, find the concept in early Greek philosophy, as well as in theologies of antiquity.

Josephson and Josephson extend the meaning of *alienation* to embrace "loss of self, anxiety, anomie, despair, depersonalization, rootlessness, apathy, social disorganization, loneliness, atomization, powerlessness, meaninglessness, isolation, pessimism, and the loss of beliefs or values" (Josephson & Josephson, 1962, p. 12). These authors point out also the prevalence of alienation in ages past, citing the complaints of an Egyptian chronicler of four thousand years ago with regard to war, breakdown in community relations, and rise in the local crime rate!

Contemporary alienation is often attributed to the rise of industrialism and the evils accompanying the advance of science and technology (Mumford, 1966; Ellul, 1964). Alienation is illustrated in families as the generation gap, in government as the credibility gap, in society as the minority-group rebellion, and in the environment as the ecological crisis (Schacht, 1970).

Lack of Commitment

Keniston has described the contemporary American stance as "non-committal" (Keniston, 1960). He notes that in contrast to times past, present-day alienation is commonly chosen as an attitude. Keniston describes a "native existentialism," characterized by a denial of inherent meaning to man's life or the universe, with a consequent emphasis on sentience, feeling, and immediate experience. This negative reaction is the result of the failure to find an adequate substitute for traditional values that have been rejected.

The transition from an industrial to a technological society, according to Keniston, has led to a fragmentation of tasks, a shattering of community, and the ascendency of technological values. "Final" values have been replaced by "instrumental" values; the why of life has been replaced with the how of life. The core of present-day technological values, therefore, is empiricism. What is real and true is the observable and quantitatively verifiable; the unobservable and the inferred (e.g., the essence of poetry, art, and religion) have been reduced to mere opinion.

Furthermore, contends Keniston, contemporary alienation has no shared conscious myth, vision, or conception of the good life. Today's myths have substituted analysis for synthesis, fission for fusion, and regression for growth. In overview, Keniston distinguishes four types of alienation: (a) "cosmic outcastness"—the loss of connection with a divinely or metaphysically structured universe that "cares" about man; (b) developmental estrangements—a sense of the loss in individual life of ties and relationships that can never be re-created; (c) historical loss—a loss caused by rapid, worldwide, and chronic social change; and (d) self-estrangement—a lack of contact between the individual's "conscious self" and his "real self," manifested in a sense of unreality, emptiness, flatness, and boredom.

Meaninglessness

Meaninglessness in modern man is a theme in many recent works. W. G. Cole (1966) contends that the world is sick, as reflected in Albert Camus' novel *The Plague*. For Cole, the plague begins within the individual, and the germ within us is meaninglessness. Painting, sculpture, and music of recent times bear out the theme of the discordant, the bizarre, and the grotesque. The theater of the absurd has enhanced perversion, degradation, and nudity. Cole attributes contemporary meaninglessness to the breakdown of religion and of traditional values, together with the emergence of a new faith in scientism and in a blind, mechanistic determinism. He characterizes twentieth-century man as living in a spiritual vacuum: God is dead and man is finding it impossible to create values out of nothing. The consequent skepticism and fear of error lead to a reluctance to commit one's self to any cause, any faith.

Rollo May (1953, 1967) sees alienation in contemporary man in terms of emptiness and a loss of personal significance. We are a hollow people, with no center of personal strength and values. The primary reason is a breakdown in societal values. Man, living in a confused society, is himself confused. Anxiety, however, is inversely proportional to values: the stronger the value-system, the less anxious an individual will be (May, 1967). The lack of personal significance and the feeling of powerlessness are strong factors underlying the prevalence of aggression and violence in contemporary society (May, 1969, 1972).

C. G. Kemp (1967) has observed that uncertainty and unawareness of where meaning may be found in life leads to "horizontal living," an expression he borrows from Paul Tillich. Contemporary man pursues superficial goals without depth or true significance. To avoid confrontation with ultimate meaning, he seeks escape in busy activities, diversion, and even repression.

Meaninglessness in present times has been the constant theme of Viktor Frankl (1966, 1963) and his school of logotherapy. According to Frankl, the inner emptiness and meaninglessness in modern man are elements of an existential vacuum, leading to existential frustration and existential neurosis. This collective neurosis of modern times is characterized by a planless attitude toward life, fatalistic helplessness, a merging with the masses, and fanaticism. To help modern man find meaning is today's greatest challenge to psychotherapy (Frankl, 1972).

Erich Fromm (1955) has described the supposed normalcy of modern society in terms of pathology. Citing the incidence of suicide, homicide, and alcoholism in the so-called progressive countries of Europe and North America, he concludes that the inhabitants of those areas are in fact largely maladjusted and pathological in their behavior. Fromm explains alienation in terms of man's original separation from nature through evolution, and the constant struggle to cope with this separateness. The failure to adjust and to fulfill certain basic human needs leads to pathological behavior in individuals and in societies at large.

Spiritual Alienation

Alienation has been analyzed also from theological viewpoints. Paul Tillich (1962), an existential theologian, dwells on the theme of anxiety as the existential awareness of ultimate nonbeing. He observes that nonbeing threatens man's spiritual affirmation—relatively, in terms of emptiness: absolutely, in terms of meaninglessness. He further describes three forms of human anxiety: that of guilt and condemnation, that of emptiness and loss of meaning, and that of fate and death. One might easily fit these three aspects of Tillich's scheme into temporal dimensions, as referring to past, present, and future anxiety, respectively.

W. J. Burghardt (1974) sees alienation as part of the human condition consequent to man's original turning away from God, as related in the Scriptures (Gen ch. 3). Through man's rebellion, four ruptures occurred: between man and God (Gen 3.24), within man himself (Romans 7.15-24), between man and man (Gen 4.8), and between man and nature (Gen 3.17). Guinness (1973) has referred to this four-fold breach as theological, psychological, sociological, and ecological.

Thus far we have painted a rather bleak picture of alienation and meaninglessness. However, even though meaninglessness is devoid of positive character, the same is not always true of alienation. As Kaufman (1970) notes, alienation need not necessarily be a self-destructive condition. To take a stand will inevitably alienate one from those who disagree; but if the stance has validity, it is worth the price of alienation. For example, theism, and particularly the traditional Christian perspective, is not the popular orientation of contemporary culture, and the authentic Christian soon finds himself alienated from the secular values of the world in which he lives.

Having surveyed the emptiness and meaninglessness associated with alienation and the human condition, and the implications for a stabilizing, valid system of values, let us next consider man's search for such values and meaning.

False Solutions

In the contemporary search for values, Keniston (1960) points out three fallacies that he thinks should be avoided. The first is the "fallacy of the psychological vise," the sense that one is trapped in a social, cultural, and historical process over which one has no control. Such despair is unnecessary, for we can and should exercise directionality in society's development. The second fallacy is termed "romantic regression," or the desire to return to the simpler pre-industrial existence. Keniston believes a return to a more primitive, agrarian society is not only escapism and an avoidance of responsibly solving the complexities of life, but a choice that would also be accompanied by endemic disease, grinding poverty, and lawlessness. A third mistake is "the fallacy of unfinished business," the belief that given time, technology can solve the problems of society, many of which it has itself created. The values we need are already in our tradition, and we have only to take them seriously, claims Keniston. We need to reconstruct commitment, and to reshape technology in the service of man, rather than vice-versa. We need an open and pluralistic society in which one can be more imaginative and creative, more courageous, and more dedicated. But how can this utopian setting be brought about? Although Keniston tells us what should be done, he does not spell out the means for this achievement.

Need for Internal Strength

Rollo May (1953), as we have seen, attributes meaninglessness in present society to the absence of any internal center of strength. Borrowing Reisman's terms, May characterizes modern man as either outer-directed and conforming to expected societal roles, or inner-directed, in the sense of the gyroscopic man of the Victorian period who functioned somewhat like a wound-up watch. In either case, the error is to accept values as one's own without reflective awareness. The outer-directed person is a will-o'-

the-wisp, attuning himself to whatever is expected of him by others, whereas the inner-directed individual is equally hollow, in that external values have become internalized without examination. The contemporary challenge to value formation is to find the sources of strength and integrity within ourselves that will serve as a core of unity. Man must build what May calls the "creative conscience," a primary function of which is to evaluate or affirm values. This assertion of the self is essential to establishing a center of values within the self. While acknowledging philosophy and religion to be sources of value, May in the final analysis would stress judgment in acceptance or rejection of values (May, 1953). This emphasis on subjective judgment places May in the humanist tradition; and in view of his operational treatment of religion, as well as his mythological interpretation of the fall of man, it appears he would favor an atheistic or possibly pantheistic humanism (Hammes, 1975b; see Appendix A).

Another writer who emphasizes the individual conscience is Frankl (1972), for whom conscience is the means by which man discovers meaning. What is good is that which fosters the meaning-fulfillment of a person; what is bad is that which deters meaning-fulfillment. However, conscience may err, says Frankl, and a person may not know for certain whether his conscience is true or false, since though truth exists, one cannot be absolutely sure he has arrived at the truth. This concession appears to place Frankl in the position of skepticism in regard to the possibility of attaining absolute meaning and absolute certitude in the value-seeking process. Nonetheless, he believes meaning can and should be found in the search for values. The essence of Frankl's logotherapy is to make man more fully conscious, thereby increasing his freedom, and as a correlative, to have him accept responsibility for this freedom. Frankl claims that man lives by three kinds of values: creative, experiential, and attitudinal. Creative values refer to productivity and achievement; experiential values include the experience of the good, the true, and the beautiful; and attitudinal values embrace one's orientation to the tragic triad of human existence, that of suffering, guilt, and death (Frankl, 1966, 1963).

Social Needs

An evolutionary perspective is that of Fromm (1955), who believes man must find new ways of relating to the nature from which he evolved and became subsequently separated. Human existence has brought with it unique human needs, different from the animal nature of which man was once a part. Fromm believes the search for values and meaning can be resolved by building a society which satisfies basic human needs. He describes these needs in terms of relatedness, transcendence, rootedness, a sense of identity, and the need for a frame of orientation or world-view. He describes the kind of society he thinks would fulfill those needs, namely, communitarian socialism. Such a society would be humanistic in character (as opposed to technological) and would guard against the dehumanization so characteristic of today's technological society (Fromm, 1968). As lofty as Fromm's humanism may be, it rejects any sanction external to man; it therefore fits the paradigm of atheistic or possibly pantheistic humanism (Hammes, 1975a). Fromm attempts to escape relativism by an appeal to universal consensus (Fromm, 1969b). However, any value-system founded on human judgment alone is reducible to the relativism of human opinion, and will never invite universal commitment (Hammes, 1975a).

Theological Approach

Finally, there is a theological approach to man's search for meaning, one that posits meaning in the appropriate relationship between God, the creator, and man, his creature. Whatever values further this relationship lead to man's self-fulfillment; whatever values distort or harm this relationship lead to man's self-destruction. Establishing the validity of these propositions will be the main thrust of this book.

We have presented psychological, philosophical, sociological, and theological comments on man's search for meaning. The next logical step is to the significance of man the seeker. What is man, that he should ask such questions?

SUGGESTED READINGS

1. Schacht, Richard. *Alienation*. Garden City: Doubleday & Co., 1970. See Walter Kaufman's introduction entitled, "The Inevitability of Alienation." Schacht presents Hegelian, Marxist, and existential views on alienation, as well as neo-analytic and sociological perspectives.

2. Josephson, Eric and Mary (eds.). *Man alone: Alienation in Modern Society*. N.Y.: Dell Publishing Co., 1962. See their introduction. Contributed articles on alienation and identity, work and leisure, politics, science, and war.

3. Burghardt, Walter J. *Towards Reconciliation*. Wash.: United States Catholic Conference, 1974. An ecumenical, theological analysis of the need for a four-fold reconciliation: of God to man, of man within himself, of man to his fellow man, and of man to nature.

4. Keniston, Kenneth. *The Uncommitted: Alienated Youth in American Society*. N.Y.: Dell Publishing Co., 1960. A classic study of alienated youth, relevant today.

5. May, Rollo. *Man's Search for Himself*. N.Y.: W. W. Norton, 1953. An analysis of the loneliness and anxiety of modern man, as well as of the roots of his malady.

6. Frankl, Viktor. *The Doctor and the Soul*. N.Y.: Alfred A. Knopf, 1966. Frankl discusses existential neurosis as the collective neurosis of modern times, together with his theory of logotherapy, an effort to help one discover meaning in life.

2

THE MEANING OF MAN

"One single spiritual soul has a greater value and a nobler destiny than a million solar systems and a billion galaxies of blindly whirling stars. In the spirituality of his soul, [man] is the crown of the universe. With his feet he is rooted in matter; but his soul reaches out beyond the uttermost boundaries of matter and space."
—C.N. Bittle, *The Whole Man: Psychology.*

THERE are diverse ways of classifying the many models of man that have emerged throughout history. For present purposes, we may conveniently divide them into four categories: scientific, philosophical, psychological, and theological. Accordingly, one might classify the prevailing models in terms of scientific humanism, philosophical humanism, psychological humanism, and theological humanism (Table 1). Let us examine each of these four points of view and see how they perceive the problem of the meaning and significance of man in himself.

Scientific Humanism

Scientific humanism may be defined as that perspective which proposes to determine the nature of man and human society on the basis of information obtained from the natural, physical, biological, and social sciences. The basis for much of this information is the scientific method. More specifically, it is the emphasis on the experimental method, together with the exclusion of philosophical and theological reflection, as well as the rejection of the supernatural. Critics of scientific humanism refer to it as an ideology that is better termed "scientism" (Giorgi, 1970). In this sense, scientific humanism is regarded as a form of religion. The primary rationale proposed for the acceptance of scientific humanism is the claim to *objectivity*, i.e., an approach to knowledge and the study of man supposedly free of bias or subjective error in human judgment, an error that is charged to be inherent in the methods used by philosophers

Table 1. The Meaning of Man.

Scientific Humanism — Systems Theory
— Behaviorism

Philosophical Humanism — Rational Humanism
— Contemporary Evolutionary Humanism
— Existentialism
— Arational Humanism
— Counterculture Humanism

Psychological Humanism — Psychoanalysis
— Humanistic Psychology

Theological Humanism — Theistic Humanism
— Christian Humanism

and theologians. Let us examine for a moment science's claim to objectivity.

Objectivity. In connection with the present discussion, two meanings of *objectivity* should be noted. The traditional meaning is "knowledge of reality"; that is, to be objective meant to know things as they are. Of course, this position recognized that man can know only in accordance with his nature. Thus, the perceptual experience of *knowing* the color "blue" is not identical with the spectral properties of the wave length of the color "blue." To know the color "blue," however, was still a legitimate contention, in that an observer could recognize blue correctly and discriminate it from other colors. "To be objective" also traditionally meant the recognition of reality apart from arbitrary, subjective opinion; impartial judgment is an instance of such objectivity. Today, this traditional meaning of *objectivity* is still held by those convinced of the human ability to grasp reality as it is. (Furthermore, we shall see that those who believe in absolute certitude and absolute truth contend that man, though finite and able to know only according to his nature, can nevertheless probe absolute reality and arrive at absolute conviction and certitude.)

A second meaning of the expression "to be objective" is that found in contemporary science, where the phrase is defined in terms of a methodology, an approach that stresses quantitative assessment and excludes reflective inference from the reality being measured. In psychology, the behavioristic approach exemplifies this interpretation of objectivity. Man is studied in terms of variables that can be quantitatively measured (e.g., the number of responses to a specified stimulus).

The reduction of objectivity to quantitative assessment, together with the exclusion of "objectivity" arrived at by other means (e.g., reflective inference about reality), is of course arbitrary. This limited concept of objectivity is better termed "objectivism" (Giorgi, 1970), leaving the term "objectivity" to refer to the traditional meaning of the word.

It remains to ask whether the scientific method is such that it can actually be totally objective, independent of the judgment, motivation, and personality of the scientist.

Subjectivity of Science. Science at one time was defined as any systematized body of truths. With science thus understood, philosophy was known as a science, and theology as the queen of the sciences. In modern times, however, science has emerged as a discipline supposedly separate from philosophy and theology. One speaks today of the natural, physical, biological, and social sciences. Unfortunately, the modern scientific approach has engendered a superstitious, reverential awe of itself, which we refer to as "scientism." Many scientists have become so enamored of their methodology that they have unwittingly described it as wholly objective, devoid of the subjective factor claimed to be characteristic of the methods of philosophy and theology. Indeed, science has become personified, or deified; one commonly reads or hears statements that begin, "Science has discovered" or "Science has indisputably established. . . ."

As Snow (1961) has observed, our culture has become divided into "subjective" and "objective" camps, the humanities on the one hand and the sciences on the other. Is science, however, as objective as many scientists and psychologists, particularly behaviorists, purport it to be?

Barbour (1966) responds that without the scientist there would be no science. Human observers construct the findings of science; there are no uninterpreted scientific data.

Scientific results and conclusions are influenced by the observer, and often the instruments of measurement interfere with the object being measured; hence Heisenberg's Uncertainty Principle concerning the impossibility of ascertaining both the position and the velocity of an electron at a given instant in time. Barbour observes that the personal judgment of the scientist enters into the formation of theories, and also affects the assessment of evidence for or against such theories.

Rogers (1965a) agrees that science does not exist "out there," but only in people, who are not cool, impartial individuals. He points out that any "purpose" (the subjective, personal choice in regard to which a scientific endeavor is carried out) is prior to the endeavor itself and not part of it. Regardless of scientific findings, the scientist must make personal, subjective choices at each decision-point, as to where the investigation will be next carried.

Furthermore, the choice of the *object* of scientific inquiry is also a personal decision, as well as the hypotheses to be explored and the methodology to be used (Rogers, 1965b). And, most important, the values that influence these decisions are outside of and prior to the scientific endeavor itself. Matson (1964) noted that Bridgman, one of the fathers of operationism, upon later reflection acknowledged that his method was not as objective as he had first believed, and that there is no escape from the personal reference-point (Bridgman, 1961).

Wyatt (1967) has pointed out that behavioristic psychology has become tied to methodology, has identified objectivity as an end rather than a means or method, and has made the experimental method absolute and indispensable. That these value-laden directions have been subjectively chosen has been forgotten. Barbour (1966) deplores the homage given to prediction as the only worthwhile goal of science and proposes the "understanding of nature" as a more comprehensive and worthy objective.

Not only is science not as objective as some scientists would claim it to be; it should also be remembered that the final product of science has the character of contingency. Scientific findings are couched in probability terms, and, in the final analysis, can yield only probability statements. Therefore, *any* observations that science may offer us on the meaning and significance of man will be restricted to hypotheses. No final answers will be found here.

Also, in relation to human values, science cannot prescribe obligatory or "ought" values. Although some believe we can scientifically arrive at values by which human beings should live (Maslow, 1964; Skinner, 1971), this conviction is necessarily based on what is known as the "naturalistic fallacy," or the "is-ought" fallacy, namely, that an observance of how people *do* behave in no way dictates how they *ought* to behave. The moral desirability or undesirability of a given human act cannot be determined without criteria *external* to the act itself (Bourke, 1951; Adler, 1965; Bittle, 1950).

Systems Theory

Two contemporary examples of scientific humanism, or scientism, are "systems theory" and "behaviorism." Systems theory is modeled after the science of physics, emphasizing factors such as steady state, isomorphism, feedback, open system, and hierarchical organization (Gray, Duhl, and Rizzo, 1969; Bertalanffy, 1968). It is based on the Gestaltist concept of the whole (in this instance the "system") as being greater than the sum of its parts. However, systems theory is descriptive, not explanatory, restricting itself to functional relationships and excluding causality. When applied to human behavior and interpersonal relationships, this view becomes a sophisticated form of mechanism, since it denies any form of life-principle in living things, and rejects their capability for self-directive teleological activity (see Hammes, 1971, for a critique of mechanism).

In regard to the meaning and significance of man, systems theory has, naturally, little to say. It is monistic and materialistic. It is also deterministic, for, even though some representatives, such as Bertalanffy (1968), stress human freedom within an open, organismic model of man, there is also the denial of an inherent life-principle, or soul, as the source of such freedom. And if freedom does not originate within such a spiritual principle, man then becomes the victim of genetic forces within and environmental forces without.

Behaviorism

A second example of scientism is behaviorism, an attempt to make of psychology an objective science. Early representatives of this attitude were Ivan Pavlov, John B. Watson, and Edward L. Thorndike; at present, the best-known spokesman for behaviorism is B. F. Skinner (Hall and Lindzey, 1970). The early behaviorists rejected the method of introspection, which was fashionable in their day (and which, incidentally, is now being popularized by phenomenologists). Radical behaviorists admit only stimulus-response (S-R) data in their study of man. The positive contributions of behaviorism lie in the refinement of the experimental method in assessing variables in human behavior, in the value of insisting upon the study of behavior on the observable level, in the quantifiable verification or rejection of hypotheses about human behavior, and in the extrapolation of experimental findings to the applied areas of human engineering, industrial psychology, and clinical psychology. As valuable as these products of behaviorism are, this model of man gives a very depressing picture of human meaning and significance. Human freedom of choice is held by behaviorists to be delusional. The individual is assumed to be determined by his environment, inner and outer. Man is thus reduced to the elements of matter, and at best is to be regarded as a very complicated machine. These tenets of behaviorism, and particularly those of the radical descriptive behaviorism of B. F. Skinner, have been adequately critiqued elsewhere (Chomsky, 1959; Koestler, 1964, 1967; Krutch, 1953; Malcom, 1964; Matson, 1964; and Hammes, 1973a—see Appendix B).

As to the meaning and significance of man, therefore, scientific humanism, despite its brilliant contributions in the study of human behavior, cannot tell us the value of man himself, and neither can it prescribe what his values should be. Let us turn now to philosophical humanism.

Philosophical Humanism*

Guinness (1973) has traced the history of humanism from early Greece through the Renaissance and Enlightenment to the humanist movement of today. According to Guinness, contemporary humanism rests on four pillars— the belief in reason, the belief in progress, the belief in science, and the belief in the self-sufficiency of man. In this country, in September 1973, the American Humanist Association published *Humanist Manifesto II*, an updating of an earlier manifesto. The preface of *Humanist Manifesto II*

---

*This section on philosophical humanism contains material earlier published under the title "A Christian Response to Atheistic and Scientific Humanism," in *J. Psychol. and Theol.* 3 (1975), 104-108.

stated, "As in 1933, humanists still believe that traditional theism, especially faith in the prayer-hearing God, assumed to love and care for persons, to hear and understand their prayers, and to be able to do something about them, is an unproved and outmoded faith. Salvationism, based on mere affirmation, still appears as harmful, diverting people with false hopes of heaven thereafter. Reasonable minds look to other means for survival" (*The Humanist*, 1973).

Principles of Contemporary Philosophical Humanism

What are the principles underlying contemporary humanism? Paul Kurtz, editor of *The Humanist* journal and a contemporary leader in American humanism, has summed up that perspective (Kurtz, 1969). In the first chapter, he outlines the basic tenets of humanism. First, contemporary humanism is "anti-supernaturalistic," a viewpoint it shares with naturalism and materialism. The existence of God is denied. There is no soul or mind separate from the brain (materialistic monism); and man has no immortal destiny beyond the grave. "Humanists accept the fact that God is dead; that we have no way of knowing that he exists; or even of knowing that this is a meaningful question. They accept the fact that human existence is probably a random occurrence existing between two oblivions, that death is inevitable, that there is a tragic aspect to our lives, and that all moral values are our own creations" (Kurtz, 1969, p. 4). Second, human values are considered to be relative; that is, they have their source in man alone and cannot be grounded in an outside absolute source, or God. This observation follows logically from the first principle of the nonexistence of God. Thus, as Kurtz says, a theory of value "cannot be derived from a metaphysics of divinity . . .; value is relative to man . . ." (p. 4). And, "What is important," as Sartre has said, "is that there are no absolute values or norms independent of what man individually and socially chooses" (p. 6). A third principle concerns the emphasis on human reason as the sole source and guide of human action; hence the rejection of divine revelation as an informational source for human conduct. A fourth principle concerns the commitment of the humanist. He is to seek the greatest happiness for the greatest number and to further the welfare of mankind. Humanists are to work toward solutions to the problems of social injustice, poverty, war, overpopulation, and ecology. These commitments of the humanists are further discussed by Anton (1969).

Let us examine each of these four principles of contemporary humanism. First, the rejection of God logically leads to Kurtz's observation that human existence is a "random existence between two oblivions," that "death is inevitable, and that there is a tragic aspect to our lives" (p. 4). But, it may be asked, where did man get the capability of *recognizing* these aspects of human existence? How could he have arrived at the notion of *randomness* unless he had first experienced purpose and order? How is it that one does recognize the *tragic* aspects of life, unless one somehow first knows that tragedy is a deviation from an appropriate order that should be, even though it is not? Such reflections, taken for granted but unaccounted for by contemporary humanism, have implications that cannot be ignored. The basic human experiences of goodness, purpose, order, and of efficient and final causality require a factor other than chance to account for them (Barbour, 1966).

The second principle of contemporary humanism, the relativity of values, results in the impasse of attempting to prove *which set* of values should be followed. Unless values are grounded in an absolute reality outside of man, they are reducible to human opinion, and as such will invite neither total commitment nor universal acceptance. We shall discuss the problem of experiencing absolute reality in the next chapter.

The third principle, the emphasis on human reason as the sole source of principles to guide ethical action, to the exclusion of divine revelation, is subject to the same criticisms directed at the second principle.

The fourth principle, the humanistic dedication to one's fellow man, is an admirable one with which few would disagree. But can this principle be effective without divine sanction—a validating basis rejected by philosophical humanism?

Meaning and Morals without God. A variant of the humanist attitude is that of Nielsen (1969), who admits the problems with which an atheistic humanism is faced. He lists the criticisms leveled against his position, namely, that secular and humanistic morality leads to ethical skepticism, nihilism, and conventionalism; that without God and religion there is no Archimedean point of how we ought to live and die; that without an overarching purpose that men were destined to fulfill, life lacks meaning, with consequent estrangement and despair; and that no purely human purposes are ultimately worth striving for. Nielsen then attempts to show that the existence of God is unnecessary to support moral convictions. He lists the "permanent" sources of human happiness existing in a secular world, such as freedom from pain and want; the simple pleasures of life; security and emotional peace; human love and companionship; creative employment and meaningful work; and the cultural enjoyments of art, music, and the dance. All of these, Nielsen contends, are achievable in a "Godless universe." With regard to human suffering and death, Nielsen, echoing the existentialists, considers this fate one to be "struggled against with courage and dignity." For the moral norm he appeals to the common good, pointing out the pragmatic and reasonable basis for such a norm. Nielsen admits that the "secularist is surreptitiously drawing on Christian inspiration" in insisting on the equality of individual rights and mutual human respect, and that the "religious man alone can justify adherence" to these considerations. Even so, he rejects the necessity of God as a basis of this ethical norm, insisting on the adequacy of human reasoning, to the point of saying that, "even if God is dead, it doesn't really matter."

Nielsen so clearly recognizes the limitations of contemporary humanism that it is difficult to understand why he defends this position. Again, one may ask, why should man "struggle against" suffering and death with "courage and dignity," unless there be some basis for believing that such should not be his fate? The contemporary humanist does not come to grips with the discrepancy between the fact of suffering, guilt, and death and the fact that man sees such realities as unreasonable. If this is a *natural* condition (and humanists do advocate the philosophy of naturalism), then why does man struggle against it?

Baier (1969) expresses clearly the problem of a theory of godless morality: "If, in the absence of supernatural beliefs, the voices of conscience, of the moral sense, and of intuition are only the impressively dressed-up demands of our society, then these voices cannot tell us what is right and what is wrong in a sense which provides an adequate reason for doing what is right and refraining from doing what is wrong. How then can we find out what is really right and what is merely supposed so by our society?" (Baier, 1969, p. 40). Baier discusses this problem and rejects "egoism," or utter selfishness, and "utilitarianism," the interests of the greatest number. The former view fails to respect the common welfare, and the latter ignores the rights of the individual. Baier, agreeing with Nielsen, appeals to a humanistic ethic that respects both the individual and the group. He even insists that this broader ethical view could be made obligatory and "absolutely binding" upon all, since it is for the good of all.

Baier's analysis is subject to the objection that it is based on a common relativistic error, namely, drawing absolutist conclusions from relativist premises. To make a norm "absolutely binding" is a prerogative not open to a relativist. He must forego his relativism and become an absolutist before he can speak of absolute obligations. And only those ethical obligations which are based on an absolute reality outside of man *and superior to him* can bind man's total obedience.

Feigl (1969), like his colleagues, recognizes that the "ought" in human behavior cannot be merely derived from the "is" of human behavior. That is, moral imperatives cannot be derived from *declarative* descriptions of human behavior. Feigl then proposes a middle ground in morals between "relativists" and "absolutists," a "golden mean" that is empirical yet universal, one that can be designated "scientific humanism." He cites the evolution of human aspirations toward the highest cultural ideals, recognizing in this process the contributions of religions but rejecting their theistic basis. Feigl holds that universal and supreme moral values can be empirically discussed as inherent in the conscience of man.

One can agree that the conscience of man can discern the difference between good and evil behavior. But can what is good and what is evil be empirically established? We have noted that scientific humanism may be able to catalogue the various cultural types of ethical behavior, but the criteria for establishing the desirability or undesirability of such behavior clearly lie outside of the scientific endeavor. Value judgments based exclusively on human reason will always remain relative to the thinking of particular individuals. Any hope of "universal" values will be realizable only when human beings universally agree that such and such values are objectively and independently based on an absolute norm independent of human creation.

Lamont (1969) notes that contemporary humanism rejects the Christian concept of personal immortality. He states that "it is impossible for the personality to continue when the body and the brain have ceased to function," and that "it is inconceivable that the characteristic mental activities of thought, memory, and imagination could go on without the sustaining structure of the brain and cerebral cortex" (p. 281). After admitting that man has a *natural* desire to live forever, Lamont accepts what he considers a realistic point of view, that death must be accepted honestly, courageously, calmly, and that the (humanist) antidote is "preoccupation with life."

Lamont, too, is subject to the criticism that he is a relativist making absolutist statements. For him, it is "impossible" for the human spirit to survive death and "inconceivable" that the human spirit can survive the demise of brain-function. These conclusions are consistent enough with the humanistic premise of naturalism, but they cannot then logically be stated as absolutely certain. All the naturalist can say is that he is not convinced of the evidence that would indicate human immortality. For the Christian, the evidence for human immortality comes from a source other than naturalism, namely, divine revelation. However, even on logical grounds alone, the Christian can ask: Why does man have the striving for immortality? If this is a *natural* aspiration, where did it originate? If man were "naturally" destined to be merely mortal, why is he not satisfied with this "natural" fate? Why, indeed, do *all* living things strive for maintenance of life against death? Contemporary humanism cannot answer these questions, preferring to fall back on a blind evolutionary hypothesis. It should be noted here that, although contemporary humanism favors an atheistic evolution, the compatibility of evolution with theistic creationism can be demonstrated (Hammes, 1971).

Existentialism

Another expression of philosophical humanism is found in existentialism. The existential model is historically represented by Soren Kierkegaard, Friedrich Nietzsche, Edmund Husserl, Martin Heidegger, Karl Jaspers, Jean Paul Sartre, and Gabriel Marcel (Barrett, 1964; Borzaga, 1966; Blackham, 1965; Collins, 1952; Kaufman, 1960; and Schrader, 1967). The positive contributions of this perspective lie in the emphasis on human freedom, man's obligation to exert choice, and the personal assumption of responsibility for self-fulfillment. One is also expected to confront his finitude and the negation of his being (death). Existence precedes essence, taking "essence" to mean what man makes of himself; and man achieves his essence in the exercise of free choice. The ultimate questions of human origin, purpose, and destiny further divide the existential model into two camps. One, an atheistic view (e.g., Nietzsche and Sartre), sees man as thrown into existence, without purpose, and concludes that human existence is therefore an absurdity. One may accept this fact stoically, or else fight, even though futilely, against such an outrageous fate (e.g.,

Camus). The other course, a theistic one (e.g., Kierkegaard and Marcel), accepts the reality of God, sees meaning and purpose in human suffering and guilt, and can be incorporated into a Christian perspective. We shall include this latter view in our discussion of Christian humanism, later in this chapter.

As for atheistic existentialism, it should be noted that Sartre's conclusion that human existence is absurd follows logically from atheistic premises (Borzaga, 1966). But it may be asked how one can arrive at the concept of absurdity and meaninglessness without first having experienced some kind of meaning and purpose. And if meaningfulness is admitted as a human experience, there must be an origin of meaning in general. The ultimate ground and source of meaning, we shall contend, is God.

Similarly, atheistic existentialism recognizes evil, justifiably fights against it (although futilely), all the while failing to recognize that the experience and understanding of evil must be preceded by an experience and understanding of good. For evil is the absence of, or the negation of, good. Once the experience of good is acknowledged to be a valid human experience, reason demands an origin for good in general. The ultimate ground of good, we shall contend, is God.

Counterculture Humanism

In addition to contemporary humanism and atheistic existentialism, a third expression of philosophical humanism is today's "counterculture." Guinness has sketched the historical roots of this phenomenon from 1918 to the present, and characterized it as "The Great Refusal" (Guinness, 1973). The Beat Movement was founded in 1948, by such individuals as Allen Ginsberg and Jack Kerouac. The term "beat" originally meant poor, down, and out, but Kerouac redefined it as "beatific," to mean offbeat, downbeat, and "cool, man, cool" (Guinness, 1973). After ten years as a bohemian movement, it rose to cultural prominence, a new society of bells, beads, and flowers, headed by such leaders as Timothy Leary and Alan Watts. Leary's admonition, "turn on, tune in, drop out," summarized the spirit of the new "hippies." Guinness notes that Leary's advice to "drop out" was self-defeating: to leave society is to leave society unchanged.

A more positive thrust emerged in the form of the New Left, composed of intellectuals and students disillusioned by American politics, and especially the U.S. involvement in Vietnam. In 1962, the Students for a Democratic Society (SDS) issued the Port Huron Statement and a plea for participatory democracy. Both SDS and a kindred organization, the Student Non-Violent Coordinating Committee (SNCC), began as peaceful movements, but, as Guinness observes, after years of frustration these groups turned to violence to achieve their purposes. Violence invited counter-violence. "Those who take up the sword perish by the sword" (Matt 26.52). These radical movements aroused the ire of the conservative American majority, which took forceful measures to control the outbreaks of aggression. The activism of young people working in radical groups can be credited for diagnosing the political ills of American society, but their impatience with the slow change inherent in the democratic process led to violence and consequent repression. The radical elements of the counterculture have largely been forced underground.

The Rise of Consciousness III. The philosophical and humanistic underpinnings of the counterculture are visible in the work of Charles Reich and Theodore Rozsak. Reich characterized the American crisis in terms of political corruption, hypocrisy, war, poverty, distorted priorities, uncontrolled technology, environmental destruction, powerlessness, artificiality of work and culture, absence of community, and the loss of self (Reich, 1970). He further sketched American history in terms of three consciousnesses. Consciousness I is represented by 19th-century industrial America, when materialism and science replaced humanistic values. According to Reich, Consciousness-I thinkers include farmers, small-business owners, immigrants, AMA-type doctors, and "just plain folks." Consciousness II emerged during the second half of the 20th century; it is essentially represented by the technological and corporate society, the liberals, the well educated, the intellectuals, and the reformers. Reich asserts that Consciousness I and II have squelched the higher aspects of human experience. For example, Consciousness I and II have alledgedly missed out on such things as adventure, sex, morality, awe, wonder, reverence, spontaneity, play, mind-expansion, growth, learning, inner life, sensuality, community, brotherhood, and liberation (Reich, 1970, p. 152). As an alternative and as a solution, Reich proposed Consciousness III. The foundation of Consciousness III is liberation, defined as the freedom of the individual to build his own philosophy and values, his own "life-style," and his own culture from a new beginning. It starts with self; or as Reich (echoing Walt Whitman) expresses it, "Myself I sing." Reich emphasizes the value of the individual over a depersonalizing, mechanistic society. Too, no one is to judge anyone else, or to use any other as a means to one's own end. Reich also advocates personal responsibility in the choice of life-style and in personal relationships. To achieve its purposes, Consciousness III draws energy from the group or the community, from eros, from the freedom of technology, and from the uninhibited self (Reich, 1970, p. 234). Reich then elaborates on the life-style of Consciousness III in terms of earthy and sensual clothes, sensual music, and psychedelic drugs. To "blow one's mind" means to become aware. The ultimate sign of reverence, vulnerability, and innocence of Consciousness III is verbalized in the expression "Oh, wow!" (Reich, 1970, p. 263).

Lofty as the goals of Reich's Consciousness III may seem, it is based on individualism and is reducible to a relativistic form of humanism. While giving lip-service to Christian ideals, Reich does not ground their validity, or obligatory nature, in an omnipotent God. Further, he caricatures Consciousness I and speaks with contempt of Consciousness II. He adulates young people as the saviors of America, who can do no wrong and who will inevitably, automatically, change the world for the better. This prideful posture seems to be a hallmark of every form of atheistic humanism.

Other criticisms of Reich's utopia also are merited. Mc-Cracken (1971) has shown that Reich's rejection of reason has the effect of opening the door to anything and everything. Kopkind (1971) points out that Reich's popularity with many young people lies in his portrayal of drugs, sex, and non-effort as attributes of a revolutionary culture that is beautiful, valuable, and inevitable. Fried (1971) faults Reich for the pretense that labor and self-discipline are not necessary to achieve social change; such change cannot be brought about spontaneously by the magical virtues of bell-bottomed spontaneity and naturalness. Starr (1971) raises this question: if, as Reich apparently believes, man by nature is whole and good, needing no controls over natural desires, how did he ever become corrupted? To displace the blame to technology is to rationalize, for it was man who fashioned the corporate society and who is accountable for its abuses. It is man who has been inhuman to man, and the young are not automatically exempt from such evil, a fact witnessed by the rising crime-rate among them, and by the violent, destructive behavior of which young people are both capable and guilty. Harrington (1971) indicts Reich's program for changing the world through a mere change of consciousness as simplistic. He observes that political involvement and hard work are necessary; otherwise nothing will be accomplished.

Counterculture Romanticism. Another contemporary spokesman for the counterculture is Theodore Roszak, whose approach differs from Reich's. Roszak is a formidable critic of scientism, and, in particular, technological science. He rejects any interpretation of reality exclusively in terms of scientific data, an endeavor Roszak calls the myth of objective consciousness (Roszak, 1969). Roszak sees the present technocracy as a form of totalitarianism, in which scientific experts rule, in which they alone know what is best for society, and beyond whose authority there is no appeal. Within such a technocratic culture, Roszak defines "education" as "machine-tooling the young," "free enterprise" as "market manipulation," and "pluralism" as "everybody's right to his own opinion as an excuse for ignoring anybody's troubling challenge" (Roszak, 1969, p. 16).

Roszak views the counterculture as a viable alternative to technocracy and scientism, chiefly because of the counterculture's emphasis on non-intellective consciousness. Roszak welcomes art, poetry, intuition, and mysticism as better ways than science for probing and experiencing "true" reality (Roszak, 1969, 1974). Hence Roszak opposes reason against passion, intellect against feeling, the head against the heart. Others have seen the conflict similarly, in terms of the rational versus the irrational (Frankel, 1973), or the Apollonians versus the Dionysians (Holton, 1974).

The difference between traditional forms of philosophical humanism and the humanism of the counterculture is that the former stressed reason or rationality, whereas the latter emphasizes feeling, emotion, and arationality. An assessment of this opposition, which is part of the human condition, is reserved for another part of this book. It is sufficient to note here that the arational thrust in humanism is generally associated with the rise of contemporary hedonism, and in the final analysis it is another expression of individualism and relativism. As to the meaning of man, this form of humanism stresses the temporary values of pleasure and esthetic pursuits. It does not confront the questions of man's origin, purpose, and destiny; nor does it provide an answer to the ultimate meaning or significance of human existence itself.

Psychoanalytic Humanism

Having looked at scientific humanism and philosophical humanism, let us now consider psychological humanism, of which psychoanalysis can be considered one embodiment.

Classical psychoanalytic thought is represented by Sigmund Freud, Carl Jung, and Alfred Adler (Hall and Lindzey, 1970; Misiak and Sexton, 1966). Freud contributed much to the understanding of human motivation, particularly unconscious motivation and the role of defense mechanisms, in both normal and abnormal behavior. Freud pioneered in the analysis of these factors, as well as of the role of early childhood experiences, in personality growth; Jung broadened the psychoanalytic perspective to include cultural variables evolving in the progress of civilization from primitive to modern times. For Jung, all historical human data was admissible, whether rooted in religion, myth, or folklore. Whereas Freud had focused primarily on efficient causality in human growth, Jung included final causality or future goal-seeking as well. Adler extended the range of analysis further—from genetic, constitutional factors in personality growth, to social factors, emphasizing the role of others in the development of the individual. Adler also broke away from the earlier concentration on unconscious motivation and gave new emphasis to conscious motivation, crediting the individual with self-awareness and self-development.

Neo-analytic thought in psychoanalysis is represented by Erich Fromm, Karen Horney, and Harry Stack Sullivan (Hall and Lindzey, 1970; Sahakian, 1965), theorists who completed the break with classical psychoanalytic theory, and mostly stressed the cultural and social determinants of personality development and human behavior.

On the subject of the nature of man, classical psychoanalysis theory is instinct-bound and deterministic. Neo-analytic theory can also be fairly categorized as deterministic, with the "determining" factors being culture and society rather than instinct. An exception among neo-analytics is Erich Fromm, who places a high value on human freedom. Together with the proponents of classical psychoanalysis, however, Fromm favors atheism. Fromm writes, "As long as anyone believes that his ideal and purpose is outside him, that it is above the clouds, in the past or in the future, he will go outside himself and seek fulfillment where it cannot be found. He will look for solutions and answers at every point except the one where they can be found—in himself" (Fromm, 1969b, p. 249). Fromm then proceeds to reject both absolutism and relativism, and seeks to establish a middle ground based on universals reached by reason. Even though Fromm repudiates relativism, his position does not escape it. If man alone is the basis for ethical norms, then ethics, as well as the meaning of man, becomes relative to human opinion, no matter how wise this opinion may claim to be. Fromm's views on the meaning and significance of man follow along the lines of philosophical humanism, and they are subject to the criticisms already made of that perspective.

Humanistic Psychology. A second expression of psychological humanism can be seen in the more recent development of a movement known as humanistic psychology. With historical roots in existentialism and phenomenology, humanistic psychology was an attempt to humanize psychology and to recover for this discipline what behaviorism had rejected (Misiak and Sexton, 1966). In America the movement has declared itself to be the Third Force in psychology, in contrast with psychoanalysis and behaviorism. Even in this country, however, the humanistic attitude was earlier championed by such personality theorists as Gordon Allport, Henry Murray, Abraham Maslow, and Carl Rogers. The humanistic model is similar to the existential model in emphasizing human freedom, uniqueness, responsibility, and self-actualization (Bugental, 1967; Severin, 1965, 1973). But the humanistic model is not as negativistic or pessimistic as the existential model, in that the inherent goodness of man and the joy of life are emphasized more strongly as over against the existential focus on evil and suffering.

In 1961, Abraham Maslow and Anthony Sutich founded the *Journal of Humanistic Psychology.* In 1962 they established the American Association for Humanistic Psychology, later renamed the Association for Humanistic Psychology, and described the movement as an attitude rather than a school. Its chief topics of concern are love, creativity, self-actualization, meaning, responsibility, and values (Bugental, 1967; Severin, 1965; Sutich and Vich, 1969).

Existential Psychology and Phenomenology

"Existential psychology" is a term used to embrace both humanistic psychology and existential psychotherapy (R. May, 1961; May, Angel, and Ellenberger, 1967). The first American symposium on existential psychology was held at the Cincinnati APA Convention in 1959; the proceedings are recorded in May's *Existential Psychology* (1961). Themes of the Cincinnati symposium included phenomenological experiencing, will and decision, the centered self, affirmation, self-actualization, anxiety, guilt, and death. Papers were presented by May, Maslow, Feifel, Allport, and Lyons.

A related event was the first symposium held by the APA Division of Philosophical Psychology at Rice University in 1963 (Wann, 1964); this symposium was largely a debate on the merits and demerits of phenomenology and behaviorism. Contrasting views were presented on the nature of consciousness, predictability, modeling, objectivity, rationality, uniqueness, relativity, and potentiality of man. Participants included Koch, MacLeod, Skinner, Rogers, Malcolm, and Scriven. This symposium was published in Wann's *Behaviorism and Phenomenology* (1964), and later abstracted in an article by Hitt (1969).

Other representative works in the area of existential psychology and phenomenology are those of Allers (1961), Buhler and Massarik (1968), Burton (1967), Byrne and Maziarz (1969), Giorgi (1970), Lyons (1963), Ruitenbeek (1962), Rogers (1969), Strasser (1967), and Van Kaam (1966).

Existential Psychotherapy. Existential psychotherapy, or existential analysis (*Daseinanalyse*), is usually associated with the leadership of Ludwig Binswanger and Medard Boss (Misiak and Sexton, 1966; Hall and Lindzey, 1970; May, 1967). It opposes reductionism, rejects positivism, and emphasizes personal responsibility and freedom. The primary theme is man-in-the-world, for existential analysis takes a monistic point of view, in contrast with the dualistic view of man separated from his environment. Man's relationships with the world (*Umwelt*), his fellow man (*Mitwelt*), and himself (*Eigenwelt*) are the existential modes explored as the therapist attempts to enter into and experience the "world" of his patient. The existentialist view that man "creates his essence through existing," that is, by actualizing his potentialities, is the basis for existential guilt; which is, therefore, the failure to do so (Knight, 1969). Several case histories of existential analysis are presented in detail in a work by May, Angel, and Ellenberger (1967).

The version of existential psychotherapy probably best known in this country is logotherapy, so-called by Viktor Frankl to distinguish it from Binswanger's existential analysis. In contrast to Freud's "will-to-pleasure" and Adler's "will-to-power," Frankl (1963, 1969) stresses the "will-to-meaning." Man lives in three dimensions: somatic, mental, and spiritual—the last distinguishing man *as human*. In addition to human spirituality, two other characteristics are essential to Frankl's theory, those of freedom and responsibility. The essence of logotherapy is to make man more fully conscious, thereby increasing his freedom, and, as a correlative, to have him accept responsibility for this freedom. Furthermore, man lives by three kinds of values, creative, experiential, and attitudinal (Frankl, 1966). Creative values refer to productivity and achievement; experiential values include the experience of the good, the true, the beautiful; and attitudinal values embrace one's orientation to the tragic triad of human existence, that of suffering, guilt, and death (Frankl 1966, 1967). Attitudinal values are the most important, for these give meaning and significance to human misery, and reflect the spiritual posture of man. For Frankl, freedom and responsibility go together; man is responsible to himself (conscience), to others, or to God. Since logotherapy sees in responsibleness the essence of human existence, value decisions are left to the patient. A famous Frankl dictum is: live as though you were living for the second time and had acted as wrongly the first time as you are about to act now (Frankl, 1966).

Although Frankl conceives of his term "spiritual" as broader in meaning than the term "religion," his philosophy of human nature is compatible with theistically oriented therapy (Leslie, 1965; Tweedie, 1961; Ungersma, 1961).

Humanistic Psychology and Behaviorism. The contrast between behaviorism and phenomenology portrayed by Wann (1964) is applicable to the differences between behaviorism and humanistic psychology in general. Following Hitt's abstract of Wann (Hitt, 1969), a comparison is given in Table 2 (p. 38).

These two points of view differ in various aspects of their approach to the study of man. Behaviorists prefer to describe man in terms of observable behavior, whereas humanistic psychologists emphasize introspective data and conscious experience. Behaviorists maintain that an individual is basically predictable, and that once the determinants of a person's behavior are established, he will be completely predictable. Humanistic psychologists, on the other hand, contend that the individual, being self-determined and capable of free choice, will always defy complete prediction.

The behaviorist sees man as a transmitter of information input, whereas the humanistic psychologist sees him as a creative, generative source of information. The person, according to behaviorists, is but another object in an objective world; but the humanistic psychologist claims that the per-

Table 2.

Behavioristic and Humanistic Concepts of Man.*

	HOW MAN IS VIEWED	
Aspects in the Study of Man:	**Behaviorism:**	**Humanistic Psychology:**
Description	In terms of behavior	In terms of consciousness
Predictability	As determined and predictable	As free, self-determined, and unpredictable
Human Output	As an information transmitter	As an information generator
Life Situation	Living in an objective world	Living in a subjective world
Mode of Behavior	Rational	Arational and rational
Species Behavior	Behaves like other men	Behaves uniquely
Study Approach	Analytically	Synthetically
Method of Study	Known adequately by scientific method	Transcends scientific method

* Adapted from Hitt (1969).

son has a subjective perception of the objective world. Whereas the behaviorist sees man as functioning on rational, logical grounds, the humanistic psychologist emphasizes the motivational roles of arational, conative, and affective variables in behavior. The behaviorist prefers to interpret individual behavior in terms of group norms, whereas the humanistic psychologist stresses the uniqueness and importance of individual behavior. The behaviorist tends to dissect man with the analytic scalpel of the experimental method; the humanistic psychologist prefers to synthesize the multiple facets of man into a meaningful whole. Finally, the credo of the behaviorist is that man can be fully understood by scientific, experimental study; the humanistic psychologist is convinced that man transcends the grasp of science and always will.

As in the case of existentialism, representations of humanistic psychology are further subdivided in terms of theism and atheism. The atheistic-humanistic model relies heavily on evolutionary theory as sufficient explanation for man's presence on earth: man is the highest form of life, and there is no life or intelligence above or beyond him. He is responsible to himself alone, and not to God. On the other hand, the theistic-humanistic model sees evolution as *directional* change, which in turn requires an Intelligence to account for it (Hammes, 1971). This version of humanistic man is compatible with the Christian perspective, which then goes further to discover the meaning and purpose in the Divine plan for bringing man into existence.

Theological Humanism

Up to this point we have presented the views of scientific, philosophical, and psychological humanism and their attempt to cope with the meaning and significance of man.

The limitations of these perspectives can be summarized as follows. First, most proponents of these views are atheistic, depending on a blind evolutionary thrust to account for man and the universe. Second, in the rejection of God and his revelation, these viewpoints focus on man alone, man for himself, man as the highest pinnacle of life and intelligence. Consequently, one view tends to adulate man's rationality, and another his arationality. Third, these perspectives are relativistic, capable only of probability and contingency statements, rather than ones of certitude. They are also descriptive rather than explanatory. Further, a relativistic viewpoint cannot prescribe obligatory values or moral norms, and does not invite total commitment. Fourth, these interpretations of life and man are unable to explain the human condition of pain, suffering, and death. Nor can they account for evil. Lastly, all of them are inadequate in explaining the meaning, purpose, and significance of man.

A perspective that can provide what has been lacking thus far will be presented in the chapters that follow, in the perspective termed theological humanism, and, more specifically, Christian humanism.

I have referred frequently to the logical opposition between relativism and absolutism. This opposition is at the heart of the difference between theological humanism and the alternative forms of humanism so far presented. The absolutism/relativism controversy bears also on the problem of the validity of meaning in general, a concept that we should examine closely before proceeding to pursue further our inquiry as to the meaning of man.

SUGGESTED READINGS

1. Guinness, Os. *The Dust of Death*. Downers Grove: InterVarsity Press, 1973. The author critiques the Establishment and the counterculture, and proposes a Third Way, that of Christianity, to the solution of societal problems. He discusses such topics as violence, drugs, and mysticism.

2. Severin, Frank T., ed. *Discovering Man in Psychology: A Humanistic Approach*. N.Y.: McGraw-Hill, 1973. Edited readings on values, love, encounter, and humanistic aspects of science. A revised edition of an earlier work, *Humanistic Viewpoints in Psychology* (N.Y.: McGraw-Hill, 1965).

3. Bugental, James F. T., ed. *Challenges of Humanistic Psychology*. N.Y.: McGraw-Hill, 1967. The nature of humanistic psychology, with contributed articles on humanistic research, encounter groups, psychotherapy, and the relationship of psychology to the humanities.

4. Darling, Harold W. *Man in Triumph: An Integration of Psychology and Biblical Faith*. Grand Rapids: Zondervan, 1968. A critique of existential, neo-analytic, and humanistic theories of man, together with a presentation of a Christian perspective. A reconciliation of psychology with Christianity.

5. Adler, Mortimer J. *The Difference of Man and the Difference It Makes*. Cleveland: World Publishing Co., 1968. A philosophical analysis of the distinction between the nature of man and that of sub-human animal life. The author indicates the significance of various viewpoints on this topic.

6. Schaeffer, Francis A. *The God Who Is There*. Downers Grove: InterVarsity Press, 1968. A discussion of the errors in atheistic existential philosophy, as well as the fallacies of the

"God-is-dead" and other radical contemporary theologies. The author then defends historic Christianity in the present age.

3

THE VALIDITY OF MEANING

"Out of flux nothing but flux can come, and out of the relativism of the human situation no permanent values can be categorically established. Only if absolutes are supplied from outside the 'human predicament' can man stand firmly...."

—J. W. Montgomery, *Where Is History Going?*

THEOLOGICAL humanism, like specifically Christian humanism, is based on an Absolute Reality, or God. It is therefore essential to the validity of any theological humanism to demonstrate the capability of man to experience this Absolute. My argument will be that absolute reality can be known on two levels of human experience, the intellectual or reflective level, and the spiritual level.

In this chapter, we shall examine the possibility of experiencing the absolute on the intellectual level, and present the opposing alternatives of relativism and absolutism. In later chapters we shall consider the other way of grasping absolute reality, that is, on the spiritual level of human experience.

Knowing Reality
There are two factors involved in the problem of knowledge—the *knower*, and *that which is known*. We can refer to the knower as the "subjective" aspect, and to the reality

known as the "objective" aspect. We can further analyze the subjective aspect, the knower, in terms of those human functions through which one comes in contact with reality.

Generally speaking, we acquire knowledge on the sensory, intuitive, intellectual, and spiritual levels of human functioning. On the sensory level, we can observe the quantitative data yielded by the experimental method of science. On the intuitive level, we can gain insight by the aesthetic methods of the arts. On the intellectual level, we can acquire knowledge by the reflective methods of philosophy. On the spiritual level, we can obtain wisdom through the study of theology and by a personal encounter with God. The various disciplines of study in science, the arts, philosophy, and theology all contribute to man's knowledge of proximate and ultimate meaning. Phenix (1964) has presented a six-fold classification of the various realms of meaning: symbolic (language, mathematics), empirics (physical, social, and life sciences), aesthetics (music, painting, dance), synnoetics (philosophy, psychology, literature), ethics, and synoptics (history, philosophy, and religion).

Probing the Absolute

The four-fold scheme of human functions by which we come to know reality can be applied to the question of the possibility of experiencing absolute reality. First we must ask: What is absolute reality? Absolute reality may be defined as that reality which is independent of change, time, space, and man (Hammes, 1971). That is, it is changeless, eternal, universal, and has not been created by the human mind. Is there such a reality, and is it knowable? Or is there only one kind of reality, that which is ordinarily experienced as changing, and in a constant state of flux? The latter reality may be described as relative rather than absolute.

The question, therefore, is whether or not there is but one kind of reality, relative reality, or whether there are two, relative reality and absolute reality.

The sensory way of acquiring knowledge is represented by science. Can science answer the question concerning the two kinds of reality? August Comte, the nineteenth-century founder of logical positivism, thought science could. Comte described the progress of civilization in terms of three "ages," the age of superstition, the age of religion, and the age of science. He believed that, in time, science could resolve any question about meaning and value. There are scientists today who believe similarly, e.g., Skinner (1971). However, we have previously demonstrated the subjectivity and relativity of science. It lacks the capability of probing even the *possibility* of absolute reality.

The intuitive way of acquiring knowledge is found in the arts, in aesthetics. However, intuition is also relativistic in the sense of being reducible to personal opinion, which is insufficiently persuasive. There remain two other levels of human functioning on which knowledge is acquired, the intellectual (or reflective) level, and the spiritual level. I shall propose that the question of the existence of absolute reality can be resolved on both of these levels of human existence. But for the present, I shall limit my inquiry to the experience of the absolute through intelligent reflection.

Definition of Terms. In relation to the act of knowledge, we have referred to *the knower* as the subjective factor and termed *the reality known* as the objective factor. The word *truth* refers to the conformity of subjective knowledge with objective reality. If our perception of objective reality is accurate, we possess truth; if it is not, we are in error. It should be noted that the validity of the distinction between the knower and outside reality is here being assumed—a perspective which in philosophy is called "realism." The contrary opinion that outside reality is merely a projection of the human mind and does not exist apart from it is called "idealism," a position that has been critiqued elsewhere (Hammes, 1971). However, within the bounds of philosophical realism we still have to contend with the claims of the alternative positions of relativism and absolutism.

To continue: we can describe the kinds of truth in human experience, referring to knowledge of relative reality as "relative truth" and to knowledge of absolute reality as "absolute truth." To restate our original problem in these terms, we must ask whether or not there is such a reality as "absolute reality," whether we can know that reality in human experiences as "absolute truth," and whether we can experience that kind of truth with total conviction or "absolute certitude." If such a reality exists, and if the experience of it is humanly possible, then both facts will bear heavily on our search for ultimate meaning and the purpose for human existence. If such a reality does not exist, or if we cannot grasp it in human experience, we will never attain final answers in the quest for meaning and values.

In short, our inquiry resolves into two logical possibilities: is "relativism" the only position possible in human knowledge, or is "absolutism" a viable alternative? There are, of course, many implications involved in this question, beyond man's search for meaning. For example, the theologian sees that the problem bears on the existence or non-existence of God, the philosopher is faced with deciding whether human knowledge must always be in terms of contingency; in ethics, the validity and obligatory nature of moral norms are open to question; and in psychology, so is the question as to the nature of man.

In the following discussion, we shall first present the alternative of "relativism," examining its vulnerabilities, and then present the rationale for "absolutism."

The Encapsulation of Man

To illustrate the relativistic approach, a work entitled *The Encapsulated Man,* by Joseph Royce (1964), will be evaluated. Royce has presented an admirable analysis of the problem of meaning. We shall restrict our discussion to his solution to the key problem of whether there can be certitude in human knowledge.

After describing the malady of meaninglessness so characteristic of man, Royce sets out to chart the paths to the discovery of a meaningful existence. He first warns, however, of a fundamental human condition that militates against the attainment of absolute answers to the human quest. Royce calls this condition "encapsulation," hence the title of his book.

By encapsulation, Royce means (a) "claiming to have the whole truth when one has only part of it," (b) "looking at life partially and proceeding to make statements concerning the wholeness of living," (c) "living partially" because "one's world-view or philosophy of life cannot embrace the larger meaning of existence," and (d) "projecting a knowledge of ultimate reality from the perceptual framework of a limited reality image" (Royce, 1964, pp. 2, 30). Why are we all encapsulated? Royce replies: (1) by virtue of being man; (2) by irrationality; (3) by limited imagination; and (4) by being determined by cultural and social factors, and also language structure; i.e., by being influenced by the *Zeitgeist* (p. 36). Royce then describes four basic ways of knowing, namely, rationalism (thinking), intuitionism (feeling), empiricism (sensing), and authoritarianism (believing). In a later work, Royce dropped "authoritarianism" from this list, presumably because he decided that the assumptions underlying the other three contain or imply this characteristic (Royce, 1964, p. 18). He also later dropped the term "intuitionism" in favor of "metaphorism" (Royce, 1967).

Royce claims that man seeks ultimate reality, the final essence of things (1964, p. 31), but can only approximate such reality, being confined to an encapsulated or finite reality-image. The barrier between finite reality and ultimate reality is impenetrable, epistemologically untestable, and therefore forever unknowable.

In view of this impasse, Royce proposes two alternative courses of action. One is to give up in despair—which Royce describes as "psychological suicide" (p. 43); and the other is to commit oneself to the search—which Royce says is "psychologically necessary" (p. 43), even though encapsulation will prevent man from ever grasping ultimate reality or ultimate truth. Royce states, "I suggest that the great adventure of life resides in the search for ultimates, but not the attainment of them" (p. 43).

Critique of Relativism

Royce has done a service in clarifying the problems faced in the search for meaning. However, his analysis is vulnerable to criticism in his rejection of absolutism and open to objection also in his sweeping statements and dogmatic assertions.

First, how can one know there *is* ultimate reality if one can know nothing ultimate? If the bridge to ultimate reality is uncrossable, how does one *know* that such a reality *exists* at all? Furthermore, how can Royce in the first place make an absolute statement that man cannot adequately penetrate the barrier to ultimate reality? As a relativist, he can only express an opinion; he cannot make absolute state-ments on any subject without contradicting his basic posi-tion. Yet he continually makes such statements in *The En-capsulated Man*: "I presume any approach to life which at-tempts to see it whole is bound to suffer from lack of cer-tainty because of the inherent impossibility of the task" (p. 26). "Those who make pronouncements about the ul-timate nature of things are doing just that—making pro-nouncements. For they are just as limited as the rest of us, and they have no special short cuts to the truth." "Until visionaries, mystics, and other claimants can make their epistemological route clearer to competent investigators, we shall have to conclude that such men are encapsulated reality seekers along with the rest of us." "We have con-cluded . . . none of them . . . [are] able to lead us to the truth in the sense of ultimate reality . . . because man is en-capsulated" (p. 30).

Royce, again going beyond purely relativistic assertion, claims that "the error in most institutionalized religions has been that of thinking they could *know* ultimate reality. At this point Tillich helps us greatly, for he points out that religion has to do with ultimate *concern* rather than ul-timate *knowledge*" (p. 44n). One could agree with Tillich that true religion manifests itself by charity in action, that is, by concern for others. But many would disagree with Tillich's denial that religion has to do with ultimate truth and knowledge. Nor can Royce logically condemn those who see religion as dealing with ultimate truth without con-tradicting his relativistic position. Royce states, "I suggest that it requires ultimate reality in order to be aware of ul-timate reality, and that, therefore, such *infinite* and all-encompassing awareness is not available to finite, limited man" (p. 34, italics added). Royce is subject here to the objection that he has incorrectly identified awareness of *ultimate* reality with that of *infinite* reality. The former is accessible to man; it can be agreed that the latter is not.

To continue, Royce states, "Our history books are filled with the testimony of what happens to a people when they become convinced they have *the truth*. They perish. And they perish because their reality image becomes frozen. After all, if you have come to the essence of things, you have reached the pot of gold at the end of the rainbow and there is no more need to search" (p. 43). This is a caricature of, and an *argumentum ad hominem* against, absolutists. No one can be bored, or be frozen, in the possession of absolute truth. Such knowledge must rather open up new vistas, new life, to those who possess it. Royce concludes that "some kind of commitment to reality is inevitable, or at least psychologically necessary. . . . The search for ultimate reality, then, is a natural and necessary part of man's being, . . . part of what it means to be human; . . . a final answer to this question can never be given, for man is limited, he is finite; . . . for him to know the infinite is impossible by definition." Man, according to Royce, has an innate compulsion to *seek* what never will be *attained*. Note again the error of equating absolute with infinite knowledge. It is true that finite man cannot comprehend the infinite; but he can know *that the infinite exists* without comprehending its nature. Finite man can also know other absolute truths and certitudes, even though he cannot possess all of them; that is, he cannot possess all (absolute) knowledge. We shall come back to this matter later.

A further point of interest is the thought that *relativism* can be regarded as actually a form of *encapsulation*, because it rules out the possibility of absolute certitude (which, as we have seen, relativism cannot logically do, for

such ruling out would be an absolutist statement itself).
Relativists can express only opinions, and any opinion is
subject to possible error. Whereas Royce attempts to avoid
both (a) absolutism and (b) solipsism (i.e., finding reality
only within the self), he concludes that man has a psychological compulsion to seek what is unattainable (p. 43). As is
true for all relativists, he cannot maintain that his position is
absolutely correct and one that must be followed. Relativists must, if they are not to contradict themselves, preface all assertions with the phrase "In my opinion . . ." or
an equivalent qualification.

Relativists claim that absolutists are encapsulated, in the
sense of not being open to change in the possession of absolute truth. Openness to change in all truth is, for the relativist, imperative if encapsulation is to be avoided. However, if absolute truth *is* attainable, it would not encapsulate
but rather free the knower and break the "bonds" of *relativistic* encapsulation in an area where relativism is in fact
mistaken.

Having surveyed the inadequacies inherent in relativistic
attempts to explain man's search for meaning, we can turn
to look at the evidence supporting the absolutist position.

Reflective Experience of Absolute Reality

"Absolute reality," defined as reality that is unchanging,
would logically possess four characteristics. It would be independent of time (eternally true), of change (immutably
true), of space (universally true), and of man (discovered by
man and not created by him). A reality not meeting even
one of these criteria would be reducible to relative reality.
Our problem is to determine whether there is reality that
meets these requirements. We have proposed that absolute
reality can be experienced on the reflective level of human

experience, and on the spiritual level as well. Let us first examine the evidence yielded by reflective experience.°

In traditional philosophy, specifically in epistemology, one meets a principle of knowledge that the average person takes for granted. It is the *principle of contradiction*, sometimes referred to as the principle of identity, or as the principle of the excluded middle (Bittle, 1936). This principle is illustrated in the following statements. "Whatever is, is whatever it is, and cannot be other than whatever it is" (principle of identity). In other words: a being is itself and not a being other than itself. A variant of this principle holds that something cannot both "be" and "not be" at one and the same time and under the same circumstances (principle of contradiction). Or again, between two such alternatives that are mutually exclusive there can be no third alternative (principle of the excluded middle).

As a practical illustration, one can select any object, a "toothpick," say, and set up the two classifications of "toothpick" and "non-toothpick." The prefix "non-" means "all things other than." It should then be obvious a) that the toothpick is whatever it is and cannot be other than itself, b) that everything that *is* must be either a toothpick or a non-toothpick (all things other than toothpicks), and c) that between the categories of "toothpick" and "non-toothpick" there can be no other category possible.

The truth of the principle of contradiction is not questioned by the average person, who uses it in daily life. For example, when one person disagrees with another's opinion, he presupposes the distinction between true and non-true statements, or accurate and non-accurate perceptions. Our laws assume the distinction between legal and non-

---

° The rationale for the experience of absolute reality on a reflective level has been given in detail in an earlier work (Hammes, 1971). This rationale is briefly reviewed in the following paragraphs.

legal behavior, between right and non-right (wrong) acts. Our very discussion of "truth" assumes the distinction between truth and non-truth (error). Among students of philosophy, however, there are those who subordinate this principle to a conjectural status, or treat it as merely one of preference among various systems of logic. The logical positivist, the operationalist, and the linguistic analyst do not generally concede the realistic validity of the principle of contradiction (Hammes, 1971). However, the principle in fact underlies all systems of philosophy, language, or logic, for it can be applied to *their own validity*. Those systems are correct or incorrect, right or not right, true or not true. Indeed, the principle can categorize those who accept or reject it, and those who agree or disagree with its validity. It describes such observers in the mutually exclusive categories of acceptance and non-acceptance, or of agreement and non-agreement. (The term "non-acceptance" or "non-agreement" includes any and all degrees of divergence from the positions of acceptance or agreement, respectively.)

Perhaps the reader has thought of the possibility of a *future* discovery of a category between two categories that are mutually exclusive. Is that really possible? The only two logical answers to this question are the affirmative and the negative. Since between *these* two there is no third alternative possible, it is seen that once again the principle of contradiction has demonstrated its self-evidence and validity.

We are now ready to see whether or not the principle of contradiction meets the requirements we have listed as necessary to absolute reality. Is the principle independent of time? We can contemplate any moment of the past or the future, and it is evident that the only two possibilities with regard to the principle's validity for any moment are: *it is valid*, or *it is not valid*. Since the principle is *applicable* to any moment in time, it follows that it is valid for any moment in time. The principle's independence of time can be illustrated also in the following statements. With regard to past time, "Whatever was, was whatever it was, and was not other than whatever it was." With regard to future time, "Whatever will be, will be whatever it will be, and will not be other than whatever it will be." Therefore, it can be stated that the principle is independent of time, or eternal.

Does the principle meet our second criterion, independence of change? Independence of time necessarily embraces independence of change. A precept that is eternally true is not subject to change. The principle of contradiction, being eternally true, will never change.

Is the principle independent of space, that is, universally true? For example, would the principle be true on some distant planet in an unknown galaxy? The only two possible descriptions of the situation on that planet are that the principle is valid there, or that it is not valid there. No third alternative is possible. Since the principle describes the situation on that planet, or anywhere else in space, it is applicable to and valid at any point in space. It is therefore independent of space, or universally true.

Lastly, does the principle of contradiction meet the criterion of independence of man? Again, being eternally true, the principle is independent of man, who is time-bound in his existence. The human mind did not create this principle, but rather has discovered it and has recognized it as grounded in a reality independent of man himself.

These, then, are the philosophical reflections that lead to the conclusion that man can come to know absolute reality on this level of human experience.°

° For a more detailed analysis of the principle of contradiction, the reader is referred to additional discussions (Hammes, 1971; Gallagher, 1964; Bittle, 1936).

The principle of contradiction is nevertheless being challenged in contemporary philosophical literature by those who deny the existence of absolute reality; these objections can be discussed later when we consider the relativists' criticism of absolutists.

The reflective experience of absolute reality illustrated in the discussion of the principle of contradiction can be described as the knowledge of an "absolute truth," to use a phrase previously defined. The individual who perceives the validity of the principle of contradiction is also impressed with its self-evidence, to the extent of total conviction or "absolute certitude." It might be noted here that certitude and the possession of absolute truth in the experience of absolute reality are not themselves static, unchanging experiences. They may deepen in appreciation and comprehension, and often do, for the reflective individual. It is the objective reality, which these subjective experiences grasp, that is eternal and unchanging.

The principle of contradiction is also useful in demonstrating that the relativist is in error in proposing relativism to be the *only* true position possible. The two mutually exclusive possibilities are (1) that relativism is the only valid posture in the quest for truth, and (2) that relativism is *not* the only valid posture in the quest for truth. It has been shown that the first alternative leads to the absurdity of relativists' making an absolutist statement; and therefore this position is untenable. The only other possibility is that relativism is not the only valid posture to take; and this is the position of the absolutist. The absolutist contends that the correct perspective is to recognize the existence of *two* kinds of reality, relative and absolute.

The principle of contradiction also puts in a clear light the logical weakness of the personal convictions of the relativist. The relativist is either (1) absolutely sure all things are relative, or (2) relatively (non-absolutely) sure all things are relative. Alternative one is self-contradictory, for in order to be absolutely sure, the relativist must first allow the possibility of knowing absolute reality, in which case he is not really a relativist. Alternative two requires the relativist to admit the possibility of the existence of absolute reality, since he is not certain of his relativistic stand. The only logical position he could then take is that of agnosticism, which deprives him of making any certain statements at all, including criticisms of the absolutist perspective.

Now let us consider some of the objections that relativists have to absolutism, and how they may be answered.

Relativists' Objections to Absolutism

First, relativists accuse absolutists of a rigidity and an inflexibility that supposedly block freedom of thought. Absolutists reply that any alternatives to absolutely certain truths can only be incorrect alternatives. Such error is the absence of truth and therefore meaningless. Freedom *from* error is a higher freedom than freedom *to* err. When one possesses absolute truth and absolute certitude, it would be foolish to reject it simply in order to be able to exercise "freedom of choice" in the matter. Rigidity and inflexibility in embracing absolute truth is reasonable and intelligent behavior. Naturally, the same attitude applied to the area of *relative* reality is rejected by absolutists with a vigor equal to that of the relativists.

Second, relativists sometimes project into the position of absolutists a "holier than thou" attitude. But the only relevant contrast between the two positions is one of evidence, not attitude. The absolutist is convinced of his position, and would be hypocritical if he pretended otherwise merely to please a relativist. The issue is one of principles, not person-alities. Again, the relativist contradicts himself in claiming that the absolutist has no right to be absolute, for the rela-tivist would then be making his *own* view absolute. Neither advocate, of course, has any right to impose his view upon the other, or to judge the sincerity of the other. Differences should always be discussed in a context of logic and reason, not emotion.

Third, some relativists point out that it is still possible to experience doubt concerning absolute certitude in regard to the absolute truth of the principle of contradiction, and they therefore withhold assent to its absolute validity. Now it is true that any truth *can* be doubted; but it does not follow that all truths *must* be doubted. Human beings have a remarkable capacity to doubt everything. In philosophy, this position is termed universal skepticism. But is such a position reasonable? For example, I may, if I wish, doubt my own existence. The error of such a reflection is immedi-ately obvious upon the further consideration that I must first exist in order for me to doubt anything at all! There-fore, it is unreasonable to doubt one's own existence. My existence is self-evident. The validity of the principle of contradiction is self-evident. It should be clear, then, that to doubt a self-evident truth is to hold to an unreasonable doubt. Such doubts are compulsive, irrational, and unwor-thy of retention.

Fourth, relativists charge that the absolutist accepts the validity of the principle of contradiction because the con-trary is inconceivable. Ignorance is thus alleged to be the basis of the conviction of the absolutist. This criticism is based on the relativists' hope that someday new evidence will indicate the falseness of the principle of contradiction. However, we have already met this challenge in demonstrating that the principle is independent of time, and will be as true in the future as it is today.

Fifth, it would appear that the temperament of Western society is relativistic. Today, many favor subjectivity over objectivity. Humanistic psychology is itself a product of this orientation. The emphasis on personal, subjectivistic, phenomenological experience has led some to reject the possibility of knowing anything other than personal impressions; the natural outcome is skepticism regarding the knowability of the real nature of the objective, outside world. A related attitude is that which rejects a subjective-objective dualism —the position that the human observer is separated from what he observes. Rather, it is contended, reality does not and cannot exist apart from the subjectivity of human experience. A current example of this perspective is usually referred to as "Eastern philosophy," which, in its pantheistic view, considers reality and the person-experiencing-reality to be one and the same thing. Such monistic theories end up in skepticism, a logical consequence of denying the dualistic distinction between the experiencing subject and the objective reality experienced.

Sixth, there is also an anti-intellectual or anti-rational view popular today (Frankel 1973; Trilling, 1972; Holton, 1974), which militates against a rational, reflective search for objective reality. We shall return to this later, in our discussion of arationality as an ethical norm.

A seventh possible reason for the reluctance of relativists to admit the capability of man to grasp absolute reality is the apprehension of the impact such insight would have on personal life. The absolutist, of course, sees such impact favorably, but the relativist, accustomed to what he considers to be unfettered freedom of thought, may feel threatened by a reality that logically permits no freedom of rejection. Too, the recognition of absolute reality, with the inevitable implications of the existence of God and a moral reckoning, would be uncomfortable for that type of relativist who prefers to create moral guidelines in accord with personal preference. The atheistically inclined relativist would not welcome a Divine Lawgiver who tells him how he should conduct his moral affairs. The evolutionary relativist would not be inclined to recognize a Mind higher than his own, to whose wisdom he must bow. These motives for rejecting absolute reality need not be consciously known, but could operate easily as an unconscious block to acceptance of absolute reality.

Eighth, a viewpoint akin to relativism is that of agnosticism, the belief that there is insufficient evidence to support either relativism or absolutism. One can sympathize with the person who has seriously studied an issue and conscientiously cannot arrive at a conclusion. The best advice for such a person is to continue his study, in hope that insight will eventually be gained. Nevertheless, it would seem that even the agnostic should be able to perceive the self-contradiction involved in the relativist's denial of the possibility of absolutism.

Proving God by Reason

What is the significance of the human capability to experience absolute truth? Earlier it was observed that if reality is but relative, changing, and in continued flux, then no ultimate answer could be found to the question of the meaning of human existence. Nor could final solutions be found for the problems of guilt, suffering, and death. Establishing the human capacity to recognize the existence of absolute reality and to grasp it by way of absolute truth was a prerequisite to further exploration of absolute reality. The next step is to relate absolute reality to Absolute reality, that is, God; for God is considered by theists to be the ground of all being and all reality.

The principle of contradiction can be used to establish, on an intellectual, reflective level, the existence of Absolute reality, or God (Hammes, 1971). A prerequisite for such a demonstration is the acceptance of the reality of cause-effect relationships in the world. To deny causality, of course, is to preclude even the possibility of finding ultimate meaning, which is essentially final causality. If we begin, therefore, by accepting the reality of causality and the validity of the principle of contradiction, it can be shown that God must of necessity exist, in that the alternative to his existing is absurd.

An essential characteristic of God is that he is necessarily prior to all other existing beings, for if he were not, some other being would have to account for his existence. But it is this very being, prior to all others, that we mean when we speak of God. Consequently, God can also be called the First Cause. The question can now be asked: Was there a First Cause? An equivalent question is: Does God exist?

When the principle of contradiction is applied, the only two possible alternative answers to that question are: *There was a First Cause*, and *There was not a First Cause*. Now, there are two ways in which one alternative of two that are mutually exclusive can be verified. The usual approach is to affirm one of the alternatives, and thus prove the other false. Another way is to prove that one of the two mutually exclusive alternatives is false, thereby necessarily confirming the remaining alternative, since it is the only other. Most of the rational arguments for the existence of God follow the first approach. The following argument pursues the latter course: Assume for the moment that the alternative, *There was not a First Cause,* is the true alternative. If so, then there would not have been a second cause, or third cause; nor, finally, in the sequential chain of causes and effects, would there be any presently existing causes. This conclusion follows logically from our starting point. However, it contradicts our basic empirical experience of causality as actually present in the world. Therefore, the conclusion must in fact be erroneous; and false too must be the premise from which it was logically drawn. That is, the proposition, *There was not a First Cause,* must be false. Consequently, the only other remaining alternative must be true, namely, *There was a First Cause.* Since the essential nature of God is that he be the First Cause, then it follows that the necessary existence of God has been demonstrated.

A frequent follow-up question is, What caused the First Cause? This question is based on a misunderstanding of the principle of causality, which states that all effects must have causes, but which does not state that every cause must itself *be* an effect. We usually experience causes that are the effects of previous causes; but the possibility of a cause whose existence is sufficiently explained by its own necessity is compatible with the principle of causality. Reflective reasoning demands, as we have seen, the existence of the First Cause, necessary for the existence of all subsequent causes and effects (e.g., the universe and all things in it, including man). This First Cause has within itself the necessity of existence; hence God is sometimes referred to as Necessary Being. All other beings are contingent or, in a sense, unnecessary. Notice that one's recognition of the necessity of the existence of the First Cause in no way implies that one understands the *nature* of the First Cause, or Necessary Being. The acceptance of the necessity of the existence of God is independent of the problems of understanding the nature of God. In the rational world, we accept the existence of many things whose nature is not understood—gravity, electricity, etc.

God, The First Cause or Necessary Being, meets the four criteria previously seen to be essentially descriptive of absolute reality. For example, the First Cause is independent of time; since it is Necessary Being, there was never a time when it did not exist; and it is therefore eternal. Similarly (following along previous lines of discussion), it is independent of change, space, and man.

Relation of the Principle of Contradiction to God. The observant reader may have wondered about the relation of the principle of contradiction, which has been used as evidence of absolute reality (with a small "a"), to God, who is Absolute reality (with a capital "A"). Even though the principle can be used to prove the logical existence of God, in actuality the principle derives its validity from God. That is, absolute reality with a little "a" is grounded in Absolute reality with a big "A."

The explanation is this: The ground of the principle of contradiction is "being," for the category of "being" is that to which the mutually exclusive alternative of "nonbeing" is posed. The ultimate ground of being is Necessary Being, required to account for the existence of all other beings, termed contingent or unnecessary beings. The capability of the principle of contradiction to posit in the first place the mutually exclusive categories of "being" and "non-being" is therefore dependent on Necessary Being. Thus the validity of the principle of contradiction as exemplifying absolute reality is seen to be grounded in the prior existence of Absolute reality, or God.

At this point the reader might well ask, How can a principle be used to prove the existence of the God who is the basis of the validity of the principle? We saw that the validity of the principle was demonstrated on the basis of reflective thought, and not in reference to God. It was then applied toward solving the question of the existence of God. Note also that the principle was used only to posit the two alternatives regarding God's existence; it did not say which of these two alternatives was true. That observation was based on the conclusions to which the alternatives led, and we saw that the absurd conclusions of one alternative led to its rejection. The principle merely pointed out that since there were only two, the remaining (unrejected) alternative was necessarily true.

We have arrived at an Absolute reality with a capital "A," but it should be noted that an intellectual or rational demonstration of the existence of God is insufficient in convincing a non-believer. Indeed it seems that one must *experience God* in a personal way in order to be totally convinced of his existence, and in order for this conviction to affect one's way of life. If rational demonstration alone was sufficient, there would be no atheists. This matter of the spiritual *experience* of Absolute reality, or God, an experience that transcends the *intellectual* level of experiencing Absolute reality, is the subject of the next chapter.

SUGGESTED READINGS

1. Hammes, John A. *Humanistic Psychology: A Christian Interpretation.* N.Y.: Grune & Stratton, 1971. The author establishes the compatibility of scientifically established psychological truth with the truths of Christianity. Topics include the origin and nature of man, the validity of absolute certitude, and human destiny.

2. Gallagher, Kenneth T. *The Philosophy of Knowledge.* N.Y.: Sheed and Ward, 1964. An analysis of human knowledge, including perceptual, conceptual, and existential truth. Gallagher discusses first principles, e.g., principle of identity, principle of sufficient reason, principle of efficient causality.

3. Royce, James E. *Man and Meaning.* N.Y.: McGraw-Hill, 1969. A book in philosophical psychology, covering such areas as human knowledge, human motivation, and theories of human nature. (Author is not be confused with Joseph R. Royce, author of *The Encapsulated Man.*)

4. Barbour, Ian G. *Issues in Science and Religion.* Englewood Cliffs: Prentice-Hall, 1966. A comprehensive study of religion and the history of science, and the relationship of religion to the methods and theories of science. Topics include evolution, indeterminacy, verification, and process theory.

5. Montgomery, John W. *Where Is History Going?* Grand Rapids: Zondervan, 1969. The author establishes the validity of absolute truth, the historical validity of the New Testament and the divine identity of Jesus Christ. These truths are applied toward a Christian philosophy of history.

6. Phenix, Philip H. *Realms of Meaning: A Philosophy of the Curriculum.* N.Y.: McGraw-Hill, 1964. A comprehensive presentation of contemporary attacks on various realms and sources of meaning. The author defends the validity of meaning and applies patterns of meaning to a curriculum for general education.

4

ULTIMATE MEANING

"No world religion can seriously consider abandoning its absolutistic claim. If it did, it would scarcely have the right to call itself a religion."
—H. J. Schoeps, *The Religions of Mankind.*

THE spiritual experience of Absolute reality, or God, is clearly the highest experience of which anyone is capable. The study of this relationship between man and God is the study of religion. The term "religion," derived from Latin *religio,* "to tie," signifies the tie between humanity and a higher power (Schoeps, 1968). We do not know when religious consciousness began. Evidence of the emergence of mankind on this earth appears to indicate that Neanderthal man, of approximately 100,000 years ago, buried his dead, thus manifesting a possible contemplation of or longing for an afterlife (Howell, 1965). Whether or not there was earlier reflection on existence and meaning, we simply do not know. However, from the time of Cro-Magnon man, approximately 50,000 years ago, there has survived much evidence in discovered cave art of possible religious practices, such as ceremonial burial, use of shrines, and animal worship and sacrifice.

The Origin of Religion

Theories explaining the origin of religion are divided as to the kind of god that early man venerated. Some writers contend that religion evolved from primitive animism into polytheism and then monotheism; others propose that man originally was monotheistic in his belief, which then deteriorated into polytheism, and finally evolved again to monotheism (Schoeps, 1968). It should be observed that all such theories are in the final analysis conjectural, since presently known records of the beliefs of man do not date early enough in human history to verify any particular hypothesis. One approach to this problem is the study of divine revelation, a source of information to be considered in a later discussion of the Judeo-Christian religious perspective.

In the previous chapter we established the existence of two kinds of reality, relative and absolute. We further analyzed the experience of absolute reality and related it in a rational, intellectual way to the existence of God. We asserted, however, that logical discourse alone was insufficient to persuade anyone of God's existence; for to be fully convinced, one must experience God in a personal way. It is this personal experience of God that we shall now consider, as well as the way in which this experience is related to the attainment of ultimate meaning. We shall consider first the ways in which mankind to the present day has perceived God; that is, we shall sketch the main religious beliefs of the past that have survived to the present.

The World's Living Religions

Religions are customarily divided into dead (extinct) and living religions. Religions become extinct when their tenets conflict with the advance of knowledge, or when a newly developed religion offers a more comprehensive perspective of God, man, and the universe. Such newer developments, however, may retain those tenets of past religions which, as we shall see, are valid concepts (e.g., monothe-

Table 3. Dates and Founders of the World's Living Religions.

Religion	Place	Founding Date	Founder	Membership°
Hinduism	India	3,000-2,500 B.C.	Unknown	524 million
Judaism	Mesopotamia	1,700 B.C.	(Abraham), Moses	14 million
Shinto	Japan	660 B.C.	First Japanese Emperor	60 million
Zoroastrianism	Persia	660 B.C.	Zoroaster	230 thousand
Taoism	China	604 B.C.	Lao Tse	30 million
Buddhism	India	560 B.C.	Gautama (alias Buddha)	250 million
Confucianism	China	551 B.C.	Confucius	186 million
Christianity	Palestine	4 B.C.	Jesus Christ	955 million
Islam	Arabia	570 A.D.	Mohammed	538 million

°*The World Almanac & Book of Facts* (N.Y.: Newspaper Enterprise Assoc., 1977).

ism, and the belief in an afterlife). Religions considered extinct today include those of ancient Babylon and Assyria in Mesopotamia, ancient Egypt in Africa, ancient Celts and Teutons in Europe, ancient Mexico and Peru in the Americas, and ancient Greece and Rome. The so-called living religions all originated in Asia. They include Hinduism and Buddhism in Southern Asia; Confucianism, Taoism, and Shinto in Eastern Asia; and Judaism, Zoroastrianism, Christianity, and Islam in Western Asia (Hume, 1959).

Estimated members of adherents of the world's living religions are presented in Table 3. The total number approximates 2.5 billion, a little more than half of the world's population of 4 billion. Christians constitute almost half of this membership in the world's living religions, and about one-fourth of the world's population in general. The founding dates of the world's living religions, together with the names of the founders, are also presented, chronologically, in Table 3.

In our analysis of the spiritual experience of Absolute reality, or God, we shall examine this concept in both living and extinct religions, as well as the relationship of man to God and the implications for the human condition of evil, suffering, and death.

The Concept of Deity

In the religions of man, deity has been viewed in various ways. First, some have proposed a monotheism, while others believe in polytheism, henotheism, and pantheism. Some religions have changed from one view to another and back again. *Monotheism* refers to belief in one God, usually an Absolute God; *polytheism* means belief in several gods; *henotheism* is the belief in one god without denying the existence of other gods; and *pantheism* is the belief that all things are part of one reality, or that all things are emanations of God.

As we understand them today, the religions stressing monotheism are Judaism, Christianity, and Islam (Table 4). Zoroastrianism proposes a theistic dualism in the opposition of a supreme being, Ahura Mazda, to the devil, Angra Mainyu (or Ahriman), both of whom have supposedly co-existed eternally. Although these two powers are in a sense co-equal, it is prophesied that at the end of the world Ahura Mazda will trimph over Angra Mainyu.

Ancient Hinduism changed from monotheism to pantheism and polytheism. Buddhism started as atheism, for Buddha himself rejected any concept of deity. His followers, however, deified Buddha, and in the course of history have

Table 4.
Concept of Deity in the World's Living Religions.

| | NATURE OF DEITY | | | |
	Monotheism	Polytheism	Pantheism	Personal Absolute
Hinduism	X	X	X	
Judaism	X			X
Shinto		X	X	
Zoroastrianism		X		X
Taoism		X		
Buddhism		X		
Confucianism		X		
Christianity	X			X
Islam	X			X

added other gods. Other polytheistic religions include Shinto, Taoism, and Confucianism. Some religions are not only polytheistic, but pantheistic as well, e.g., Hinduism and Shinto. Of the extinct or dead religions, most were polytheistic, although there is evidence that the early Egyptian religion, the Babylonian religion, and others were monotheistic. In time, however, they all lapsed into polytheism.

The Relation of God to Man

Another distinction in the way religions view God or the Absolute is in terms of his relationship with man. The three monotheistic religions, Judaism, Christianity, and Islam, together with Zoroastrianism, view God as a *personal* God; that is, he is actively interested in human welfare and the individual. He is also good and just, and therefore will reward the good and punish the wicked. Judaism and Zoroastrianism tend to stress the omnipotence and power of God, who is to be feared. Islam adds to this concept of God a capricious and unpredictive quality. Christianity, while keeping in mind an omnipotent God, perceives him primarily as a Heavenly Father, and all human beings as the children of this loving Father. This concept was taught by Jesus Christ, in what has come to be called the Lord's Prayer (Matt 6.9-13).

The other living religions, in addition to being polytheistic or pantheistic, conceive of any absolute in impersonal terms. For Hinduism the ultimate and unchanging reality is Brahma, into which someday the individual, Atman, will be absorbed. Man is considered but an emanation of this impersonal absolute, and man is expected to save himself in this world without Brahma's help. Although Hinduism added personal gods (Vishnu, Siva, Kali, etc.), those gods are but pantheistic emanations of Brahma.

We have already noted that Buddha was an atheist, and that his followers later deified him. Buddhism lacks any concept of the absolute; the Buddhist teaching that comes closest to acknowledging any absolute is that of Nirvana. The individual is regarded as chained to the Wheel of Life, undergoing transmigration in endless series of births and deaths, until finally one achieves Nirvana, the negation of life and existence.

Lao Tse, the founder of Taoism, had no intention of founding a religion, and considered himself but a philosopher, which his name connotes. A thousand years after his death, the followers of Lao Tse deified him. The central concept of this religion is Tao, variously translated as Way, Path, or Road. It can be further interpreted in philosophical, ethical, and religious terms. Tao has sometimes been seen as equivalent to God; and to achieve Tao is to achieve heaven. However, this goal is seen negatively, in terms of quiescence, restfulness, and calm, an escape from the world's suffering and turmoil. Historically, Taoism has degenerated into polytheism, witchcraft, and occultism.

Confucius was a contemporary of Lao Tse, whom he visited. The teachings of Confucius encouraged an interest in practical affairs; Lao Tse attempted to persuade Confucius to give up that orientation in favor of meditation on the Tao. Confucius, like Lao Tse, had no intention of founding a religion. He was interested primarily in social ethics and social reform. But he did acknowledge a Supreme Being, Shang Ti, a concept subsequently lost when Confucianism lapsed into polytheism.

Another living religion, Shinto, also has lacked any concept of the absolute, and has defined God in terms of polytheistic nature deities, e.g., the sun-goddess, Ama-terasu. Such worship came to be extended to the Mikado and his successors.

Sacred Religious Writings

Most of the world's living religions clearly claim their writings and directives for human behavior as having come from their deity, or deities. These sacred writings are listed in Table 5. Some kind of divine incarnation is usually associated with the founders of these religions; such claims are made by their followers many years after the founders' deaths. The founder of Hinduism is unknown, but several of the Hindu gods are believed by their followers to have become incarnate in men, called "avatars." None of them, however, are presented as morally perfect. Too, other founders (such as Zoroaster, Lao Tse, Buddha, and Confucius) were men with defects in character and personality. Only one founder of the world's living religions appears to

Table 5.
Sacred Writings of the World's Living Religions. °

Religion	Writings
Hinduism	Vedas (Knowledge); Upanishads
Judaism	Old Testament; Torah; Talmud
Shinto	Ko-ji-ki (The Records of Ancient Matters); Nihon-gi (The Chronicles of Japan)
Zoroastrianism	Avesta (Knowledge)
Taoism	Tao-Teh-King (The Canon of Reason and Virtue)
Buddhism	Tripitaka (Three Baskets of Wisdom)
Confucianism	Five Classics; Four Books
Christianity	Bible (The Book)
Islam	Koran (The Reading)

° Adapted from Hume (1959).

be without fault and without sin, one who also claimed to be God and was put to death for that reason; that person was Jesus Christ.

Nature of Man

What do the various living religions have to say about man? Human nature is worthless or insignificant according to the beliefs of Hinduism, Buddhism, and Shinto. Taoism sees human nature as good; so also does Confucianism, which is actually a form of philosophical humanism. Judaism, Zoroastrianism, Christianity, and Islam agree on the goodness of man, while also acknowledging human sinfulness. Judaism and Christianity see man as made in the "divine image," Christianity going further to stress the need for man to empty himself to become even more Godlike. Both Judaism and Christianity acknowledge that man can, and has, sinned, and that he has done so to the extent of requiring divine redemption and forgiveness. We shall return to this theme later.

Nature of Evil and Suffering

Whence came the world? And evil? All ancient religions, having acknowledged a deity or deities, attribute the creation of the world to them. Included is the concept of conflict between the gods, such that evil is attributed to one god, and good to another. Man is usually seen as subservient to the gods, serving them in fear. The theme of human rebellion against the gods likewise is often found (e.g., in the Greek concept of imprisonment of mind or soul in the body as punishment for that transgression). The universal flood, another instance of divine punishment, is also narrated in various ways, as in the epic of Gilgamesh in Assyrian documents (Abbot, 1969).

Among the world's living religions, Hinduism accepts evil and suffering as part of the human condition, from which one attempts to escape in some future pantheistic unity with Brahma. For Buddhism, suffering is consequent to selfish human desires, which must be suppressed to achieve happiness. Buddha, an atheist, had no religious explanation for the existence of evil in the world. Taoism does not explain the existence of evil and suffering, but rather accepts it and attempts to escape it, as well as world involvement in general. Confucianism, being more a practical philosophy that avoids speculative theology, offers no adequate explanation for evil and suffering. Shinto, immersed in nature deities and primarily a religion of the natural world, has become intermingled with Buddhism and Confucianism. Its solution to evil and suffering lies in self-purification.

Judaism and Christianity believe the devil, a fallen angel, to be evil personified. Original man succumbed to the devil's temptation and was responsible for the present human condition of suffering, guilt, and death. However, all human beings, through personal sin, contribute to evil and suffering. Zoroastrianism and Islam have similar concepts of the devil and of personal responsibility for moral evil.

Human Purpose

What is man's goal in life? We have already seen the negative view of human existence in Hinduism and Buddhism, for which one's goal is escape from this life. Shinto stresses self-purification, whereas Confucianism emphasizes social propriety. Taoism advocates withdrawal from world involvement. Judaism, Zoroastrianism, Christianity, and Islam all relate the goal of present human existence to the afterlife awaiting man upon death. Meanwhile, it is contended that man is to love and obey God in this life, so as to enter into eternal bliss with him in the next.

The Golden Rule in either a positive or negative form is found in all of the world's living religions (Hume, 1959). Ideal, just, good, and peaceful relationships among men are endorsed—at least until the neighbor turns into an enemy meriting just punishment.

Social Involvement

The various living religions have differing ideas about the structure of society and its betterment. Hinduism, with its caste system, is not oriented toward solution of social ills. Buddhism seeks escape from, rather than confrontation with, social evils; so also does Taoism. Shinto has no goal of social betterment. Confucianism stresses social propriety and natural humanistic obligations toward others; these objectives, however, are not based on divine sanction. Zoroastrianism prescribes good treatment of good people, but ill treatment of the wicked. Presumably, social betterment would occur as a secondary result of the primary Zoroastrian thrust against evil in the world. Judaism has historically tended to be more concerned with the welfare of its own people than that of society in general. The same is true of Islam. Christianity, by contrast, proposes concern for the welfare of all, even to the unique teaching that one should love one's enemies.

The attitude of a religion toward society is related to its claim to universality. The writings of Buddhism, Christianity, and Islam include a plan for a universal missionary effort. Zoroastrianism has historically dropped that orientation. The founder of Christianity claimed his teachings were for all people of all ages, and prophesied that before the end of the world there would be one flock and one shepherd.

Comparative Religious Claims

Those, then, are some of the primary characteristics of the world's living religions. It is beyond the scope of this book to give detailed consideration to the contributions that each has made to human civilization. The limited purpose here is to relate religion to the spiritual experience of Absolute reality, and the comprehension of ultimate meaning.

Each religion claims some kind of communication of God to man, and the faithful adherents of each religion claim the personal experience of God, or Absolute reality. However, we have seen that existing religions offer different interpretations of the nature of God, and of human origin and destiny; they differ also in their explanations for the present human condition of suffering, guilt, and death. These different interpretations lead to different concepts of what constitutes ultimate meaning. How, then, to discriminate the true from the false?

We shall follow a procedure already established. Without in any way presuming to judge the sincerity of the convictions of the adherents of different religions, we shall examine the evidence for the *validity* of the truths which different religions of man propose. We shall begin by delineating those of the world's living religions which have the higher, nobler, and more idealistic claims, and then evaluate the credibility of and the evidence for such claims.

With regard to the nature of deity, the claim of *monotheism* is higher than that of either polytheism or pantheism. The concept of one Supreme Being governing all of creation is a nobler concept than that of various deities bickering among themselves. The concept of an Absolute reality transcendent to the flux of relative reality is similarly a higher concept than that of pantheism, which reduces God to divisible terms and often to confusing, contradictory relationships among the components, whether they be gods or humans.

Hinduism once held to monotheistic belief but historically lapsed into polytheism and pantheism. Zoroastrianism, in proposing the co-eternality and co-existence of two principles of good and evil, was not a pure monotheism, and later developed into polytheism. Only Judaism, Christianity, and Islam can therefore be regarded as truly monotheistic religions.

We have seen that the relationship of God to man has been perceived as either personal or impersonal in religious doctrines. The concept of a *personal* God is a higher aspiration than the concept of him as impersonal, unconcerned, and uncaring about his creatures. Judaism claims a personal God, but has historically tended to stress his power and omnipotence, and the fearful posture man should assume toward God. Islam stresses this attitude even more, as the term *Islam* ("submission") connotes, and adds a capricious unpredictability to God's nature, rendering him less trustworthy. Christianity sees the personal relationship of God to man as Father to children, a Father who is loving, caring, and so concerned for man as to send his only-begotten Son to earth to redeem man and teach him how to live. In those religions claiming a *personal* God, Christianity emerges as having the most idealistic concept of the nature of this personal relationship.

Let us consider next the founders of the monotheistic religions. Judaism was founded by Abraham and given structure by Moses. Islam was founded by Mohammed, who claimed to be Allah's prophet. Jesus Christ alone claimed to be more than man. He identified himself as the Word of God, and equal to God, as the Second Person in the Trinity. It was for this claim that the Jews accused him of blasphemy, and on this account that he was killed. The *claim* of the founder of Christianity, then, was higher than the claims of the founders of the world's other living religions.

What do the monotheistic religions teach about the nature of man and the destiny of society? All propose that human nature is good, while acknowledging that human freedom includes the option of evil behavior. However, the superiority of men to women is evidenced in both Jewish and Islamic beliefs. On the other hand, Jesus Christ taught equality in the dignity of the two sexes. The *call to human perfection* is also greater in Christianity than in Judaism or Islam. Christians are to be totally perfect, as their Heavenly Father is perfect (Matt 5.48). To be Christian is to empty oneself and become more like God, in whose image man was made. Society, too, was more widely encompassed in Christianity than in Judaism or Islam. Judaism was for a specified segment of the population, the "chosen people." Islam lacked any thrust toward the solution of social ills and the betterment of society. By contrast, Christianity was a religion for all people of all ages, of all civilizations, to which all are *universally* called and united. Its social emphasis is on establishing the Kingdom of God on this earth in this life, in the sense of working toward a society based on principles of peace, justice, and love. One is to love one's neighbor with a love equivalent to love of oneself, and to implement this love in action. The Christian is even expected to *love his enemies*. Therefore, with regard to human nature and society, Christianity proposes ethical ideals higher than those of Judaism and Islam.

As for the human condition of suffering, guilt, and death, Islam has no explanation, but rather stresses acceptance and submission. For Islam there is no need of human salvation, nor need for penitence in the Judeo-Christian sense. The Judeo-Christian explanation for the human condition, in terms of the original fall of man, has already been given in outline. (Also see Appendix A.) It can be noted here that Judaism looked forward to a promised Messiah or Redeemer to deliver the Jewish people from bondage, material and spiritual. Jesus Christ claimed to be that Messiah, and furthermore, to be God as well.

What do the monotheistic religions propose about life after death? All three accept the concept of bodily resurrection after death. Islam, however, conceives of paradise in terms of sensual delights. Judaism and Christianity both present heaven in *higher, spiritual* terms, such as "light" and "glory."

In summary: with regard to the nature of God, his relationship to man, the personality of the founder, the nature of man, the historical destiny of society and civilization, the ethical obligations among persons, the human condition, and life after death, Christianity emerges with the highest idealistic *aspirations* and *claims* of all of the world's living religions. Our next step is to examine the tenets of Christianity as to their validity. If these tenets can be demonstrated to be credible, they can be used as the ground for establishing ultimate meaning, as well as the meaning of man.

SUGGESTED READINGS

1. Hume, Robert E. *The World's Living Religions.* N.Y.: Charles Scribner's Sons, 1959. A presentation of the world's living religions, together with a comparison to Christianity and a critique.

2. Schoeps, Hans-Joachim. *The Religions of Mankind*. Garden City: Doubleday & Co., 1968. A historical analysis of the world's religions, living and extinct, of the East and the West.

3. Lewis, John. *Religions of the World Made Simple*. Garden City: Doubleday & Co., 1968. A discussion of psychology, anthropology, and religion, followed by descriptions of and selected readings from the world's religions.

4. Gaer, Joseph. *What the Great Religions Believe*. N.Y.: New American Library, 1963. An account of the basic beliefs of the world's historic religions, with selections from their sacred literatures.

5. Fabro, Cornelio. *God in Exile: Modern Atheism*. Westminster: Newman, 1968. A study of contemporary atheism, from its roots in Cartesian thought to the present day.

5

THE MEANING OF CHRIST

"I am the light of the world . . ." — John 8.12, 9.5.
"I am the Way, the Truth, and the Life . . ." — John 14.16.
"I am the resurrection and the life . . ." — John 11.26.

W E have seen that Christianity presents the highest, most idealistic claims of all of the world's living religions. It remains for these claims to be substantiated. Our approach will be to examine the historical validity of the New Testament, what it tells us of the life and claims of Jesus Christ, and then to see whether or not he validated those claims. We shall then examine the significance of Christ in relation to the human quest for ultimate meaning and the meaning of man.

The New Testament

The first point to be established is the historical validity of the New Testament, and specifically that of the four Gospels; for these writings are our primary source of information about the founder of Christianity. Scholars generally agree that the Gospels were written between 70 and 100 A.D., the earliest being that of Mark, and the last that of John (Bruce, 1974a). The oldest surviving manuscript copy of any of the Gospels is the Rylands Papyrus, recording a section of John's Gospel, and dating from around 135 A.D. This partial copy of John's Gospel, therefore, dates only 35 years or so after the writing of the original, an interval that allows little time for copyists' errors to enter.

Consider also that it was the Jewish custom to memorize the teachings of the Rabbi. Jesus' followers would certainly have reacted if the written Gospels were not in accordance with his teachings (Montgomery, 1969). There were also early Christian writers who verified the Gospel teachings. St. Irenaeus (*c.* 135-203 A.D.), a disciple of St. Polycarp, who in turn was a disciple of the Apostle John, quoted various New Testament passages approximately 1,800 times (Alexander, 1954). St. Ignatius (*c.* 50-109 A.D.), Bishop of Antioch, and friend of Polycarp, was another early writer who quoted the Gospels in his several letters. St. Clement of Rome, the third successor of St. Peter, wrote his epistle to the Corinthians around 95 A.D., citing Gospel teachings. The *Didache* (Teachings of the Twelve Apostles), written around 150 A.D., extensively presents Jesus' teachings (Glimm *et al.* 1947). Tertullian (*c.* 155-220 A.D.) quoted the New Testament about 7,200 times; and St. Clement of Alexandria (*c.* 150-211 A.D.), about 2,400 times (Alexander, 1954). Other early Christian writers who quoted the New Testament are Origen (*c.* 185-254 A.D.; a pupil of Clement of Alexandria), St. Justin Martyr (*c.* 100-165 A.D.), and the latter's pupil, Tatian, the author of the *Diatesseron*, a harmony of the four Gospels, written in 150 A.D. (Alexander, 1954).

Non-Christian writers also give testimony to the historical validity of the person of Jesus Christ and his teachings. Those writers include Josephus (*c.* 70 A.D.), Tacitus (*c.* 55-120 A.D.), Pliny the Younger (*c.* 62-113 A.D.), and Suetonius (*c.* 100 A.D.) (Bruce, 1974b; Fremantle, 1953). It can therefore be concluded that the New Testament is a collection of written documents that has come down to us substantially intact (Bruce, 1974a).

The Promised Redeemer

According to the Judeo-Christian tradition, at the time that original man turned away from God and lost his friendship, God promised a redeemer (Gen 3.15). Throughout Jewish history, the people looked for that savior, later referred to as the "Messiah," a word translated in Hebrew as the "Anointed One" and in Greek as the "Christ." Although the Jews came to anticipate a political figure to save them from the oppression of their enemies, Jesus did not fulfill such an image. Nonetheless, he claimed to be the Messiah, the savior of his people. On one occasion he challenged his disciples to say who he was. Simon Peter replied, "You are the Messiah, the Son of the living God." Jesus replied, "Blest are you, Simon son of John! No mere man has revealed this to you, but my heavenly Father" (Matt 16.17).

In another instance, Jesus converses with a Samaritan woman at Jacob's well. She has come to draw water, and Jesus tells her he can provide the water of eternal life. He then identifies himself as the Messiah (John 4.4-41). To a blind man whom he cures, Jesus says he is the Son of Man, a messianic title (John 9.35-37). Before the synagogue itself, he announces he has fulfilled the messianic prophecy (Luke 4.16-28).

On other occasions, Jesus asserts he has come to save what was lost (Luke 19.10), and he compares himself to the good shepherd, who lays down his life for his sheep (John 10.7-18). Earlier, he was acclaimed by John the Baptist as the "Lamb of God who takes away the sin of the world!"

(John 1.29). In addition, there was the angelic salutation to
Mary that she is to conceive the Son of God (Luke 1.26-38),
Elizabeth's recognition of this event (Luke 1.26-38), as well
as the angel's reassurance to Joseph (Matt 1.18-23), and the
angelic message to the shepherds, heralding Jesus' birth
(Luke 2.8-20).

Even the powers of darkness acknowledged Christ. On
three separate occasions, Jesus exorcised devils that acclaimed him to be the Messiah and the Son of God (Mark
1.23-28 and Luke 4.33-37; Mark 3.11-12 and Luke 4.41;
Matt 8.29, Mark 5.7, and Luke 8.28).

Jesus' Claim to Divinity

But Jesus went further than his claim to be the Messiah.
He also made himself out to be equal to God. To Nicode-
mus, the rabbi who through fear of the Jews came to con-
verse with him at night, Jesus revealed his divinity — "God
so loved the world that he gave his only Son, that whoever
believes in him may not die but may have eternal life"
(John 3.16). Jesus identified himself with the Father, and
claimed power over life and death (John 5.16-47). On one
occasion, Jesus asserted his eternity of existence: "I solemnly declare it, before Abraham came to be, I AM" (John
8.58); and at another time, he reiterated his identification
with God the Father — "The Father and I are one" (John
10.30). The Jews who heard him make such statements fully
understood his words, for we are told that in these instances
they attempted to stone him for blasphemy. At a later time,
Jesus described the end of the world and the manner in
which he, as Son of God, would come in great power and
majesty to judge the world (Matt 24.21-31, Mark 13.19-27,
and Luke 21.25-27).

Jesus used various self-descriptions to communicate the
fact of his divinity. He declared to the man born blind,

whom he healed, "I am the light of the world" (John 9.5); and he also said that those who follow him will not be in darkness (John 12.46). Jesus, before raising Lazarus from the dead, declared to Martha, "I am the resurrection and the life: whoever believes in me, though he should die, will come to life; and whoever is alive and believes in me will never die" (John 11.26). And, on the night before his death, he said to his disciples, "I am the way, the truth, and the life; no one comes to the Father but through me" (John 14.6). Jesus called himself the bread of life: "I myself am the living bread come down from heaven. If anyone eats this bread he shall live forever; the bread I will give is my flesh, for the life of the world" (John 6.54). We are told that the Jews were troubled at hearing that statement, for it appeared cannibalistic to them. Yet Jesus continued, "He who feeds on my flesh and drinks my blood has life eternal, and I will raise him up on the last day. For my flesh is real food and my blood real drink" (John 6.54-55). Little did his listeners understand that he would accomplish this claim at the Last Supper — a topic to which we shall return.

At his trial, the Jews could not validate charges of sedition against Jesus. The only charge substantiated was his claim to be God. To their questioning, he once again affirmed himself to be the Christ, the Son of God; they therefore accused him of blasphemy and judged him liable to death (Matt 26.63-66, Mark 14.61-64). Pilate examined Jesus and found him innocent of all charges of sedition (Luke 23.13-15). He became fearful, however, when the Jews demanded the death sentence for one who claimed to be God (John 19.6-8); and he finally handed Jesus over to be crucified. Even on the cross, Jesus was not free of such accusations; for onlookers and the Jewish leaders dared him, as Son of God, to save himself and come down from the cross (Matt 27.39-43, Mark 15.29-32, and Luke 23.35-

37). As a historical fact evidenced by written texts, therefore, there is no doubt that Jesus Christ claimed to be God, and that for this claim he was put to death.

We come now to the final question: Did Christ prove he was God? Whenever a claim is made, we look to the evidence. What is the evidence presented by Jesus? It was the power he manifested, a power that could only be God's. Jesus accomplished things that only God could. The evidence he gave consisted of miracles, performed for the purpose of proving his claim to be God. He demonstrated his power over nature, over sickness and disease, over the powers of darkness, and over death. Let us consider the evidence.

His Power over Nature

In the order of nature, Jesus' first miracle was performed at the request of his mother, upon the occasion of a wedding feast at Cana. The wine ran out, and Mary, wishing to save the newlyweds from embarrassment, brought their plight to Jesus' attention. He instructed the stewards to fill six stone jars with water, then to draw the liquid. To everyone's amazement, the water was changed to wine (John 2.1-11).

On at least two occasions Jesus fed the large numbers of people who came to hear him. With five loaves and two fish he fed a crowd of five thousand (Matt 14.13-21, Mark 6.31-34, Luke 6.10-17, and John 6.1-15); and from seven loaves and a few fish he fed a crowd of four thousand (Matt 15.32-39, Mark 8.1-10).

The disciples were mostly fishermen. In two instances, Jesus astounded them with his power over nature. At both times they had been unsuccessful through an entire night's labor. At Jesus' word they lower their nets, and their catch is overwhelming (Luke 5.1-11, John 21.1-11). At another time, the disciples had need of money to pay the temple tax. Jesus instructs Peter to go fishing and says that he will find a coin in the first fish he catches, and with this coin he is to pay the tax (Matt 17.23-26).

Two of the more impressive examples of Jesus' power over the forces of nature involved storms on Lake Gene-sareth. On the first occasion, we are told, a great storm arose, such that the disciples' boat was being overwashed by the waves. Alarmed, they awake Jesus, who apparently was asleep. Jesus rises, and at his command the wind and sea become still. Marveling, the disciples exclaim, "What sort of man is this, that even the winds and the sea obey him?" (Matt 8.23-27, Mark 4.35-40, Luke 8.22-25). On the second occasion, the disciples were alone at night when a storm arose. From the shore, Jesus sees their plight and comes to them, walking on the sea. Seeing what they believe to be a ghost, the disciples are further frightened. Jesus identifies himself, whereat impulsive Peter attempts to walk to Jesus on the water. His confidence fails, and Jesus rescues him. As Jesus gets into the boat, the storm ceases, and the disciples are astonished (Matt 14.22-23, Mark 6.45-52, John 6.16-21).

In each of these miracle-stories, there are human characteristics that add to the narrative's credibility. The people at that time acted and reacted very much as we might. For example, when Jesus turned water into wine, the chief steward remarked to the groom that the good wine, contrary to custom, has been kept until now (John 2.10). When Jesus fed the five thousand, they were so impressed with this man who could end their daily labor for food that they wanted to make him king (John 6.15). The evangelists went to the extent of specifying the number of loaves and baskets of frag-

ments remaining *after* the feast. In the one fishing narrative, Peter reluctantly lowers the net once more (Luke 5.5);
and in the other, the disciples give the exact count of fishes
caught (John 21.11). In the one narrative of the storm on
Lake Genesareth, the disciples complain to Jesus that he apparently does not care that they are all about to be drowned
(Mark 4.38). In the other storm incident, impulsive Peter
walks to Jesus on the water, loses his faith in Jesus' word,
and begins to sink (Matt 14.27-31). Earlier, the disciples
had thought they saw a ghost in the night when Jesus comes
to them upon the water (Matt 14.26, Mark 6.49). Would we
not have reacted similarly to such events?

His Power over Disease

In addition to displaying his control over the environmental forces of nature, Jesus showed his miraculous power
over illnesses and disease. He had much compassion for the
sick and the afflicted, particularly the blind and the paralyzed. We are told of several specific occasions on which he
healed the blind (Matt 9.27-38, Mark 8.22-26, John 9.1-41,
Matt 20.29-34, Mark 10.46-52, Luke 18.35-43). One of the
more interesting cures is related at length by John (9.1-41):
Jesus and his disciples encounter a man blind since birth.
The disciples assume he had been punished for sin, but
Jesus tells them that the blindness is rather an occasion for
the works of God to be shown. He then heals the blind man,
a cure that brings on the man the wrath of the Pharisees,
who were hostile to Christ. The man cannot understand
why the Pharisees do not accept the miracle, and tells them,
"It is unheard of that anyone ever gave sight to a person
blind since birth. If this man were not from God, he could
never have done such a thing" (John 9.32-33). The Pharisees, enraged, expel him from the synagogue.

We are told also of several specific paralytic cures Jesus worked in order to demonstrate his divinity; he first forgave the person's sins, then cured the paralysis (Matt 9.1-8, Mark 2.1-2, Luke 5.17-26). At other times, he cured a man who had been paralyzed thirty-eight years (John 1.1-15) and a centurion's servant at a distance (Matt 8.5-13, Luke 7.1-10), as well as a woman bent over for eighteen years (Luke 13.10-17). A woman afflicted with hemorrhage for twelve years was healed by merely touching Jesus' cloak (Matt 9.18-21, Mark 5.21-34, Luke 8.26-39). We read of two occasions on which he cured leprosy (Matt 8.1-4; Mark 1.40-45; Luke 5.12-16, 17.12-19). On the second occasion, only one of ten lepers returned to thank him (Luke 17.12-19). Other specifically narrated cures include a withered hand, healed on the Sabbath, thus angering the legalistic Pharisees (Matt 12.9-13, Mark 3.1-5, Luke 6.6-10); a case of dropsy, again on the Sabbath (Luke 14.1-6); a deaf and dumb man (Matt 15.29-31, Mark 7.31-37); a lunatic (Matt 17.14-20, Mark 9.13-28, Luke 9.37-44); a man whose ear Peter cut off in Jesus' defense (Luke 22.47-53); the ill son of a royal official (John 4.46-54); and Peter's ailing mother-in-law (Matt 8.14-15, Mark 1.29-31, Luke 4.33-37). Indeed, we are told that Jesus healed everyone who came to him, each suffering from some other illness or disease (Matt 8.16-17, Mark 1,32-34, Luke 4.40-41; Matt 9.35; Matt 4.24, Mark 3.10, Luke 6.19; Luke 7.21; Matt 14.34-36, Mark 6.53-56; Matt 15.30-31; Matt 21.14).

His Power over Evil

Jesus also demonstrated his divinity by his power over evil spirits. On three occasions when he exorcised devils, they acknowledged his divinity (Mark 1.23-28, Luke 4.33-37; Matt 8.23-27, Mark 5.1-20, Luke 8.26-39; Luke 4.41,

Mark 3.11-12). In two other instances, he drove the devil out of deaf and dumb men (Matt 9.32-34; Matt 12.22, Luke 11.14); and once he exorcised the devil at a distance (Matt 15.21-28, Mark 7.24-30). (We shall consider the question of the existence of evil spirits in a later chapter regarding occultism.)

His Power over Death

Jesus' strongest evidencing of his divinity is seen in his power over death. We are told of his compassion on the widow of Naim, whose only son had died. Jesus interrupted the burial procession, and said, " 'Young man, I bid you get up.' The dead man sat up and began to speak" (Luke 7.11-17). At another time, he raised from the dead the daughter of a ruler of the synagogue (Matt 9.23-26, Mark 5.35-43, Luke 8.49-56). An event more widely known concerns Lazarus, the brother of Mary and Martha, all close friends of Jesus. In this instance, as in the occasion of the ruler's daughter, Jesus speaks of the deceased as but "asleep." By this word he plainly means death (John 11.11-14), but he uses it to emphasize the ease with which divine power can wake one from the dead, and possibly also to mean that bodily death is temporary (like sleep) until the resurrection. Jesus also tells his listeners that he was glad he was not with Lazarus when he died, so that they may come to believe in him in view of what he was about to do (John 11.15). At Lazarus' tomb, we meet again an expression of the human compassion of Christ, who weeps over the death of his friend (John 11.15). Here also we find a natural, "human" response on the part of his observers. When Jesus tells them to remove the stone, Martha objects, "Lord, it has been four days now; surely there will be a stench!" (John 11.39). However, Jesus, after a prayer to his heavenly Father, calls for Lazarus to come forth from the tomb. "The dead man came out, bound hand and foot with linen strips, his face wrapped in a cloth. 'Untie him,' Jesus told them, 'and let him go free'" (John 11.44). This miracle, of course, alarmed the Pharisees to the extent that they plotted to kill Jesus, fearing that "the whole world will believe in him" (John 11.48).

His Resurrection

The miracles described thus far, performed publicly before crowds of people, would themselves be sufficient to establish and verify Jesus' claim to be divine. He went even further, however, to prophesy victory over his own death (John 2.19-22). St. Paul tells Christians that if Christ did not resurrect from the dead, their faith is worthless (1 Cor 15.16), for Christ came to redeem man from sin and the consequence of sin, death. The greatest miracle Jesus performed, therefore, was his own resurrection, the ultimate proof that he was God (Matt 28, Mark 16, Luke 24, and John 20 and 21; 1 Cor 15.1-8).

The Gospels record several significant events related to the resurrection of Christ. We are told of the women who, at dawn on the first day of the week, go to anoint the body of Jesus. In their concern, they did not think about the problem of moving the entrance stone—another example of the human element in the Gospel narratives. But upon arriving they find the stone rolled back, and the tomb empty (Matt 28.1, Mark 16.1-4, Luke 24.1-2, John 20.1). They are frightened at the appearance of an angel, who reassures them that Christ has indeed risen and will appear before them in Galilee (Matt 28.1-7, Mark 16.1-8, Luke 24.1-8, John 20.1-2). We are told also that the guards, posted earlier at the tomb to prevent Jesus' friends from stealing the body and falsely claiming his resurrection (Matt 26.62-66), are terrified by the vision of the angel and paralyzed with fear (Matt 28.4). It is significant that the women were the first to hear of the risen Christ. It was they who informed the disciples. These same women had remained faithfully by the cross (John 19.25-27) when all of the disciples except John had abandoned Jesus (Matt 26.56).

Mary Magdalene excitedly told Peter and John of the news (John 20.2), whereafter the two men ran to the tomb to see for themselves. Here again we come upon human elements in the Gospel story. John, the younger of the two, runs faster than Peter and arrives at the tomb before him. However, out of deference, John waits and allows Peter to enter the tomb first (John 20.3-10). John's Gospel meticulously describes the empty tomb, pointing out that the head cloth was not lying with the other linens but was rather folded and set apart. The men then depart, satisfied that the women's report was true. Mary Magdalene, however, still confused and upset by the disappearance of Jesus' body, is not yet convinced of his resurrection. She believes the body has been stolen. Jesus appears before her near the tomb, but in her tears she does not recognize him, thinking he is a gardener. He asks her why she weeps, and she replies, "Sir, if you are the one who carried him off, tell me where you have laid him and I will take him away" (John 20.15); as if she could carry a heavy corpse! It is then that Jesus pronounces her name, and immediately Mary recognizes him. In her joy she apparently embraces Jesus, for he tells her not to cling to him (John 20.17). Jesus tells Mary to inform his disciples, and she does so: but they did not at first believe her (Matt 16.10-11).

Meanwhile, some of the guards reported their experience to the chief priests, who decide to bribe the men to tell the people that Jesus' disciples came and stole his body (Matt 28.11-15).

We read of another encounter of the resurrected Jesus with two disciples, on the way to Emmaus (Luke 24.13-32). Here, as with Mary Magdalene, he appears unrecognized. In the ensuing conversation, Jesus pretends ignorance of recent events, and the two men narrate the crucifixion and the reported resurrection, about which they are perplexed. Jesus gently reprimands them for their unbelief, and, beginning with Moses and all of the prophets, he interprets the scriptural passages concerning himself—a marvelous conversation. As they neared Emmaus, Jesus acts as if he were going farther, but they persuade him to sup with them. It was in the breaking of the bread that they recognized Jesus, whereupon he vanished from their sight (Luke 24.31-32). Excitedly, they exclaim, "Were not our hearts burning inside us as he talked to us on the road and explained the Scriptures to us?" (Luke 24.32).

Another post-resurrection story is that concerning Thomas, one of the Apostles. After Jesus' death, the disciples, for fear of the Jews, kept themselves hidden behind locked doors. Jesus suddenly appeared to them, thoroughly frightening them, for they thought they saw a spirit (Luke 24.36-43, John 20.19-23). Jesus reassures them to be at peace, then invites them to feel his hands and feet, and asks them for food to eat, so that he can convince them he has truly risen from the dead. He then proceeds to confer upon them the power to forgive sins (John 20.21-23). It happened that Thomas was not with them, and he refused, later, to believe their testimony (John 20.24-25), stating he would never believe unless he could place his finger in the place of the nails, and his hand into Jesus' side, the place of the wound caused by a soldier's lance while Jesus had hung on the cross (John 19.34). Jesus again appeared to his disciples: this time while Thomas is present. He invites Thomas to touch him in his wounds, whereupon Thomas exclaims his faith in the risen Christ (John 20.20-29). Jesus' next statement to Thomas has important significance for Christians of today: " 'You become a believer because you saw me. Blest are they who have not seen and have believed' " (John 20.29).

At another time, Jesus encounters his disciples while they are fishing. After a fruitless night, as dawn broke, they saw Jesus standing on the beach. Again, as in previous instances, we are told they did not recognize him. Jesus asked them about their fishing, and tells them to cast the net again. It becomes so heavy with fish that they cannot pull it up. Thanks to this miracle, John recognizes Christ and tells Peter. Peter impulsively leaps into the sea and swims to land, followed by the others dragging the net. John makes two detailed observations: the catch numbers one hundred fifty-three, and the net amazingly was not torn by the load. The disciples breakfast with Jesus on the meal he has already prepared for them. Then, Jesus engages Peter in conversation and instructs him three times to feed his flock, an emphasis on Peter's leadership and authority, reminiscent of the time Jesus referred to Peter as the rock on which he would build his church, and to whom he would give the keys to heaven (Matt 16.18-19).

After his resurrection, Jesus spent forty days with his disciples (Acts 1.3), instructing them to baptize and to teach all nations (Matt 28.19-20). He also told them to wait for the coming of the Holy Spirit (Luke 24.49, Acts 1.4-5). Finally, the time came for him to leave. We are told he was lifted up before them and a cloud took him from their sight. While they were gazing up into the heavens, two men in white (angels?) chided them for standing there so long, and told them Jesus would return in the same manner in which he had left (Acts 1.9-12).

The Gift of Faith

We have surveyed the evidence that Jesus Christ claimed to be the Messiah, and to be God as well. We cited the miracles performed publicly as substantiation of his claim. We saw that for his claim to be God he was put to death, but that he conquered death through his resurrection, the crowning proof of his divinity. We observed the skepticism of his disciples, to whom he had to give many proofs that he had indeed risen from the dead (Acts 1.3). Through the Gospel narratives, we observed the authentically human reactions of the people in Jesus' day, behavior with which one can easily identify. The skepticism, fears, sufferings, joys, and hopes of Jesus' followers are not so unlike the experiences in our own lives; and it is possible and often easy to transcend time and project ourselves to his day. The New Testament narratives can thus become alive and exciting.

But it requires more than a merely rational examination of the Gospels to arrive at a belief in the divinity of Jesus Christ. That belief rests on a faith that only God can give; for that reason, Christians refer to their faith as a gift. Furthermore, Christians believe that God will bestow this gift, an illuminating insight, on all who openly and earnestly seek it. It is the hope of Christians that modern-day wise men will come to follow his star, to arrive at an understanding and acceptance of the Word made flesh, who came that mankind might have life, and have it more abundantly (John 1.1-14, 10.10).

We have compared the world's living religions and have seen that Christianity presents the highest *aspirations*, and that its founder, Jesus Christ, made the highest *claims*. We studied the credibility of the historical Gospel account, as well as the evidence that Christ presented in support of his unique claim to be God. Even though the evidence is, to the Christian, overwhelming, the personal acceptance of Jesus Christ as God and savior finally rests on the gift of Christian faith, a gift only God can give, but which can be obtained by all who honestly and sincerely seek it.

The Significance of Jesus

We have already noted that Jesus claimed to be the Son of God, and equal to God. He further developed this claim in his revelation of the Trinity. Jesus taught that there are three persons in God, the Father, the Son, and the Holy Spirit, in whose name his disciples were to baptize all nations (Matt 28.19). We saw also that, as Son of God and the second Person in the Trinity, Jesus proclaimed his mission as savior and redeemer of mankind. If Jesus is God, and if he truly was, as he claimed to be, mankind's savior, then it follows that the scriptural story of man's rebellion against God is a still-valid explanation of the present human condition.

The steps we are following here are these: We start with Jesus Christ as a person who historically existed, then examine the validity of his claim about his identity, and use the facts thus ascertained to confirm the scriptural revelation of the original "fall" of man, a fall that was the occasion for God's becoming incarnate in order to redeem mankind (John 1.1-14). Since Christ chose to confirm and fulfill the Jewish tradition, it would follow, too, that among the pre-Christian revelations made by God and contained in the various religions of antiquity, it was the Jewish revelation, embodied in the Old Testament, that was favored as having the fullest and most complete interpretation of God's initial covenant with man.

Burghardt (1974) presents a concise summary of the Christian perspective on the fall of man and his redemption by God; and in that connection he points out four significant facts concerning the history of mankind. First, in God's original plan, there were perfect unity and tranquillity in human existence. Man was harmoniously related to himself, to his fellow man, to nature, and to God. Second, this fourfold unity was disrupted when original man rebelled against God, a sin that brought on the present human condition. Third, God restored unity by becoming man, thereby reconciling man to God, and enabling man, through divine grace, to overcome the fourfold rupture brought about by the original rebellion against God.

These observations are worth examining closely. The primeval story of the creation of man is related in Genesis, the first book of the Old Testament scriptures. God established a garden of delight (Eden, Paradise) for the first human beings he created. He permitted them to partake of all its fruits except that of one tree, the tree of knowledge of good and evil. The serpent tempted Eve by telling her that the reason God forbade that particular fruit was that it would give her and Adam powers equivalent to God's. Eve succumbed to this temptation, and so did Adam. They were consequently banished by God from the garden (Genesis 1-3). The concept of the "fall of man" is found in all ancient theistic theologies. The common theme is that God created man with intelligence and freedom, but man abused his freedom by turning away from God and was subsequently punished. The resulting alienation of man from God is the root of the present human condition, one of suffering, guilt, and death.

God, however, had compassion on man. In the same breath of pronouncing punishment, God promised redemption. A future son of woman was to crush the head of Satan (Genesis 3.14-15). This future redeemer was Jesus Christ, the Word made flesh (John 1.14, 3.16). God would become man to redeem man, to restore him to the state of justice or sanctifying grace, to reconcile him once more with divine love, and thus to enable man to accomplish his original destiny of immortal life with God.°

Christians believe that Jesus Christ was the Messiah, the one who came to take away the sin of the world (John 1.29). He achieved this redemption by his passion and death on the cross. Why God the Son, incarnate, chose that means of showing redemptive love is a mystery, for God could have achieved it in some other manner. Nevertheless, Jesus' redemptive act succeeds in communicating two profound truths, the depth of God's love (John 3.16), and the hideousness of sin (1 Peter 2.22-24). The theme of redemption from sin was constant, not only in the four Gospels, but also in the additional writings of the Apostles. John reiterates the fact that Jesus offered Himself for the sin of the world (1 John 2.1-20). Peter stresses the value of Christ's blood as greater than that of silver or gold (1 Peter 1.18-19). Paul speaks of mankind's being rescued from the power of darkness (Col 1.13-14), and of Christ as the mediator between God and man (1 Tim 2.5-6).

Thus we finally came to the nature of ultimate meaning, arrived at by an analysis of the Christian perspective, yet nonetheless pertaining to all of humanity: for the Christian message is intended for all mankind. It is simply the "gos-

---

°A further analysis of the Adam and Eve story can be found in Appendix A, which includes also a comparison of the Christian interpretation with that of atheistic humanism.

pel" *(good news)* that God became incarnate in the person of Jesus Christ, for the purpose of restoring the initial friendship that original man enjoyed with God and then lost. It is the message that through the redemptive love of God man need no longer be alienated from God, from himself, from his fellow man, or from nature. For even though man will never recover the original natural paradise he once enjoyed, the grace and strength received from Christ's redemptive love will be sufficient to enable every person to endure the hardships and sufferings of the human condition. That is the point of St. Augustine's well-known phrase: "Happy fault which won for us such a meritorious Redeemer!" Christ's redemptive love also helps us in a positive way by encouraging the spirit of selflessness to alleviate the sufferings of our fellow man.

Moreover, those sorrows and tragedies over which man has no control are thought by Christians to take on new meaning when offered in prayer and penance for personal sin. The future becomes bright with new joy, as one works toward the Kingdom of God on earth, one of justice, peace, and love, while anticipating an immortal afterlife with God forever.

Jesus in the Eucharist. Jesus, knowing that his message was for all ages, and that only his generation would have the privilege of seeing and hearing him, went further to provide mankind the strength and solace that his followers received. Jesus, again from the depths of Divine Love, gave himself to all people in a unique and perpetual manner. Recall the occasion on which Jesus multiplied five loaves and two fish to feed the multitude of five thousand (Matt 14.13-21, Mark 6.31-34, Luke 9.10-17, John 6.1-15). At a later time, Jesus, referring to that event, admonishes his listeners not to work for perishable food, but rather to seek the food of eternal life, a food that he will give them (John 6.26-27). They entreat him for this food, and Jesus replies, "I myself am the living bread come down from heaven. If anyone eats this bread he shall live forever; the bread I will give is my flesh, for the life of the world" (John 6.51). The Jews are disturbed by these words, and wonder how a man can give his flesh to eat. Jesus continues, "Let me solemnly assure you, if you do not eat the flesh of the Son of Man and drink his blood, you have no life in you. He who feeds on my flesh and drinks my blood has life eternal, and I will raise him up on the last day. For my flesh is real food, and my blood real drink. The man who feeds on my flesh and drinks my blood remains in me, and I in him" (John 6.53-56). Jesus' listeners are further upset; we are told that many of his disciples left him. Jesus, instead of recalling them, turned to the twelve, asking, "Do you want to leave me, too?" (John 6.67). Whereupon Peter responds with a magnificent profession of faith, "Lord, to whom shall we go? You have the words of eternal life. We have come to believe; we are convinced that you are God's holy one" (John 6.68). Peter did not understand how Jesus would give men his flesh, but he had the faith to believe that in some way Jesus could, and would.

That moment came on the evening before Christ died, when he had his last meal with his disciples. Jesus took bread, blessed it, broke it, and gave it to his disciples, telling them to eat of it, for it was his body. Likewise, he blessed some wine, telling them to drink of it, for it was his blood, which was to be shed for the forgiveness of sin. And, most significantly, he instructed them to repeat his action in memory of him (Matt 26.26-28, Mark 14.22-24, Luke 22.19-20, John 22.19-20). Thus Christ, the Son of God, performed by Divine power another miracle, the changing of bread and wine into his own body and blood. To all appearances, visually and chemically, the bread and wine did not appear to change; but intrinsically, in some miraculous manner, they were now indeed the body and blood of Christ. If one accepts the other miracles of Christ, then it is not difficult to accept this one. If the human body can, through natural processes, convert bread and wine into living tissue, then why cannot Jesus, as God, do so in a miraculous manner?

The early Christians took Jesus' teaching literally, and believed that Christ also gave his Apostles that same power, so that from their time on, Jesus was to be with men always in the consecrated bread and wine. Indeed, Paul warned the Christians of his day: "This means that whoever eats the bread or drinks the cup of the Lord unworthily sins against the body and blood of the Lord" (1 Cor 11.27). The early Christian community commemorated this eucharistic ("thankful") meal (Acts 2.42; 20.7), which Paul describes as the sign of unity among them (1 Cor 10.17). And in the first centuries of Christian history, the Church Fathers wrote of the literal partaking of the body and blood of Christ in the consecrated bread and wine (Glimm *et al.*, 1946). Among Christians today, however, there are many who consider Jesus' words at the Last Supper symbolic rather than literal in meaning. The latter understanding was the common belief in the early centuries of Christianity; and that original belief is still held today in traditional Catholicism and traditional Protestantism.

Second to his becoming incarnate and redeeming mankind from sin, God's gift of himself in the Eucharist is the most wondrous. If Christians truly comprehended the significance of this gift, their behavior would be so exemplary as to attract the entire world to the Christian faith.

Jesus' Second Coming. Another teaching of Christ that gives meaning to the life of the Christian was his promise to "come again." The night before he died, Jesus detected his disciples' sadness, and promised them that he would prepare a place for them, and would come again to take them there, to be with him (John 14.1-3). He had previously referred to a second coming at the end of the world (Matt 24.21-31, Mark 13.19-27, Luke 21.25-27). The early Christians thought the latter event would occur with the destruction of Jerusalem, and they eagerly anticipated this second coming, or "Parousia" (the Greek term).

These are the more important factors that constituted ultimate meaning for the early Christians—their redemption from past sin by Jesus' sacrifice on the cross, the gift of God himself in the Eucharist to strengthen their present lives, and their future reunion with Jesus forever in his heavenly Kingdom. For the Christian, these truths give significance to the totality of time—the past, the present, and the future.

The four-fold alienation of man from God, man from man, man from himself, and man from nature had been remedied by Jesus Christ, who reconciled man with God and healed the breach of alienation. The human condition of suffering, pain, guilt, and death became meaningful in the shadow of the cross and in the light of the resurrection.

Doctrine of the Cross

As we have seen, Jesus redeemed humankind and reconciled all with the Father, but did not restore the initial state of happiness in Eden. Whereas the human condition of suffering, guilt, and death remains, it is now endurable. Essential to this fact is Jesus' teaching on the necessity for each Christian to carry a personal cross of suffering, tragedy, and hardship in the attempt to reach moral perfection. Jesus told his hearers, "If a man wishes to come after me, he must deny his very self, take up his cross, and follow in my steps.

Whoever would preserve his life will lose it, but whoever loses his life for my sake and the gospel's will preserve it. What profit does a man show who gains the whole world and destroys himself in the process?" (Mark 8.35-36; also Matt 16.24-27, Luke 9.23-26). "He who will not take up his cross and come after me is not worthy of me. He who seeks himself brings himself to ruin, whereas he who brings himself to nought for me discovers who he is" (Matt 10.38-39; also Luke 14.27). Jesus' followers embraced their cross willingly and in love. Paul writes, "I have been crucified with Christ, and the life I live now is not my own; Christ is living in me. I still live my human life, but it is a life of faith in the Son of God, who loved me and gave himself for me" (Gal 2.19-20). Again, "May I never boast of anything but the cross of our Lord Jesus Christ! Through it the world has been crucified to me and I to the world" (Gal 6.14). Jesus reassures us of help in carrying our cross. "Come to me, all you who are weary and find life burdensome, and I will refresh you. Take my yoke upon your shoulders and learn from me, for I am gentle and humble of heart. Your souls will find rest, for my yoke is easy and my burden light" (Matt 11.28-30).

Without the gift of Christian faith, the doctrine of the cross is incomprehensible. Paul observes, "Jews demand 'signs' and Greeks look for 'wisdom,' but we preach Christ crucified—a stumbling block to Jews, and an absurdity to Gentiles, but to those who are called, Jews and Greeks alike, Christ the power of God and the wisdom of God. For God's folly is wiser than men, and his weakness more powerful than men" (1 Cor 1.22-25).

What Jesus expects of his followers is indeed much. "In a word, you must be made perfect as your heavenly Father is perfect" (Matt 5.48). We have seen the means he has given men to enable them to reach such perfection. Paul sums it up in another way: "My point is that you should live in accord with the spirit and you will not yield to the cravings of the flesh. The flesh lusts against the spirit and the spirit against the flesh; the two are directly opposed. This is why you do not do what your will intends. If you are guided by the spirit, you are not under the law. It is obvious what proceeds from the flesh: lewd conduct, impurity, licentiousness, idolatry, sorcery, hostilities, bickering, jealousy, outbursts of rage, selfish rivalries, dissensions, factions, envy, drunkenness, and the like. I warn you, as I have warned you before: those who do such things will not inherit the Kingdom of God! In contrast, the fruit of the spirit is love, joy, peace, patient endurance, kindness, generosity, faith, mildness, and chastity. Against such there is no law! Those who belong to Christ Jesus have crucified their flesh with its passions and desires. Since we live by the spirit, let us follow the spirit's lead" (Gal 5.16-26).

Christian Humanism

Earlier in this book we examined the different versions of humanism and their attempts to explain the meaning of man. One may summarize the Christian perspective on the human condition and on human significance as follows: (1) Man was made in the image of God and was originally intended to live in friendship with God. (2) Man turned away from God, meriting the human condition of pain, suffering, evil, and death. (3) These hallmarks of the human condition are "non-rational," that is, "unreasonable," or against the natural human propensity toward survival, health, goodness, and happiness. (4) Explanations on the level of reason, or philosophy, including evolution and atheistic humanism, are therefore bound to fail, precisely because the facts to be explained are "unreasonable," or beyond natural analysis. (5) The Christian alternative to explain the human condition is based on divine revelation, as recorded in the Scriptures. (6) Whether one accepts the Christian interpretation or the atheistic-humanistic explanation of the Fall of Man and the present human condition depends ultimately on whether or not one believes in the existence of God and divine revelation as recorded in the Scriptures. (7) Faith in divine revelation is a gift of God, accessible to all (Hammes, 1971, ch. 15). (8) The human condition has been remedied, though not removed, by the Incarnate Word and by redemption. Man is consoled by the promise of eternal happiness after death; and lifetime on earth is but a moment when compared to that eternal existence. (9) Ultimate meaning for man is personified in Jesus Christ, the Second Person of the Blessed Trinity incarnate in human flesh, true God and true man, the gift of the Father. (10) In response to this Divine Love, man in this life is to know and to love God, giving of himself in service to his fellow man. The Christian is to put on Christ (Gal 3.27) in bringing peace, love, and justice to all he encounters, so that eventually God's kingdom will come to the world. Christian humanism, therefore, provides a complete answer to the human search for meaning.*

The Promise of the Spirit

Jesus Christ left his followers something besides the gift of himself in the Eucharist. In his plan to ensure the accurate transmission of his teachings to others of his generation

---

*For additional commentaries, the reader is referred to such works as Armerding (1968), Barbour (1966), Bube (1968), Cell (1967), Darling (1969), Guinness (1973), Hammes (1971), Raughley (1962), Schilling (1969), and Williams (1965).

and generations to come, he promised to send his Apostles the Holy Spirit, the Third Person of the Trinity. "I will ask the Father, and he will give you another Paraclete—to be with you always; the Spirit of truth, whom the world cannot accept, since it neither sees him nor recognizes him; but you can recognize him because he remains with you and will be within you" (John 14.16-17). "The Paraclete, the Holy Spirit whom the Father will send in my name, will instruct you in everything, and remind you of all that I told you" (John 14.26). The fulfillment of the promise of the Spirit has an important bearing on the Christian perspective on the human condition—the subject of the next chapter.

SUGGESTED READINGS

1. The New Testament: it is helpful to read and compare the various translations for a better appreciation of the faith of the early Christians. *The New American Bible* (N.Y.: P. J. Kenedy and Sons, 1970); *The New Testament of the Jerusalem Bible* (Garden City: Doubleday & Co., 1969); *The New English Bible* (N.Y.: Oxford University Press, 1970); *The Living Bible* (Wheaton, Ill.: Tyndale, 1971).

2. Bruce, F.F. *The New Testament Documents: Are They Reliable?* Downers Grove: InterVarsity Press, 1974. A defense of the historical validity of the documents of the New Testament.

3. Bruce, F.F. *Jesus and Christian Origins outside the New Testament.* Grand Rapids: Wm. B. Eerdmans Publishing Co., 1974. Evidence from Jewish and Roman writers of the historical validity of Jesus Christ, his early followers, and the events recorded in the New Testament.

4. Perrin, Norman. *Rediscovering the Teachings of Jesus.* Harper & Row, 1967. A defense of the historical validity of the New Testament against biblical "form critics."

5. Glimm, F., J. Marique, and G. Walsh, eds. *The Fathers of the Church: The Apostolic Fathers.* N.Y.: Cima, 1947. Selections from early Christian authors during the first three centuries following Christ.

6. Fremantle, A., ed. *A Treasury of Early Christianity.* N.Y.: Viking, 1953. Chosen works from Christian writers spanning the first 600 years of Christianity.

7. Alexander, A.F. *College Apologetics.* Chicago: Regnery, 1954. A defense of the historical validity of the New Testament and of the Christian revelation. A separate part presents the traditional Catholic perspective.

8. Goodier, A. *The Passion and Death of Our Lord Jesus Christ.* N.Y.: Kenedy, 1944. A moving account of the events surrounding the last days of Jesus.

6

THE MEANING OF THE HOLY SPIRIT

"Your body is the temple of the Holy Spirit, who is in you since you received him from God" — 1 Cor 6.19.

THERE are two ways in which Jesus planned to be with his followers always—in the Eucharist and in the Holy Spirit. The Eucharist was the gift of himself; the Holy Spirit was the gift of the Third Person in the Trinity. Let us consider further the personality of the Holy Spirit in relation to the Christian outlook on the meaning of human existence.

The Holy Spirit in the Scriptures

In the Old Testament, the Holy Spirit is described in the Book of Isaiah as being poured out upon men, from on high (Is 32.14-18; 44.1-4; 59.21). The prophet Joel writes, "In the days to come—it is the Lord who speaks—I will pour out my spirit on all mankind. Their sons and daughters shall prophesy, your young men shall see visions, your old men shall dream dreams" (Joel 3.1-2). Peter cited these verses in reference to the disciples' reception of the Holy Spirit on Pentecost (Acts 2.1-8). The Old Testament contains innumerable passages referring to the "spirit of God" (e.g., Gen 1.48; Num 24.2; 2 Chron 15.1; 24.20; and Job 33.4) and to the "spirit of the Lord" (e.g., Judges 6.34; 14.6; 11.6; 16.13; Is 11.2; and Ezek 11.5).

In the New Testament, the Holy Spirit is revealed by Christ to be the Third Person in the Trinity. Jesus instructed his disciples, "Go, therefore, make disciples of all the nations; baptize them in the name of the Father and of the Son and of the Holy Spirit . . ." (Matt 28.19). The nature of the Trinity was earlier manifested in Jesus' baptism by John. "As soon as Jesus was baptized he came up from the water, and suddenly the heavens opened and he saw the Spirit of God descending like a dove and coming down on him. And a voice spoke from heaven, 'This is my Son, the Beloved; my favor rests on him'" (Matt 3.16-17). From then to the present day, in Christian religious art, the dove has been a common symbol of the Holy Spirit.

The Spirit Is Divine Love

Theologically considered, each person in the Trinity has been traditionally associated with a particular relationship to the world and to men. God the Father is associated with creation, God the Son with redemption, and God the Holy Spirit with sanctification. The Holy Spirit played a dominant role (a) in the Incarnation of Christ, (b) in the sanctification of those who followed him, and (c) in the preservation of his teachings. Let us consider these three "works" of the Holy Spirit.

The Holy Spirit is the bond of love between Father and Son; and the Father's giving of his Son to the world, as the Word made flesh (John 1.14), was motivated by Divine Love, i.e., by the Holy Spirit (John 3.16). God became incarnate by asking a woman to conceive and give birth to him; and God accomplished it expressly through the Holy Spirit. Luke narrates this event: "In the sixth month the angel Gabriel was sent by God to a town in Galilee called Nazareth, to a virgin betrothed to a man named Joseph, of the House of David; and the virgin's name was Mary. He went in and said to her, 'Rejoice, so highly favored! The Lord is with you.' She was deeply disturbed by these words and asked herself what this greeting could mean, but the angel said to her. 'Mary, do not be afraid; you have won God's favor. Listen! You are to conceive and bear a son, and you must name him Jesus. He will be great and will be called Son of the Most High. The Lord God will give him the throne of his ancestor David; he will rule over the House of Jacob for ever and his reign will have no end.' Mary said to the angel, 'But how can this come about, since I am a virgin?' 'The Holy Spirit will come upon you,' the angel answered, 'and power of the Most High will cover you with its shadow. And so the child will be holy and will be called Son of God' " (Luke 1.26-35).

Since God chose to become flesh through a woman, Mary is introduced as a necessary part of the Incarnation plan. Her freely given consent made that plan a reality. One can only imagine the plenitude of grace and love that was Mary's. The Holy Spirit, the spirit of Divine Love, espoused Mary, and through his power the Word became flesh. Her unique role in the eternal plan of redemption is the reason why Christians have venerated Mary through the ages.

Second, the Holy Spirit is the source of sanctification to those who have received him. Justification, or grace, was won for mankind by Christ, and is available to all through the Holy Spirit. Through grace, man participates in divine life, becoming a child of God, an heir to heaven (John 1.12; Rom 8.14-17), and, as Paul wrote, temples of God: "Didn't you realize that you were God's temple and that the Spirit of God was living among you? If anybody should destroy the temple of God, God will destroy him, because the temple of God is sacred; and you are that temple" (1 Cor 3.16-17).

The "gifts" commonly attributed to the Holy Spirit include wisdom, understanding, counsel, strength, knowledge, and fear of the Lord (Is 11.2-3), and his "fruits" are love, joy, peace, patience, kindness, goodness, trustfulness, gentleness, and chastity (Gal 5.22-23). The so-called charismatic gifts of the Holy Spirit include preaching, healing, miraculous powers, prophecy, distinguishing of spirits, speaking in tongues, and interpretation of tongues (1 Cor 12.7-11).

Third, the Holy Spirit is instrumental in preserving Christ's teachings for generations to follow. We have seen that at the Last Supper, Jesus promised to send the Holy Spirit. "I shall ask the Father, and he will give you another Advocate to be with you forever, that Spirit of truth whom the world can never receive since it neither sees him nor knows him . . ." (John 14.16-17); "but the Advocate, the Holy Spirit, whom the Father will send in my name, will teach you everything and remind you of all I have said to you" (John 14.26). After his death and resurrection, Jesus again mentioned his promise: "John baptized you with water, but you, not many days from now, will be baptized with the Holy Spirit" (Acts 1.5); "you will receive power when the Holy Spirit comes on you, and then you will be my witnesses not only in Jerusalem but throughout Judea and Samaria, and indeed to the ends of the earth" (Acts 1.8).

On Pentecost, fifty days after Jesus' death, the Holy Spirit descended upon Mary, the mother of Jesus, and the Apostles, as they were gathered together to await him: ". . . when suddenly they heard what sounded like a powerful wind from heaven, the noise of which filled the entire house in which they were sitting; and something appeared to them that seemed like tongues of fire; these separated and came to rest on the head of each of them. They were all filled with the Holy Spirit, and began to speak foreign languages as the Spirit gave them the gift of speech" (Acts 2.2-4). We are told that in the power of the Holy Spirit, Peter went out and converted three thousand persons that very day (Acts 2.41).

Authority of the Spirit

Both traditional Protestantism and Catholicism believe that the Holy Spirit resides within those who love God and wish to respond to Christ's teachings. Catholicism goes further to assert that the Holy Spirit resides also in the authoritative teaching of the Apostles, and in their successors to this day. This religious and moral authority was initially invested by Christ. On one occasion, Jesus said to Peter, "You are Peter and on this rock I will build my Church. And the gates of the underworld can never hold out against it. I will give you the keys of the kingdom of heaven: whatever you bind on earth will be bound in heaven; whatever you loose on earth will be loosed in heaven" (Matt 16.19).

This element of divine authority, together with the human element of membership in the Church, can be seen as one interlocking reality, mirroring the close union of the divine and the human in Jesus Christ, the founder of the Church (Abbott, 1969, "The Church," sec. 8, p. 22). The concept of the moral authority of the Church is replete in the writings of the Church Fathers during the first 400 years of Christianity. St. Clement, the third successor to St. Peter, wrote a letter to the Corinthians about 97 A.D., in which he mentions that the Apostles appointed bishops as their successors, and these passed on the succession (Glimm *et al.*, 1946). St. Ignatius, martyred around 109 A.D., wrote several beautiful letters to the Ephesians, Magnesians, Trallians, Romans, Philadelphians, and Smyrnans, urging his fellow Christians to regard the bishops as they would Christ. St. Irenaeus, martyred about 190 A.D., was a disciple of St. Polycarp, who in turn was a disciple of John the Apostle. Irenaeus, in a work entitled "Against the Fake Gnosis," speaks of the succession of bishops from Peter and Paul, and lists Peter's successors, the early popes, down to the year 175 A.D., when Pope Eleutherious ruled (Fremantle, 1953). Peter's first three successors, Linus, Anacletus (or Cletus), and Clement, reigned during the lifetime of John the Apostle. St. Cyprian, martyred in 258 A.D., wrote of the primacy of Peter and Peter's successor, as well as of the duty of Christians to follow their teachings as authoritative doctrine (Fremantle, 1953). In 400 A.D., St. Augustine compiled a list of Peter's successors to his day (Alexander, 1954). The complete listing, from Peter to Paul VI, can be found in *The World Almanac and Book of Facts* (1977). A contemporary exposition of the divine authority that Christ invested in Peter and the Apostles, and which the Holy Spirit has preserved in their successors, can be found in the documents of Vatican Council II (specifically sections 2 and 3 of the "Decree on Ecumenism," and section 14 of the "Declaration on Religious Freedom": Abbott, 1966).

The Body of Christ

The Holy Spirit plays an important role in the human element of the Church, its members on earth. We have seen that Christ's second great commandment was love of neighbor (Matt 22.39), which implies a specifically Christian community. Indeed, Christians are to be an extension of

Christ in the world. Jesus used the image of a vine to illustrate the closeness he desired to have with his followers: "I
am the vine, you are the branches. Whoever remains in me,
with me in him, bears fruit in plenty . . ." (John 15.5). He
prayed to his Father for unity among "his own"; "May they
all be one. Father, may they be one in us, as you are in me
and I am in you. . . . May they be so completely one that
the world will realize that it was you who sent me and that I
have loved them as much as you have loved me" (John
17.21, 23). On the occasion of Paul's conversion, Jesus identified himself with the Christians whom Paul was persecuting: "Suddenly, as he was traveling to Damascus and just
before he reached that city, there came a light from heaven
all round him. He fell to the ground, and then he heard a
voice saying, 'Saul, Saul, why are you persecuting me?'
'Who are you, Lord?' he asked, and the voice answered, 'I
am Jesus, and you are persecuting me' " (Acts 9.3-6). In his
writings, Paul describes the Church as the body of Christ:
"Now the Church is his body, he is its head" (Col 1.18);
"And may the peace of Christ reign in your hearts, because
it is for this that you were called together as parts of one
body" (Col 3.15); ". . . so all of us, in union with Christ,
form one body, and as parts of it we belong to each other"
(Romans 12.4-6). With reference to the Eucharist, Paul
writes, "And is not the bread we break a sharing in the body
of Christ? Because the loaf of bread is one, we, many
though we are, are one body, for we all partake of the one
loaf" (1 Cor 10.16-17; also 12.12-13, 26-27). Stressing the
unity of the Church, Paul urges, "Do all you can to preserve
the unity of the Spirit by the peace that binds you together.
There is one Body, one Spirit, just as you were all called
into one and the same hope when you were called. There is
one Lord, one Faith, one baptism, and one God who is Father of all, over all, through all and within all" (Eph 4.3-6).

It is within the context of this community, as members of the body of Christ, that Christians implement the twofold commandment of love of God and love of their fellow men. It is the Holy Spirit who gives the spiritual wisdom, motivation, and strength to the body of Christ, enabling its members to achieve good works in this life and, by example, to draw others to Christ.

The Remaining Task

This draws to an end both our analysis, and the resolution we have proposed concerning man's search for ultimate meaning, including the meaning of himself. However, to know human purpose and destiny is but the beginning. There remains the need to implement Christian values in day-to-day life. The following chapters present a Christian perspective on some of the moral and ethical problems encountered in contemporary society.

SUGGESTED READINGS

1. The Acts of the Apostles (New Testament): written by Luke, the Acts tell of the role of the Holy Spirit in the founding of the early Church, including the story of Paul's conversion.

2. Abbott, W. M., ed. *The Documents of Vatican II*. N.Y.: Herder, 1966. See documents entitled "The Church," "The Church Today," and "Ecumenism." The first document discusses the Holy Spirit in the Mystical Body of Christ, the Church; the second considers the work of the Christian in the modern world; and the third is an appeal to Christians of all denominations to work together in Christ.

3. Boylan, E. B. *This Tremendous Lover*. Westminster: Newman, 1954. An exposition of the meaning of Christ and the Holy Spirit in the Church, from a Catholic perspective.

PART II

CHRISTIAN ETHICS & VALUES

7

ETHICAL AND MORAL PRINCIPLES

"The Lord said to Moses, 'Come up to me on the mountain. . . . I will give you the stone tablets on which I have written the commandments' "
—Ex 24.12.

THE word "ethics" is derived from the Greek word *ethos*, meaning custom, practice, or constant mode of behavior. In philosophy, ethics is the study of how men should behave, of their rights and duties or obligations. Some philosophers think the study of ethical norms should be restricted to include only those arrived at by rational reflection; others contend that ethics should embrace also helpful information obtained from divine revelation, e.g., the Ten Commandments (Bourke, 1966). Whether the latter constitutes the subject matter of moral theology or of ethics is the subject of a debate that need not concern us here. Since we have undertaken to establish the existence of God, his divine revelation (the Bible), and his Incarnation in Jesus Christ, we shall use these realities as a foundation for our discussion of Christian values related to ethical and moral behavior.

The Norm of Morality

God, as Creator, established a divine order in things. This divine harmony and orderliness is manifested in the beauty of the earth and the universe. "The heavens declare the

119

glory of God, and the firmament proclaims his handiwork"
(Ps 19.2). This order is generally spoken of in terms of law.
In reference to inanimate things and to living things lacking
freedom, we say their activity or behavior follows natural
physical laws. Examples include the laws of physics and
chemistry for inanimate bodies, and the laws of instincts in
subhuman animal species. Man, too, has a nature to be fulfilled, actualized, or realized in his lifetime. However, he is
uniquely different from other living beings in that he has
been fashioned in God's image. "God created man in his
image; in the divine image he created him; male and female he created them" (Gen 1.27). Intelligence, self-
awareness, and freedom are characteristic of this image
(Hammes, 1971). But God did not give man absolute, un-
limited freedom. We have seen how original man was given
a prohibition, which he chose to violate, bringing upon
himself the human condition of guilt, suffering, and death.
Man, then, was subject, from the beginning of his existence, to moral obligation, and is so to the present day. We
can refer to the basis of this obligation as the moral law.
Philosophers customarily refer to the knowledge of basic
natural moral law, the embodiment of God's expectations of
man, as something knowable through simple cognitive reflection. For example, the precept "Do good and avoid
evil" can be arrived at apart from divine revelation. Paul
speaks of the law written in the hearts of all, in their
conscience (Rom 2.15). However, God saw fit to declare
clearly what he expected in human moral behavior, in the
Ten Commandments (Ex 20.1-17; Deut 5.1-21). These
commandments were expressed as negative precepts in the
Old Testament. Jesus, as we have seen, restated them positively in the two-fold command to love God and to love
neighbor, but in no way abolished or set aside the original

ten. Paul, for example, had occasion to combine the positive and negative precepts of the commandments (Rom 13.8-10). Thus we may conclude that (a) God has clearly outlined the moral law, and (b) man perfects his nature, realizes his potential, and fulfills his destiny by living in accord with it. In departing from it, man dehumanizes and depersonalizes himself, and perverts the divine plan.

Traditional Christian ethicists have held to moral absolutes regarding human moral obligation. These absolutes are expressed as precepts that hold true universally, for all time for all persons; and no circumstance or condition permits moral exemption from them. The negative precepts forbidding idolatry, blasphemy, murder, adultery, and theft, for example, are seen as absolutely and always binding. Human acts violating such precepts are considered *intrinsically* evil, that is, evil in themselves, and never morally justifiable. Another example of an absolute prohibition is the principle that a good end cannot justify an evil means of achieving that end (Rom 3.8). Some contemporary radical Christian moralists have proposed the rejection of absolute, unconditionally binding moral precepts. This position has come to be called the New Morality, or situational ethics. As we shall explain in detail later, this view is a departure from traditional Christian teaching.

Another way of viewing intrinsic morality is to see it as independent of human opinion. Murder, the intentional destruction of innocent life, is always morally evil, regardless of whether anyone wishes it were otherwise. Thus a statement of intrinsic goodness or intrinsic badness is *objectively* grounded and independent of any *subjective* opinion of its validity. The reason is that intrinsic goodness or badness rests in the divine plan. God is the validating base of moral absolutes. Since he has not changed his revelation concerning the commandments, we can conclude that the moral absolutes contained therein are unchangeable and eternal. Philosophers therefore refer to God's divine plan of moral obligation as the *eternal* moral law, and man's reception and understanding of it as the *natural* moral law.

With regard to the human response to the obligations of the moral law, it should be remembered that this response is free. That is, God in creating man did not fashion a robot, but rather a creature in his image, possessing freedom of choice. He endowed man with conscience, the subjective judgment as to what is morally correct behavior and the prompting to act accordingly. The demands of the moral law are morally binding but not coercive. Man *can disobey*, even though he *should not*. Human motivation in obeying the moral law should be love and gratitude to a Creator who saw fit to bring into existence creatures to enjoy the goodness of this life and the eternity of an afterlife. Why God did that is indeed a mystery, for he had no need of that which he created. The Christian attributes creation to the expansiveness of Divine Love, and, having said that, remains silent.

Upon reflection upon the moral law and the Ten Commandments, one can infer the correlative relationship existing between rights and duties. For example, the commandment prohibiting the destruction of innocent life implies the human right to life, and a corresponding duty or obligation to respect such life. The commandment rejecting theft implies the right to possess property, as well as the duty or obligation to avoid damaging the rightful possessions of another person. The commandment condemning adultery bespeaks the right to marital integrity and the duty of marital faithfulness. The balancing of rights and duties is an important aspect of justice. We consider an individual to behave unjustly if he claims rights that are not really his to claim, or if he denies the legitimate rights of another.

Characteristics of a Moral Act

Having seen that there can be a subjective-objective analysis of reality, we can see also that moral behavior involves the same two aspects. The *subjective* aspect involves the opinion one has of the rightness or wrongness of a moral act. The *objective* aspect concerns whether or not in fact a particular moral choice is right or wrong. The subjective aspect involves the judgment of conscience, and the presence or absence of moral guilt. The objective aspect considers the correctness or incorrectness of moral choice independently of whether the doer feels guilty or innocent. This subjective-objective distinction is a reasonable one. For example, the subjective factor is taken into consideration in the legal sentencing of a murderer, in terms of first-, second-, and third-degree murder, contingent on a judgment of the guilt factor. Objectively speaking, all murders are equally to be condemned, as acts, regardless of the state of mind of the murderer.

In the discussion to follow, we shall evaluate the objective aspects of moral behavior, reserving the study of subjective aspects to a later examination of situational ethics and of the nature of conscience.

Even though one can ascertain several factors involved in a moral act, it should be remembered that the final evaluation is of the act as a whole. If any one aspect of the act is evil, the entire act is evil. Furthermore, a moral act can be considered in relation to (a) what is actually done, and (b) why it is done. The second factor is the end or purpose the act achieves, or was intended to achieve. A third factor is (c) the set of circumstances that affect the degree of objective goodness or badness of the moral act.

Let us consider the first objective factor in a moral act, namely, *that which is done*. We might first ask, Is it possible for human acts, that is, acts freely done, to be morally indifferent? Or are all volitional acts either morally good or morally evil? Traditional Christian moralists are divided in opinion (Bittle, 1950; Bourke, 1966). However, if one sees volitional activity (any decision to act) in relation to self-realization, it would follow that every willed act contributes to or detracts from such fulfillment. Be that as it may, moral acts can be considered *intrinsically* good or evil, or *extrinsically* good or evil. Intrinsically evil acts are by nature evil; extrinsically evil acts are so in virtue of some external circumstance. Intrinsically evil acts involve rights that no human being may claim; extrinsically evil acts involve rights that humans may claim under certain conditions. The deliberate and intentional destruction of innocent life is intrinsically evil, and no one can claim such an act as a right. In that sense it is no right and cannot ever be a right. Disobedience, on the other hand, can be extrinsically morally evil; for while parents have the right to expect obedience from their children, children do not have such a right in regard to their parents. In general, the commandments that are negatively stated refer to intrinsically evil acts, acts that no one can ever claim as moral rights.

The second factor in a moral act is *the end or purpose served by the act*, objectively recognized in the act. Here enters a moral principle: "A good end does not justify an evil means." We shall later see, in the discussion of situational ethics, that this principle applies not only to the "end" of the act as objectively recognized, but also to the subjective intention of the agent. Thus the principle is two-fold and would include the principle, "A good *intention* does not justify an evil means." An example of the objective violation of this principle is therapeutic abortion, the intentional and deliberate destruction of the unborn child as a means to save the mother's life. (See Chapter 8.) The end is good, but the means are evil. An example of the subjective violation of this principle is the appeal to the motive of love (intention) as justification of adultery (means).

It can also be noted, in regard to subjective intention, that an evil intention is sufficient to render a human act morally evil, even though the intended end of the act is not achieved. If someone shoots a gun at another with the intention to murder, the act is morally evil even if the gun misfires or he misses the intended victim. As we have already seen, Christ taught that even in one's thoughts the commandments can be broken (Matt 5.27-28; 1 John 3.15).

The third factor in a moral act is *the set of circumstances*, which determine how good or how evil the act objectively is. The murder of a pregnant woman would be doubly evil. Adultery wherein children of the concerned parties are affected is more evil than adultery between those who are childless. The theft of a million dollars would likely be more evil than the theft of ten dollars.

Moral Permissibility of an Evil Consequence

Even though it may be granted that a good end (objectively, the end of a moral act; subjectively, the intention of the agent) can never justify the use of immoral means toward its achievement, the question can still arise: Suppose an action results in two foreseeable effects or consequences, one good and the other evil? Can the foreseen evil end be permitted to occur, in the interest of achieving the good end? That is, even though moral evil residing in the *means* is forbidden, is it ever permissible to allow moral evil to occur as an *end* or consequence to a human act? Some Christian moralists answer in the affirmative, if certain conditions are first met. These conditions are four in number, and taken together they compose what is known as the *principle of the double effect*. Let us state the four conditions and apply them to two medical situations, one involving therapeutic or "direct abortion," and the other a case of "indirect abortion." First, some clarifications: Therapeutic abortion is a form of direct abortion; that is, the fetus is *intentionally* destroyed. The purpose, let us assume, is to save the mother's life, in that allowing the fetus to come to term would apparently result in the mother's death. "Indirect abortion" may be illustrated by the case of uterine cancer in a pregnant woman, where removal of the diseased uterus results in the death of the fetus it contains. In both these instances, there is a two-fold effect, one good and one bad. In both instances, the unborn child is lost and the mother's life saved. For purposes of the present discussion, we shall assume that fetal life is human and therefore equal in value to the mother's life. °

The Principle of the Double Effect

What is morally permissible or impermissible in the two situations just described can be evaluated by an application of the four conditions contained in the principle of the double effect (McFadden, 1967; Healy, 1956):

Condition One: The action itself must be morally good or morally indifferent, but never evil.

Intrinsically evil acts are those forbidden by the negative precepts of the moral law and are absolutely forbidden. Extrinsically evil acts relate to the affirmative precepts of the

---

° A closer analysis of abortion is contained in the next chapter.

moral law and are circumstantial, that is, are evil in some instances and not in others. The question of the morality of an act that produces both good and bad effects arises only in regard to affirmative concepts; moral permissibility is immediately and totally excluded by negative precepts.

Another way of stating the first condition of our principle is that the action itself, *considered apart* from the concomitant evil effect, must be morally good or morally indifferent. The "considered apart" qualification emphasizes the requirement that the action not be necessarily related to the evil effect, so that it could be taken in other instances without the evil effect necessarily resulting. (An *intrinsically* evil act, by contrast, always and necessarily includes the evil effect.)

Now therapeutic abortion as an operation is the direct, intentional destruction of innocent, unborn human life and, being therefore an act of murder, violates a negative moral precept. It is therefore intrinsically evil and is never morally permissible. However, the removal of a cancerous uterus as an operation is in itself morally good, one that is not necessarily related to the destruction of a fetus, inasmuch as removal would be indicated even if the woman were not pregnant. An operation for the removal of a cancerous uterus is not by necessity related to the death of a fetus, as *is* the case with therapeutic abortion.

Condition Two: There should be no causal relationship between the good effect and the bad effect.

That is, the bad *effect* cannot be the *means* by which the good effect is achieved. Both effects must remain as coordinate ends of the action. If the bad effect does become the means, the moral principle that "a good end cannot justify an evil means" is violated. This principle is violated in the case of therapeutic abortion, wherein the evil effect, destruction of the fetus, becomes the means by which the good effect, preservation of the mother's life, is achieved. However, in the case of removing the cancerous uterus, fetal death is not the means by which the mother's life is saved.

Condition Three: The evil effect must be but tolerated and never directly intended.

The principle that an evil intention always renders any moral act evil applies here. It should also be noted that whenever the evil effect is used to achieve the good effect, the evil effect is intentionally chosen as the means. The direct destruction of the fetus in therapeutic abortion expresses the intention to murder and renders this act immoral. On the other hand, the fetal death resulting from the removal of a cancerous uterus is foreseen but is neither directly intended nor approved; the good effect alone is intended in this case.

May (1975), in a discussion of the principle of double effect, refers to the good effect as "directly intended" and the evil effect as "indirectly intended," and cites Grisez (1970) as maintaining that both effects flow so immediately from the act, although not necessarily simultaneously in time, that the act may be considered unitary. Grisez still retains, however, the distinction between the two effects, as stated in the principle.

To critics who would consider both good and bad effects "directly intended," Grisez correctly points out a distinction between "foreseen" consequences and "intended" consequences. For example, following Grisez: in visiting the dentist, one may foresee the pain (evil effect) but not intend it. In taking medication, one may foresee adverse side effects (evil effect) but not intend them. In the final analysis, both Grisez and May insist that the evil effect, whether it is considered unintended or indirectly intended, must remain an undesired effect and never be the *means* by which the good effect is achieved.

Condition Four: The good and evil effects must be proportional.

The good effect may be equal to or greater in value than the evil effect, but never less in value. Thus there must be a *sufficient reason* (the good effect) for permitting the evil effect to occur. This condition naturally presupposes that there is no other alternative than to place the two-fold effect. In our medical examples, all other means of saving the mother's life must have first been exhausted. This condition is met in both therapeutic and indirect abortion, in that the mother's life and the child's life are equal in value.

In summary, it can be seen that therapeutic abortion, and all forms of direct abortion, whether for reasons of health, rape, economics, or personal whim, violate conditions one, two, and three of the principle of the double effect.

Let us now consider the application of this principle in other moral situations. Suppose, for instance, a ship at sea accidentally strikes a mine. The ship begins to sink, and the captain knows that he must immediately shut off and secure bulkheads in a certain part of the vessel. He knows too that this action will result in trapping several men below decks who will not have sufficient time to reach topside. Let us assume also there is no other way of saving the ship and the rest of the crew from a watery death. Would it be morally permissible in this situation for the captain to secure the necessary bulkheads? The four conditions are applied as follows: First, the captain's action is not intrinsically related to the death of the men below decks, i.e., their presence there is incidental to the action. The action in itself is therefore not evil. Second, the evil effect of the loss of life is not causally related to the good effect, the saving of life. That is, the death of the men below decks is not the means by which the other lives are saved. Third, the intention of the captain is to save life; the evil effect is tolerated and not desired. Fourth, there is proportionality between the good and evil effects; both involve human life. In this situation, therefore, the captain's action is morally licit.

An Operational Alternative. It should be noted that in all of the cases involving double effects, we have evaluated what is morally permissible. Moral permissibility does not, however, mean the action must be taken. For example, the mother with the cancerous uterus may wish to refuse the operation, if such would permit the fetus in time to become viable and be delivered. Even though, in the order of justice, she has a right to an operation that would remove the cancer and save her life, nevertheless in the order of charity (love) she could surrender this right so that her child might live. "There is no greater love than this: to lay down one's life for one's friends" (John 15.13). Also, the principle of the double effect could be applied to such a decision. First, to permit natural death to occur through cancer would be a morally indifferent act. Second, her death (bad effect) is not the means by which the child's life is saved (good effect). That is, the continuing development of the fetus to term is independent of the fact of a cancerous uterus. Third, her intention is not to die. The bad effect is but tolerated; her intention is that her child live. Fourth, the good and bad effects are proportional. Consequently, there would be no moral objection to the mother's decision not to have the operation, even though her death was thus unavoidable. In the same way, she could justifiably postpone the operation until her child is born, even though her chances of survival would thereby be reduced.

Self-Defense

The morality of defending oneself against an unjust aggressor to the point of killing that aggressor is related to "just war" theory. Let us first consider this question on the level of the individual person. Can I kill someone who is trying to kill me? In answering this question, of course, the distinction between "killing" and "murder" must be maintained. Taken in context, the commandment "Thou shalt not kill" actually forbids the intentional and deliberate destruction of innocent life; in other words, murder. Murder is prohibited by a negative moral precept and absolutely forbidden. Killing, as we shall use the term, is the taking of life under conditions that exclude murder. The only occasions on which killing *can* be separated from murder are those in which an aggressor has forfeited his right to life. The innocent do not forfeit their right to life; but it is the opinion of some moralists that an unjust aggressor may. Capital punishment, for example, is justified on that basis. On that basis also, one may kill a personal unjust attacker, *if* that is the only way he can be stopped. If someone attacks my life, I may defend my life to the necessary point of taking his, since by his attack he has presumably forfeited his right to life. On a national level, a similar forfeiture of the right to life renders it morally permissible for one nation to protect itself against the unjust attack of another; hence "just war" theory. Note that in either the case of the individual or the case of the nation, two conditions must be met: (a) the attack must be unjust, and (b) killing the aggressor must be the *necessary*, and therefore the *only*, means of defense.

Referring again to the instance of therapeutic abortion: one may be inclined to see the fetus as an unjust aggressor who forfeits his right to life. But in fact the medical problem is essentially the fault of the mother's anatomical or physiological condition, resulting in the difficulty of bringing her pregnancy to term. The fetus or embryo merely finds itself where it is, not because of any fault of its own. As the innocent party, it does not forfeit its right to life.

It should be noted that the right of self-defense to the necessary point of killing an unjust aggressor is a morally permissible act but not one that is required. The victim may, for reasons of charity, refrain from killing his assailant. Some Christian moralists hold that the right to life cannot be forfeited; and they therefore conclude that all killing is prohibited, not just murder alone. Such moralists would logically reject also capital punishment, as well as any "just war" theory (Barnette, 1967; Grisez, 1970).

Situational Ethics*

We have seen that traditional Christian ethical teaching holds to moral absolutes, precepts that contain the reality of intrinsic evil. Such precepts were negatively stated in the Ten Commandments, forbidding absolutely and unconditionally certain immoral acts. In recent years, the absolute character of certain moral demands has been challenged by a view variously referred to as the New Morality, situational ethics, contextual ethics, existential ethics, transcendental ethics, phenomenological ethics, antinomianism, and nominalism (Cunningham, 1970; Gleason, 1967). This perspective accuses the traditional view of Christian morality of being legalistic, Pharisaical, and antihumanistic. It rejects natural-law theory and substitutes love as the only norm. The rational, cognitive elements in moral judgment are replaced by an emphasis on affective, intuitionistic elements. The primary premise underlying the new rejection

* For an earlier summary of the criticisms that have been directed at situational ethics, see Hammes, 1975c.

of moral absolutes is that there is no such thing as intrinsic evil. All moral acts are seen as but extrinsically good or evil, or circumstantially good or evil. There are no moral acts that are intrinsically or absolutely evil at all times and in all circumstances. As Joseph Fletcher, a leading contemporary situationist, has declared, "No action is good or right in itself. It depends on whether it hurts or helps people, whether or not it serves love's purpose—understanding love to be personal concern—in the situation." "Adultery, for instance—could be the right and good thing" (Fletcher, 1970). Logically, situational ethicists justify, at times, other acts, such as fornication and active euthanasia, that traditional Christian ethical teaching regards as intrinsically evil.

Historical Roots of Situational Ethics

The fundamental root of situational ethics is evolution theory. *Change,* the basic tenet of evolution theory, is logically opposed to the stable, the eternal, the unchanging. For evolution ethics, there are no eternal moral absolutes; even God, the only possible basis of moral absolutes, is therefore subjected to change (as portrayed in so-called process theology). Other historical roots of situational ethics are found in existential philosophy and phenomenology (Bourke, 1970). The emphasis in these perspectives is on subjective experience, to the point of rejecting the subjective-objective distinction that is basic to traditional Christian ethics. The phenomenological, subjectivistic aspect in situational ethics is best seen in the importance it assigns to intuition and the personal encounter with God in moral conflict. Decisions as to good or evil are based primarily on this personalistic encounter rather than on moral precepts divinely revealed. Furthermore, the situational ethicist does not agree that human judgment in fallen human nature is impaired and is in need of an absolute moral norm, a view basic to traditional Christian ethics.

Love Alone as the Moral Norm

We have already seen the importance of love in the Christian life. "God so loved the world that he gave his only Son" (John 3.16). "God is love, and he who abides in love abides in God, and God in him" (1 John 4.16). "There is no greater love than this: to lay down one's life for one's friends" (John 15.13). But traditional Christian morality saw love as needing direction, and this guidance was received from a source external to man, the divinely revealed moral law. Situational ethicists, however, see love as a sufficient moral norm in itself. Bultmann contends that to love another as one wishes oneself to be loved is adequate; and Robinson speaks of love as having a built-in moral compass (Barnette, 1967).

Those who champion the concept of love alone as being directive, like a compass, ignore fallen human nature or deny that it is fallen and show an inability to see clearly what authentic Christian love demands. Love without "content" is reducible to relativism and subjective whims of opinion. Furthermore, if love is but the good intention, purpose, or end of the agent (according to Fletcher), then anything and everything could be justified as morally good. However, one cannot do the "loving thing" unless one can distinguish loving things from unloving things. Even terrorists, rapists, and murderers could defend their behavior as a loving action, according to their personal value systems (Lutzer, 1972). Love as personal intention can lead to contradictory courses of action. Lutzer cites the example of the pagan informing a British officer, "My conscience tells me to burn a widow with the corpse of her husband." The officer replied, "My conscience tells me to hang you if you do" (Lutzer, 1972). It is obvious that both of these men cannot be objectively correct. Subjective judgment indeed relates to guilt or innocence, but the morality of the act itself must be evaluated on objective grounds, apart from mere personal opinion.

Traditional moral theologians and ethicists have always recognized that man has the right (1) to judge whether circumstances change the applicability of the law (with the exception of those absolute demands forbidding intrinsically evil moral acts), and (2) to decide conscientiously the degree of subjective, personal moral guilt or innocence (Bourke, 1966; Bittle, 1950; Connell, 1958). Indeed, one must always follow the dictates of a certain (undoubtful) conscience, even when, objectively considered, they are erroneous.

However, traditional moral theologians did not hold that man has the prerogative of deciding also the objective binding validity of the law. That prerogative has been claimed by the situational ethicist. For example, if one conscientiously thought that fornication or direct abortion was permissible for some purpose envisaged as good, and acted accordingly, both traditional and situational moralists would agree that there was an attenuation or absence of subjective guilt. But the traditional moralist would contend that the person was still bound (obliged) by the law, in that the person's conscience is in fact erroneous (Harvey, 1975). The traditional moralist has held that intentions, however good or noble, do not determine the binding (obligatory) power of the moral law. The situational ethicist, on the other hand, claims that where the intention is good, the binding power of the law is lifted, and that the individual is free of moral absolutes whenever he conscientiously judges he is.

If the *objective* binding (obligatory) power of moral absolutes is a matter of personal choice, then indeed it is illogical to go on speaking of moral absolutes. The logical consequence is moral relativism, a facet of atheistic humanism, in which the validity of moral precepts is reducible to subjective opinion. The Ten Commandments become mere guidelines, contingent on the interpretation of the individual, who feels free to transcend the law whenever he (conscientiously) feels he is illumined to do so, by way of an intuitionistic, immanent, internal light.

Another way of seeing the basic inconsistency of situational ethics is in terms of the two-fold command of Christ, to love God and to love neighbor (Matt 22.37-40; Mark 12.29-31). Situational ethics ignores the first commandment, to love God (and his absolute moral precepts), which is higher than the second commandment, to love others as one loves oneself; the first command *directs* the second and keeps it from being perverted into moral relativism. The second command can be seen as the horizontal dimension of morality, love among men, whereas the first command is the vertical dimension of morality, love of God and therefore of his moral law, a law that is absolute because it rests in the Absolute.

Love and the Law

Situational ethics is essentially a reaction to legalism, or Pharisaism, and is best understood as a historically conditioned phenomenon. Although Jesus had some friends among the Pharisees (for example, Joseph of Arimathea, in whose tomb Jesus was laid), they represented a legalistic attitude that Jesus condemned. That attitude tended to substitute the letter of the law for the spirit of the law, and it was common enough among the Pharisees to warrant Jesus' response to it. The term "Pharisaism" also includes, in terms of moral theory, substitution of legalism and ritualism for true morality, pride in one's own moral righteousness together with rejection of others judged to possess less moral virtue, and use of religious ceremony as an occasion to glorify oneself rather than to glorify God (von Hildebrand, 1955).

Situational ethicists rightfully reject Pharisaism, or legalism. But in rejecting that abuse of moral law, they have gone to the extreme of rejecting the moral law itself, at least in regard to its absolute character. In effect they have gone to the extreme of making the spirit of the law and the letter of the law essentially irreconcilable. Then too, their assertion that love supercedes law to the extent of dispensing with it is open to challenge. The nature of the moral law and its relationship to Christian love both need to be brought into a harmonious, balanced view of the meaning of human life.

The Mosaic law of the Old Testament contained three types of laws or commandments: ceremonial, judicial, and moral (Wu, 1967). The first two types, ceremonial and judicial, were dispensed with by Christ in the New Covenant between God and man; and specifically Christian ceremonial and judicial proceedings were established accordingly. The third aspect of the Mosaic law, the moral law or the Ten Commandments, was not dispensed with by Christ, but rather clarified. As we have already seen, Jesus summed up the Law and the prophets in his two-fold command to love God and to love neighbor (Matt 22.36-40). Even though these two precepts are found in the Old Testament (Deut 6.25, 10.12, 11.13; Lev 19.18), it was Christ in his divine wisdom who pointed out their importance as the ultimate moral precepts. In no way did Christ negate the absolute moral demands of the Ten Commandments; indeed, his own two commands are themselves absolute moral precepts summing up completely and in a positive way both the positive and the negative absolute precepts of the Ten Commandments. Love, then, does not negate the moral law, but rather fulfills the moral law (Kovach, 1970). Christian liberty is freedom to fulfill the law in love, rather than freedom from the law to do as one wishes.

Situational ethicists are prone to quote certain passages in the writings of St. Paul to support their view of Christian freedom from the law (Gal 5.13; Romans 6.14). However, when those passages are read in fuller context (Romans 2.12-16; Gal 5.13-26), Paul is rather saying that the love of Christ enables us to fulfill the law, not grudgingly, not in letter only, but in the spirit of love. Love renders any burden light (Matt 11.29-30; 1 John 5.3). Even in the Old Testament, the psalmist speaks of loving God's commandments to the point of delighting in them (Ps 119.47). To maintain, as situational moral theologians do, that love frees one from the absolute demands of the Ten Commandments is to distort the relationship between true Christian liberty and true Christian love. Paul sums up this relationship of love to the moral law: "He who loves his neighbor has fulfilled the law. The commandments, 'You shall not commit adultery; you shall not murder; you shall not steal; you shall not covet,' and any other commandment there may be are all summed up in this, 'You shall love your neighbor as yourself.' Love never does any wrong to the neighbor, hence love is the fulfillment of the law" (Romans 13.8-10). If law and love are complementary, not antagonistic, certain things follow in consequence: Love is enhanced by law, which is essential to giving love authentic direction; law in turn is enhanced by love, which renders obedience joyful.

Situational ethicists have made a positive contribution in alerting us once more to the dangers of legalism and Pharisaism. But they have also departed from the path of traditional Christian morality in several ways, which may be summarized under four heads. First, situational ethics denies the binding obligatory power of negative moral absolutes in all moral acts. This denial of intrinsic evil leaves only extrinsic evil, circumstantially determined. Second, situational ethics assumes unimpaired human judgment and claims that love alone can result in correct moral decisions, without any need of negative moral absolutes, or moral law. Third, situational ethics, in making intention, end, and purpose the sole criteria of moral legitimacy, rejects the traditional Christian principle that no end, no matter how worthy, can ever justify evil means. Fourth, situational ethics, by defining love in terms of subjective intent, falls prey to relativism and thus ends in moral chaos.

Conscience

"Two things fill the mind with ever-increasing wonder and awe, . . . the starry heavens above me and the moral law within me." Thus wrote Immanuel Kant in his *Critique of Pure Reason*. We have discussed the natural moral law as grounded in divine revelation, yet accessible in its primary principles to human reason. The freedom to obey or disobey moral precepts involves conscience and the experience of guilt.

Guilt. The human condition is characterized by the experience of guilt. Human guilt is encountered when one contributes to the alienation or estrangement within oneself, or between oneself and others, or between oneself and God. It may occur, too, when one feels he has abused the environment of which he is but the steward rather than absolute owner. In formal terms, guilt is that experience consequent to one's doing what he believes he ought not to do, or failing to do that which he believes he ought. It is a universal human experience, attested to in all ages, and in peoples of varying culture and degrees of civilization. There has been no human society yet found that did not have rules of ethical and moral conduct (or "taboo").

When the Christian speaks of guilt, he speaks also of sin, in reference to human acts that have produced the experience of guilt. Unfortunately, our contemporary culture has rationalized the guilt of sin as something resulting from imperfect evolutionary development, or from genetic weakness; similarly responsibility for evil has been shifted to others, to "the system," or to society as a whole (Menninger, 1973).

Nature of Conscience. The human capacity that enables man to experience guilt is called conscience. The term *conscience* is occasionally found in the Scriptures, but the word used far more often is *heart* (Knight, 1969). Conscience can be defined as moral awareness. As such, it is an intellectual activity which involves both the ability to distinguish between moral right and moral wrong and the ability to learn the kinds of behavior that are morally good or morally evil. The learned or acquired component of conscience is contingent on the society or culture within which one is reared. Thus taboos and ethical rules may differ from culture to culture, and from one civilization to another. The innate aspect of conscience, however, is universal among people of all ages and civilizations, for it involves (a) the intellectual discernment of the difference between morally right and morally wrong behavior, (b) the recognition that one should do what is perceived to be morally good and to avoid what is perceived to be morally evil, and (c) the personal awareness of guilt following a moral transgression (Hammes, 1971).

The state of a person's conscience can be described as vincible or invincible, correct or incorrect, and certain or doubtful. (a) Vincibility refers to the possibility of being morally educated. A person living beyond the reach of Christian civilization would be invincibly ignorant of the Incarnation, the Gospel, and the expectations of a Christian-formed conscience. (b) One's conscience may be correct and true, or incorrect and false, contingent on the degree of conformity of one's conscientious judgment to true morality. We shall return later to this objective consideration of the rightness and wrongness of conscientious conviction. (c) Conscience may be certain or doubtful; and Christian ethicists are generally agreed that a doubtful conscience should be clarified before one decides to act. Not to take the pains to clarify a doubtful conscience is to be willing to risk moral evil, an attitude that in itself is sinful. A doubtful conscience is to be distinguished from a doubtful law (to be discussed later).

Occasionally moralists speak of a scrupulous and a lax conscience, the former referring to an irrational understanding or exaggeration of what is expected in moral behavior, and the latter describing a devaluing of moral obligations. In contemporary society, it would appear that laxity is much more prevalent than scrupulosity.

The Correct Conscience. When an individual attempts to live a morally good life, it soon becomes apparent that many opposing moral options are available, with contradictory choices sincerely championed. Today, for example, both pro-life and abortion advocates claim their particular position to be morally correct. The question naturally arises, which position *is* morally correct? For correct moral judgment, a sincere conscience is a necessary but an insufficient condition. It is not enough for every person to be *convinced* that his acts are morally good; it is equally necessary to determine objectively whether those acts *are* good. We have already seen the moral chaos that logically results from claiming that good intentions are sufficient for correct moral judgment. According to traditional Christian teaching, human judgment was impaired as a consequence of man's original rebellion against God. No one questions that man can make, and has made, many mistakes in human judgment—in personal life, community life, national and international history, and in the development of civilizations. It is puzzling, therefore, that some deny the need for direction in human moral judgment, and the need for objective guidance independent of mere human opinion. Some even would use a statistical average as a moral norm. Since "everybody does it," it must be permissible, as if in a consensus of human error the individual errors composing it would disappear. The atheist, of course, in the denial of the existence of God, leaves man on his own to devise a moral norm. But then men disagree, and atheism proves to be but another expression of relativism.

The only alternative to a relativistic norm of moral guidance is an absolutist norm. For the Christian, this norm is divine revelation, by which God has communicated to man the moral direction he is to follow. Objectively speaking, there is no longer any *rational* ground for rejecting this revelation, which was summed up finally and completely in the communication of God himself as the Incarnate Word. "If I had not come to them and spoken to them, they would not be guilty of sin; now, however, their sin cannot be excused" (John 15.22). The fundamental moral norm, therefore, is Jesus Christ and his teachings. Traditional Protestant Christians hold the Gospel as their sole moral norm; traditional Catholic Christians believe further that Christ established a visible Church with moral authority, to preserve and interpret his teachings for his followers after he was gone, to the end of time. In one instance during his ministry, Jesus queried his disciples as to who people thought he was. Simon replied, "You are the Messiah, the Son of the Living God" (Matt 16.16). Then Jesus said, "Blest are you, Simon son of Jonah! No mere man has revealed this to you, but my heavenly Father. I for my part declare to you, you are 'Rock,' and on this rock I will build my church, and the jaws of death shall not prevail against it. I will entrust to you the keys of the kingdom of heaven. Whatever you declare bound on earth shall be bound in heaven; whatever you declare loosed on earth shall be loosed in heaven" (Matt 16.17-19). This moral authority of the Church, biblically based, was accepted by the early Christians, and today is still upheld by traditional Catholic Christians. Be that as it may, all traditional Christians believe in an absolute moral norm, contained in the Ten Commandments of the Old Testament, and in the personal communication of Jesus Christ, the Second Person in the Trinity.

Freedom of Conscience. The Christian insistence on an objective, absolute, moral norm as a guide to correct moral judgment in no way infringes on freedom of conscience. One is bound to follow a certain conscience, even if, objectively speaking, that conscience is incorrect and false. It should be obvious, however, that for one's conscience to be certain and true is a far better state of affairs than for one's conscience to be certain but incorrect.

Suppose, however, that one is faced with deciding whether a moral precept applies in a particular instance.

For example, if one found an old, rusted box full of money while digging, would it be considered theft if one made no attempt to determine ownership? This is a question of doubt as to whether a moral law applies, and it is not to be confused with a doubtful conscience. A doubtful conscience, as we have seen, must be clarified before taking a moral action. When there is a doubt as to whether a moral norm or law applies, one may choose to act even if the applicability of the law is in doubt. A moral judgment can be made if it is reasonably probable that it is correct (Connell, 1953), but only in those cases where the doubt as to the applicability of the law cannot be resolved in some other way (O'Donnell, 1956).

Impediments in Human Acts. In view of fallen human nature, the degree of guilt for immoral acts may vary from one situation to another. Factors that impair perfect moral knowledge and perfect moral consent can be referred to as impediments to human acts (Bittle, 1950). First, it will be assumed for present purposes that freedom in behavior is a human capability.* Two prerequisites for a free human act, including moral acts, are deliberation upon the available options, and awareness while making a choice. Insufficient awareness and deliberation attenuate human freedom. This consideration, for example, is what distinguishes temptation from sin. Other factors, or impediments to freedom, that may reduce the degree of guilt or responsibility for moral choice include (a) inured habits, (b) concupiscence (the tendency of fallen human nature to commit sin generally), (c) passion, or emotional excitement, (d) fear, and (e) violence or torture (Bittle, 1950). Even though habits, once established, may lessen culpability, they are not inevitably

---

*Evidence for the reality of such freedom has been presented elsewhere: Hammes, 1971.

determining; and Christians believe that habits can be changed by actively cooperating with God's grace. With regard to passion or emotional excitement, two situations may arise. Antecedent passion, prior to moral choice, arises spontaneously and if experienced to a great degree may diminish guilt considerably. Consequent passion, or emotional excitement following a deliberate moral choice, does not lessen the responsibility or guilt for that choice. In all these instances, of course, one must guard against unconscious defense mechanisms, such as rationalization and displacement of responsibility, by which a person deceives himself into thinking he was innocent of committing moral evil. There is also the tendency to ease conscience by seeking moral doctrine commensurate with what one would like to do rather than with what one should do. "For the time will come when people will not tolerate sound doctrine, but, following their own desires, will surround themselves with teachers who tickle their ears. They will stop listening to the truth and will wander off to fables" (2 Tim 4.3-4).

Conscience Formation. We have observed that conscience embraces not only the innate intellectual ability to discern moral good from moral evil, but also an acquired or learned content of what is morally good and what is morally evil. As the individual matures, therefore, conscience also matures, as a function of both innate intellectual maturation from childhood to adulthood and the study and learning of moral truths. The psychological aspects of moral development have been studied (Kohlberg, 1968) and adapted to Christian education (Duska and Whelan, 1975). However, the judgment of what constitutes "high" and "low" moral maturity is subject to the value system of the researcher; and often the role of divine grace is ignored (Hammes, 1976a). For the Christian, progress in moral development is attained by prayer, study of the Scriptures, and active service toward the welfare of one's fellow man. The obligation to educate one's conscience, however, should be apparent to everyone, not only to the Christian. To neglect this obligation is to deceive oneself.

SUGGESTED READINGS

1. Bourke, Vernon J. *Ethics: A Textbook in Moral Philosophy.* N.Y.: Macmillan, 1966. An outline of ethics, including the moral law, conscience, and ethical problems of society.

2. Bittle, C. N. *Man and Morals: Ethics.* Milwaukee: Bruce, 1950. An introductory ethics on ethical norms, rights, and duties, and ethical problems on community, national, and international levels.

3. Barnette, Henlee H. *The New Theology and Morality.* Phila.: Westminster, 1967. A critique of "God is Dead" theology, situational ethics, and secular theology; and a discussion of Christian attitudes toward war.

4. Cunningham, Robert L., ed. *Situationism and the New Morality.* N.Y.: Appleton-Century-Crofts, 1970. Presents pro and con arguments on situational ethics.

5. Lutzer, Erwin W. *The Morality Gap: An Evangelical Response to Situation Ethics.* Chicago: Moody Press, 1972. A critique of situational ethics, followed by an alternative view based on Scripture.

6. Knight, James A. *Conscience and Guilt.* N.Y.: Appleton-Century-Crofts, 1969. A presentation of various views on the nature of conscience, together with a discussion of normal, neurotic, and existential guilt.

8

RESPECT FOR LIFE

"You shall not kill an unborn child or murder a newborn infant."
— *The Teaching of the Twelve Apostles,* 2nd century A.D.

THE simplest way to make clear the Christian perspective on human life is to contrast it with alternate views on the genesis of life, life once conceived, and life after birth. The major moral issues involved in these three stages of human life are contraception, abortion, and euthanasia; so we shall discuss the value and meaning of human life in relation to them.

Contraception

Contraception, or artificial birth control, is the contravention of conception, through such measures as condoms, foams, jellies, diaphragms, and pills (McFadden, 1976). A contraceptive device prevents a conception that would ordinarily follow sexual intercourse. Hence it is a frustration of a natural process. The "IUD" (intrauterine device) is mistakenly called a contraceptive insofar as it acts instead to prevent the implantation of a fertilized egg (zygote) in the uterine lining: it is actually an abortifacient.

To raise the matter of the morality of contraception appears ridiculous to the contemporary mind, which has accepted this practice and no longer questions it. However, contraception is intimately related to the issue of respect for life. There is still today a viewpoint that venerates human life to the extent of considering the use of the generative powers to be sacred, and subject to certain moral norms. Such a view at one time was the common Christian tradition. Today it is held by traditional Catholics and a few traditional Protestants. We can conveniently distinguish the two outlooks as the "traditional Christian view" and the "modern view" of the morality of contraception.

Proponents of both views share many common life-related concerns, such as the worldwide population explosion, social and financial problems, family hardship, and health considerations, all of which act to encourage limitation of fertility or procreation. There is usually no quarrel between the two positions about the reasons why parents wish to limit the number of children they will bring into the world. The parting of the ways comes in the election of means by which the limitation is achieved. The traditional Christian view is that artificial contraception is a morally evil means. The modern view is that any form of contraception is morally good or at least morally neutral. Even if some moderns view contraception as evil, they contend it is justifiable for certain reasons; that is, they argue that a good end can justify immoral means.

Traditional Christian View of Procreativity. The traditional Christian view, shared by almost all Christians up to the 20th century, sees man as a steward of his powers and capabilities. This stewardship extends in a special way to the generative powers, which are to be used in accordance with divine law, as mirrored in the natural moral law. The natural moral law points to the primary (or mediate) purpose of marriage, and therefore of intercourse, as being procreative. The unitive (love) aspect of marriage and intercourse is equally beautiful and valuable; but neither end of marriage should overshadow the other. Reflection on the nature of marriage shows that the purposes of marriage depend on each other and imply one another (Wallace, 1977). Although the procreative consequence is itself biological, it is not a biological law that is revered here, but rather the divine law, or divine intention, that underlies the biological law, and to which the biological law points. It is the inherent nature of an act, manifested biologically, that constitutes the natural moral law, itself a reflection of the divine law (Shehan, 1973; Monden, 1965). St. Paul, for example, recognized this meaning of the natural moral law (Romans 2.14-15) and condemned unnatural sex acts as examples of violations of the natural moral law (Romans 1.26-28).

The traditional Christian view is based also on reflection on the nature of the generative power, which has the potential of participating with God in extending life to a new human being. The divine creation of an immortal human soul, a soul that is priceless and worth more than the entire universe of lifeless matter, a soul one day ordained to spend an eternity of happiness with God, accompanies the biological generation of every new human being. The reverence for this co-creating with God leads to the desire never to frustrate the generative power, never to interfere with or frustrate the natural processes inherent in it. Artificial contraception is thus seen in the traditional Christian perspective as intrinsically evil, that is, evil in itself, and consequently never morally permissible, not even for good intentions, purposes, or ends, no matter how worthy and noble the latter may be. A kindred view on the immorality of contraception is that it violates the covenant between God and man, in the separation of the unitive from the procreative aspect of marriage (Kippley, 1970).

Modern View of Procreativity. The philosophy underlying the modern point of view contains several factors. First, there is the separation of the unitive and procreative aspects of marriage, such that the unitive (love) component has come to be held as a primary consideration overruling the procreative component. Second, the contemporary emphasis on subjectivity and the rejection of objectivity have led to the rejection of moral laws that supposedly hinder rightful human freedom, as well as a natural law that appears to be impersonal. Third, there is the current rejection of the very concept of intrinsic evil, a concept founded on objective moral absolutes. Fourth, the repudiation of the principle, "A good end cannot justify an evil means," has led to the belief that good intentions, purposes, and ends can justify anything. We have already examined several of these considerations in connection with our analysis of situational ethics. Fifth, there has been an increasing tendency to view man as the absolute judge of how he is to use his human capabilities, and to see him as not bound or limited in the exercise of human freedom. We shall evaluate this perspective when we come to examine the issues involved in biogenetic engineering and bioethics (Chapter 9).

The Basis for Moral Decision

On the philosophical level, therefore, one can find appealing rationales to support either a traditional Christian view, which regards contraception as immoral, or a modern view, which finds it morally permissible. The final personal decision will rest, not on grounds of philosophical persuasion, but on grounds of the moral authority on which the arguments rest. The moral authority for the modern view seems to be man himself. The moral authority for the traditional Catholic view was, and is, the teaching authority of the Church. For the traditional Protestant, it was the voice of conservative theologians and clergymen.

Protestantism has become more individualistic in moral authority, and today the Catholic Church appears to be the sole voice opposing ethical and moral pluralism. The traditional Catholic view of contraception was again presented at Vatican Council II and reaffirmed by Pope Paul VI: "Therefore, when there is question of harmonizing conjugal love with the responsible transmission of life, the moral aspect of any procedure does not depend solely on sincere intentions or an evaluation of motives. It must be determined by objective standards. These, based on the nature of the human person and his acts, preserve the full sense of mutual self-giving and human procreation in the context of true love." Furthermore, Catholics "may not undertake methods of regulating procreation which are found blameworthy by the teaching authority of the Church in its unfolding of the divine law" (Abbott, 1966, p. 256). Pope Paul VI reserved to himself the further elaboration of the Church's moral position on artificial contraception, which he subsequently presented in the encyclical *Humanae vitae* ("Of Human Life," 1968).

There are contemporary Catholics, both theologians and laymen, who have opposed the Church's position on contraception. Such disagreement is not new in the history of the Church. For example, the majority of Catholics for 300 years, from the sixteenth to the nineteenth century, ignored papal teaching on the evils of slavery. The Catholic Church does not base its teachings on popular vote, but rather on the moral issue as perceived by the Church, regardless of whether the consequent pronouncements are popularly acclaimed.

Natural Birth Control. One criticism so often aimed at natural birth control is no longer deserved; it is the objection that this method does not work. Over the last ten years, a method known as the cervical mucous (or ovulation) method has been developed by a team of physicians (Billings *et al.*, 1973). This procedure has been demonstrated experimentally to predict ovulation accurately. It is morally acceptable to all, and has the additional practical advantages of avoiding the side effects attendant on artificial contraceptive methods.

Abortion

The next life-related topic we should consider is human life *after* it has been conceived; this issue may be profitably examined in connection with the moral character of abortion.

"Abortion" is here used to include the expulsion of a living embryo or fetus before it is capable of living apart from the uterine environment, or the killing of a fetus before birth. Abortion may be spontaneous, indirect, or direct. *Spontaneous abortion*, or miscarriage, refers to the situation in which an embryo or fetus is expelled from the womb in a process initiated by the laws of nature. *Indirect abortion* is the expulsion of the embryo or fetus consequent to some action taken for purposes other than abortion, e.g., surgery on the mother for a pathological condition. *Direct abortion*, or induced abortion, is a deliberate and intentional attack on the embryo or fetus, resulting in its death. Our examination will be directed primarily at direct abortion, considered as a human act.

In common parlance today, there are three categories of direct abortion: abortion on demand, therapeutic abortion, and eugenic abortion. Abortion on demand is associated with situations in which the fetal child is not wanted. Therapeutic abortion refers to the destruction of the fetus for reasons of maternal health, psychological or physiological. Eugenic abortion is killing of the fetus because of the medical prediction that the child will be born defective.

In the discussion to follow, the distinction between *subjective* innocence or guilt and the *objective* rightness or wrongness of a moral act should be kept in mind. We are not concerned with making a judgment of the person advocating or having an abortion. The issue to be examined here is the objective morality of abortion, that is, its moral rightness or wrongness apart from personal opinion. (Whether conscience alone, that is, subjective experience, is adequate to establish the objective morality of moral behavior has been treated in the previous chapter; and that discussion will be assumed here.)

Legalized Abortion. On January 22, 1973, the U.S. Supreme Court, in a 7-to-2 decision, approved abortion as a legal medical procedure. The decision, based on an interpretation of the 14th Amendment, held that the right to privacy encompassed a woman's right to terminate her pregnancy. The court further stated that legal personhood did not extend to the unborn, and that therefore the unborn have no legal right to life. In applying this ruling, the court divided the nine-month pregnancy period into three trimesters. During the first trimester, or first three months, the abortion decision was to be left to the woman and her physician. During the second trimester, the state would be permitted to regulate the abortion procedure in order to ensure maternal health; and for the third trimester, the state law regarding abortion will prevail.

Abortion on demand, that is, abortion for any reason a pregnant woman may have, is legal for the first three months of pregnancy. Concern only for the mother's health is shown in regulations governing the second and third trimesters. At no time is the life of the fetus considered a relevant factor; for the unborn are decreed to have no legal right to life. One of the two Supreme Court judges who dissented from the decision, Justice Byron White, characterized the decision as an "exercise of raw judicial power." This criticism seems fully merited in view of such statements in the decision as: "We need not resolve the difficult question of when life begins. When those trained in the respective disciplines of medicine, philosophy, and theology are unable to arrive at any consensus, the judiciary . . . is not in a position to speculate as to the answer." The Supreme Court ruling on the legality of abortion has been compared with the Dred Scott decision of 1857, when Chief Justice Roger Taney held that black slaves, though human biologically, had no constitutional rights. This judicial and social attitude toward black-skinned humans was upheld for almost 100 years. Paradoxically, the same Supreme Court that in 1973 decreed the legality of killing the unborn had earlier lifted the death penalty as a legal punishment.° Another paradox is that a sizable segment of American society can become enraged at the annual harvest-killing of baby seals for their pelts but complacently accepts the slaughter of millions of the unborn of its own members. It has been pointed out that in the two centuries since the inception of the United States, all American wars have accounted for some 667,000 deaths; in 1972 alone, 600,000 unborn were aborted (Durand, 1973). This toll is increasing annually, e.g., 763,000 in 1974, and over 1,000,000 in 1977.

Infanticide. The implications of abortion for the welfare of the common good are extensive. In January 1973, the U.S. Supreme Court legalized abortion; and in May of that year, James Watson, co-discoverer of the double helix and a

---

° This decision of 1972 was reversed in July 1976.

Nobel prize winner, extended the court's logic by proposing that it would be even better if a child were "not declared alive" until three days after birth (*Time* magazine, 1973). His reason was that some birth defects were not discoverable until after birth, so the three-day extension would permit legal killing of a defective child. Watson suggested that the doctor could "allow the child to die if the parents so chose"—leaving unsettled the criteria for how defective a child must be in order to merit such a judgment. The phrase "not declared alive" implies that we can determine by mere declaration whether the newborn is to be recognized as alive. Watson was obviously referring to the legal definition of what constituted human life; and since the Supreme Court had decided the fetus had no legal right to life, Watson was astute enough to observe a logical extension of that loss of privilege.

Another implication of treating abortion as a morally good or neutral act is that if respect for life is lost at one end of the life continuum, the door is open to disrespect for life at any point along the continuum. Infanticide and euthanasia can logically be justified for the same reasons used to justify abortion (Atkinson, 1974; Grisez, 1972).

The primary question in determining the moral permissibility of abortion is whether or not the embryo or fetus is a human being. If it is, then the issue becomes one of murder, and we then return to the question whether murder can ever be justified. If the embryo or fetus is not human, one must still contend with the problem of whether or not it is permissible to interfere with life that will eventually become human. In the latter case, one would logically be dealing with the problem of the morality of contraception, which concerns the permissibility of interfering with the generative powers of life.

Let us pursue the question, Is the embryo or fetus

human? Is the zygote human all the while in its development, or does it become human along the way? There are three frames of reference commonly used as the basis for answering such questions, namely, religion, science, and philosophy.

Religious Views on Abortion

Religious views on abortion are summarized in an excellent book by Germain Grisez (1972). In early Hinduism, Egyptian religion, and Zoroastrianism, abortion was condemned as the destruction of a human being. The Old Testament refers to God as at work in the womb: "Thus says the Lord, your redeemer, who formed you from the womb" (Is 44.24). "The Lord called me from birth, from my mother's womb he gave me my name" (Is 49.1). "Before I formed you in the womb, I knew you, before you were born I dedicated you" (Jer 1.5). In Genesis we read of Isaac's entreaty to the Lord on behalf of his wife, Rebekah, who was sterile. The Lord heard Isaac's prayer and Rebekah became pregnant. But she was troubled because the two "children" jostled each other within her womb, whereupon the Lord comforted her, saying, "Two nations are in your womb" (Gen 25.23). In addition to maintaining sacred respect for uterine life, the Old Testament repeatedly prohibits the shedding of "innocent blood" (Ex 20.13, 23.7; Dt 5.17, 19.13, 21.9, 27.25; Mac 7.22-23; Prv 6.16-19; Wis 12.3-7; Jer 22.3; Dan 15.23). Abortion as such is not explicitly mentioned in the Old Testament, but the sense of reverence and respect for innocent life strongly implies its prohibition (Grisez, 1972; Morgan, 1970). The traditional Jewish view at the time of Christ permitted therapeutic abortion, but nonetheless recognized abortion as the killing of a human being (Grisez, 1972).

Traditional Christian View. In the New Testament, the dignity and sacredness of the unborn child are illustrated in the annunciation to Mary (Luke 1.35), and in Elizabeth's experience when Mary visits her (Luke 1.39-44). The early Christians explicitly condemned abortion. The *Didache,* or *Teaching of the Twelve Apostles,* is a second-century document that describes a much earlier tradition of the "two ways" one may follow, the way of life and the way of death. The way of death is explicitly described and condemned. "You shall not commit murder. You shall not commit adultery. You shall not corrupt boys. You shall not commit fornication. You shall not practice sorcery. You shall not kill an unborn child or murder a newborn infant" (Glimm *et al.,* 1947). In the Letter of Barnabas, around the first century A.D., the author writes, "You shall not murder a child by abortion, nor kill it after birth." Thus the uterine life of the unborn child was recognized by the early Christians as human life.

Catholic and Protestant Viewpoints. The Catholic Church has always taught that abortion is gravely sinful and that not even therapeutic abortion could be morally justified (Grisez, 1972; Sacred Congregation for the Doctrine of the Faith, 1975). The Church restated its teaching during the second Vatican Council when it described "any type of murder, abortion, euthanasia" as examples of "infamies" that "poison society" and are a "supreme dishonor to the Creator. . . . Therefore from the moment of its conception life must be guarded with the greatest care, while abortion and infanticide are unspeakable crimes" (Abbott, 1966, "The Church Today," art. 27, 51).

The Protestant tradition, according to Grisez, differed from the Catholic tradition in that it regarded therapeutic abortion as morally permissible. Those Protestants who hold that abortion is sometimes justifiable base their stand on the belief that the early fetus is non-human, or that, if it is indeed human, there can nevertheless be overriding circumstances that justify the killing of innocent life. Whether or not the latter belief is defensible depends on the validity or invalidity of the principle that a good end can never justify an immoral means.

Ensoulment. In later centuries in the Christian tradition, increased interest was taken in the question whether or not the fetus is ensouled from the moment of conception. The verbal distinction was expressed as "formed" and "unformed," or vivified and nonvivified, as applied to the fetus. The latter viewpoint is referred to as "delayed hominization" (Donceel, 1970). Some of the early Christian theologians (e.g., St. Basil the Great and St. Jerome) concluded it was impossible to know whether the human soul was infused at the moment of conception or at some later time. They further believed, however, that since infusion was an unknowable factor, it was not morally permissible to destroy the fetus at any moment of its development. To do so was to admit the willingness to kill what may well be human. This observation continues to be a trenchant objection to the delayed-hominization theory and the sanctioning of abortion at the earliest stages of fetal life. The early Christian writers not only condemned abortion but also analyzed the question of whether or not it could ever be justified by some overriding purpose or intention. St. Augustine treated the question at length and concluded that a good intention or end can never justify an immoral means. As Grisez points out, the Fathers of the Church condemned abortion because it was an inhumane act, an expression of undisciplined and erotic impulses, a cruel homicide inasmuch as parents should especially love and care for the helpless life they have generated, and a violation of the work of God and his commandment not to shed innocent blood.

Phenomenon of Twinning. The phenomenon of twinning would at first appear to be evidence against the belief that ensoulment takes place at the first moment of conception. Identical twins result from one fertilized egg, and the twinning process is observed sometime between the seventh and fourteenth day. Those advocating delayed hominization assert this as evidence that ensoulment takes place later in fetal development, presumably about the seventh day or thereafter. However, the fact that the process of zygotal splitting is observed to occur around the seventh day does not necessarily mean that two souls could not have been infused prior to that time, even as early as the moment of conception. It could well be that twinning, in the sense of the infusion of two souls, actually occurs at the moment of conception, with the effects not being *visually* observed until seven days later. Therefore, the fact of twinning is not incompatible with immediate hominization. Another explanation of twinning is that the zygote was ensouled for the first week of zygotal growth by one soul, with the second soul being infused a week later, resulting in the twinning split (Atkinson, 1974; Grisez, 1972; Morgan, 1970; and Hellegers, 1970). It may at first seem implausible that two souls could share the same zygote. However, are there not instances of Siamese twins sharing the same organs? No one doubts that these are two individual souls, two individual personalities. If two souls can share organs, why could they not also, at the zygotal stage, share the same body?

A related problem is the apparent recombination of twins into a single individual after initial twinning has occurred (Hellegers, 1970). Although it is observed on the subhuman level, e.g., in mice, the occurrence of this phenomenon is still debatable on the human level. Nonetheless, the immediate-hominization theorist could claim that (a) the twinning was in fact only apparent rather than real, or (b) if real, it was possible that one of the two individuals died, and the other survived. In conclusion, it can be said that both hypotheses, immediate and delayed hominization, are compatible with the phenomenon of twinning, and twinning cannot be brought to bear against the concept of immediate ensoulment.

Biological Analysis of Human Life

Next, let us consider from the viewpoint of science the question, Is the fetus considered to be human? To answer this question, we shall examine the facts discovered in the science of microbiology. Biologically considered, the fertilized egg, or zygote, contains within it the genetic blueprint of 46 chromosomes, 23 from each parent. At the moment of conception there is introduced a being that is separate from the mother, one that is not a part of the mother. The mother's body provides the environment necessary for the zygote's nourishment, survival, and development till the moment of birth—birth being merely a transition from the uterine environment to that of the external world. (In lower, less complex forms of life, there is no need for the uterine environment. The frog egg, for example, is fertilized outside of the mother's body, and develops into the tadpole and finally into the recognizable frog.)

Moreover, the zygote is continually active from the moment of conception. From microbiology we know that accelerated division and growth begin, even while the growing zygote or blastula is traveling on its way to implantation in the uterus, an event that occurs within a week or ten days after conception. The cellular division of the zygote, called mitosis, is rapid—two cells within one day, twelve cells within three days, fifty-eight cells in four days, etc. Already within four days the cells begin to arrange themselves into a characteristic shape, a sphere with an inner cavity. Most of these early cells develop eventually into the accessory structures necessary for immediate survival, e.g., the placenta and umbilical cord. Later the formative cells of the new individual predominate. Thus nature ordains first things first. Also, at the time of implantation, the placenta cells release hormones that prevent the mother's menstruating, which would destroy this new life.

After implantation, the further cell development includes not only multiplication but also differentiation and movement from place to place, together with opening and closing of passages and folding and unfolding of surfaces. Within three weeks, *less than a month's time*, the embryo has developed the beginnings of eyes, spinal cord, nervous system, thyroid gland, lungs, stomach, liver, kidney, and intestines. A heart begins to beat around the eighteenth day. This complex development is taking place in an organism that is but one-fourth of an inch in size.

At four weeks, or *one month*, the heart, in proportion to the whole, is nine times as large as an adult's. At five weeks the eyes become delineated, with retina and lens; and a skeleton begins. The embryo is now one-third of an inch in length. At six weeks, responses to tactual stimuli are made. The eyes are wide open, ears are developing, and fingers and toes are visible. There is a little mouth with lips, an early tongue, and buds for twenty milk teeth. The sex organs have begun growth. At *eight weeks*, there is readable electric activity emitted by the brain. Bone replaces cartilage. (In earlier days, this was the time that the embryo became visually recognizable as human, and its name was changed to "fetus." "Embryo" comes from a Greek word meaning "to swell"; *fetus* means "fruitful" in Greek, and "offspring" in Latin. Some writers prefer to use one term, fetus, to describe the individual from conception to birth, since nomenclature is actually arbitrary.)

The embryo develops continuously, not abruptly in sudden stages. About two and one-half inches in size, the fetus is now developing more detailed structure (e.g., finger and toenails). Internal organs become further refined; the kidneys can secrete, and sexual organs are visually recognizable. The brain structure is complete. At sixteen weeks, or *four months,* the fetus is about five and one-half inches in length, and its limb movements may be felt by the mother. This experience is referred to as "quickening," the time when the mother becomes bodily aware of the activity of the life in her uterus. At eighteen weeks, or four and one-half months, the fetus may suck its thumb, clench its fist, kick, and display facial activities associated with crying. Its vocal cords are complete, but without air the fetus cannot make a sound. At twenty-eight weeks, or *seven months,* the fetus is approximately a foot in length, and if prematurely delivered is capable of surviving. Two months later, normal delivery occurs.

The zygote, then, from the moment of conception, is certainly a living, distinct organism equipped with the genetic blueprint to become what in nine months is a newborn child. In no way, and at no time, can it be considered merely "tissue," and never is it part of the mother's body. The circulatory systems of mother and fetus are completely separate, with the exchange of nutrients and waste occurring between thin walls in the placenta, and transmitted through the umbilical cord.

Philosophical Reflections

What does philosophy say in answer to the question, Is the fetus human? We have already touched upon the speculation of theologians regarding the possibility that the human soul is infused in the embryo or fetus at some time later than the moment of conception. Since we simply do not know the answer, all hypotheses are purely arbitrary. If we wish to be scientific and follow the law of parsimony, we should prefer the hypothesis that ensoulment occurs at conception, and thus avoid a needless multiplication of life-forms; for to postulate a later human life-form requires the existence of a prior life-form to carry out fetal development up to some point.

Related to the problem of when human life begins is the question, Is such rudimentary human life equivalent to personhood? Some anthropologists would agree that possibly fetal life, and certainly newborn life, is human, but assert that such life does not acquire personhood until socialized (e.g., Ashley Montagu). Grisez cites Montagu as saying, "The embryo, fetus, and newborn of the human species, in point of fact, do not really become functionally human until humanized in the human socialization process. Humanity is an achievement, not an endowment" (Grisez, 1972, p. 277). The obvious difficulty here is the arbitrariness of the definition of "person." If a baby were to be raised by wild animals without ever contacting other human persons, he would presumably never become a "person" in Montagu's sense; and killing that child would therefore not be murder. Others making this distinction would admit abortion as the killing of a human *life* but not the killing of a *person*, and therefore as morally permissible. The same reasoning can logically be extended to permit infanticide, as well as the destruction of the mentally retarded and the senile aged.

Of these various observations on the nature of fetal life, which is correct? The evidence of biological science and philosophical analysis rather clearly points to and supports the hypothesis of immediate ensoulment, and human personhood at the moment of conception. That also has been the constant teaching of traditional Christianity. But even among those who agree, there are some who see abortion as morally justifiable. That is, there are some who grant that the fetus from the moment of conception is human, with a claim to the right to life equal with that of those already born, but still say there can be moral justification for abortion. Such justification is based on the belief that a good intent, purpose, or end may justify an evil means. Thus, even though abortion is granted to be the destruction of innocent human life, this action is said to be morally justifiable for good reasons. Reasons that are given include the psychological or physical health of the mother, economic hardships, rape, genetic fetal defects, population control, and rights of a woman over her own body (Atkinson, 1974). The belief that a good end can justify the use of evil means is, of course, a rejection of the concept of *intrinsic evil*, i.e., the position that some actions are absolutely evil, forever prohibited. The concept of intrinsic evil does not permit exception. The position that a good end may justify immoral or evil means is a premise of situational ethics. According to its proponents, commandments are not absolute and permit exceptions. Situational ethicists thus justify abortion, euthanasia, fornication, adultery, and other violations of the commandments in the name of good intentions or extenuating circumstances. Such, however, is not the position of traditional Christianity. Augustine's condemnation of the view that a good end justifies evil means has already been mentioned. This condemnation is found also in Scripture (Romans 3.8). The logical implications of this principle, as we have seen, are such that all moral evil can be justified by good intents and purposes. Consequently the foundation of morality would collapse; there would be no such thing as "moral evil."

Indirect Abortion

To this point in the discussion on abortion, we have considered the moral character of *direct abortion*, the deliberate and intentional attack on the life of the fetus. Let us now consider another kind of abortion, known as "indirect abortion," whereby the abortion is brought about, not directly, but indirectly as a consequence of another action not intended to cause it. For example, a pregnant woman who is found to have a malignant growth in the uterus may have the uterus removed, even though this action also results in the death of the fetus. The moral permissibility of indirect abortion is evident from the application of the principle of the double effect (Bittle, 1950; Bourke, 1966). We have seen, in the previous chapter, the application of this principle to the case of indirect abortion.

An Alternative to Abortion

Abortion has come to be considered the easiest solution to an unwanted pregnancy. However, in view of the evidence presented to show its immorality, other alternatives should be sought and followed. Society should provide the mother reassurance and opportunities for having her child brought to term. This care and concern should be extended to mother and child after the birth, e.g., by liaison with adoption agencies. The "Birthright" organization, which originated in Canada and has spread to the U.S. and England, provides counseling and care for pregnant women, as well as adoption procedures for the newborn child. Abortion cannot be defended as a social necessity when humane alternatives are available.

A Person Is a Person

It is common practice for "abortion clinics" to refer to early embryonic growth as "tissue." This depersonalized terminology is adopted in order to assure the pregnant woman that abortion is equivalent to the removal of a mole or a tumor. We have already reviewed the biological evidence opposing this way of viewing the embryo. But, by way of analogy, we can consider the meaning of a Dr. Seuss television program entitled "Horton Hears a Who." Horton, a personable elephant character, one day hears a faint voice crying, "Help!" The voice comes from a dust speck that has floated down from the sky, landing on a nearby flower. Sure enough, Horton learns that a tiny colony of celestial creatures, called "Whos," live on the dust speck, which is their planet. Horton makes friends with the speaker, "Dr. Who." It appears that the good professor is having difficulty persuading his fellows that their world is but a part of a larger universe, inhabited by other living beings. As the story develops, Horton cannot convince the other jungle animals that he hears a voice on the dust speck. They, thinking him mad, decide to cage him, and to boil the troublesome dust speck. The professor, hearing of their plan, convinces the colony that, to be saved, they must make themselves heard. He manages to have everyone shout out in unison, "We're here!" The jungle animals then hear the voices; and in the nick of time, the dust speck is saved. Both parties rejoice over the discovery of each other, as the jungle animals finally acknowledge in rhyme and verse, "After *all* . . . a person's a person . . . no matter how *small!*" Similarly, the new speck of unborn human life cannot be heard in a desperate plea, "Help! I'm here! I'm here!" Pro-abortionists have thus far been slow to accept, much less to sing, that "a person's a person . . . no matter how small."

Euthanasia

Euthanasia, or "mercy killing," especially of the aged,

the incurably ill, and so forth, also has its proponents today. Let us begin by citing an example of the outlook of traditional Christianity on this matter: "Whatever is opposed to life itself, such as any type of murder, genocide, abortion, euthanasia, or willful self-destruction . . . all these things and others of their like are infamies indeed" (Abbott, 1966, "The Church Today," art. 27). "We have begun to tolerate, if not encourage, abortion as a partial means of population control. Soon we shall institutionalize the removal of olders under the excuse of euthanasia. Next comes culling, removal of misfits, both physical and psychic, and finally we shall issue licenses for procreation with appropriate fees, safeguards, and penalties. This will cover the situation: abortion, culling, termination. So shall we return to the world of the primitive, the so-called savage who with natural nonchalance kills off the unwanted newborn, the useless oldster, and lets natural enemies take care of misfits. In fact, an old civilization like one prior to Mao followed similar customs. That's what you face: nothing new this side of the gates" (Sutter, 1970).

Motives for Mercy Killing. The term *euthanasia* comes from the Greek, meaning "easy death" or "happy death." It is synonymous with the more common expression, "mercy killing." It refers to one human being terminating the life of another for what are considered worthy motives. These motives include killing the incurably insane, the retarded, the newly born with physical defects (infanticide), the hopelessly crippled, the very aged, the dying, and people considered a burden on society or who are unwanted for other reasons (Bittle, 1950; Wertham, 1966). Those who advocate euthanasia usually concede they are terminating a human life. The ethical principle to which they appeal is that a good end may justify an immoral means. Two familiar problems are encountered here. First, what is to be considered a good end, purpose, or intention? Second, once judged to be good, can such an end, purpose, or intention be used to justify immoral means toward its accomplishment?

Most people would probably disagree with the statement that people can morally be killed because they happen to belong to a particular social or ethnic group. When couched in such terms, euthanasia is seen to be really a misnomer. Many people might also balk at killing senile and mental patients "for their own good." However, one purpose or end on which nearly everyone would agree as really worthwhile is the alleviation of pain and suffering in the terminally ill patient. The next question is whether such relief can be brought about by killing the patient. The answer to this question hinges on moral absolutes. If the destruction of innocent life, or murder, is considered to be absolutely and always prohibited, then it would follow that no good purpose could ever justify it. If the commandment prohibiting murder is seen to allow exceptions, then relativism and situational ethics prevail; that is, in some circumstances it would be held that absolute moral precepts can be violated for good reason, intentions, purposes, or ends. We have already seen the moral chaos that results from the acceptance of the principle, a good end can justify an immoral means. If this principle is accepted, then any and all immorality can be justified or defended. The traditional Christian contends that termination of innocent human life is a prerogative belonging to God alone, and that man has no grounds for assuming that right. For that reason, the Christian condemns suicide, as well as mercy-killing.

Withdrawing Extraordinary Life-Support. There has risen the ethical question of whether the decision to withdraw, or not to use, extraordinary means of preserving the life of a dying person is an act of murder (McFadden, 1976). This withdrawal of artificial life-support (e.g., artificial respirators, electrolytic balance fluids, blood transfusions, and kidney machines for the terminal patient) is sometimes referred to as "passive euthanasia," in contrast to "active euthanasia" or direct intervention to kill the patient. It is an ethical error, however, to consider these situations as merely two kinds of euthanasia. There is a radical difference between allowing nature to take its course, a way in which God takes human life, and deliberately killing an individual. To allow the terminally ill person to die is a morally indifferent act; to kill him is murder. To allow one to die a natural death does not preclude, however, the alleviation of pain and suffering. Drugs may be used to the point short of being lethal (but not beyond that point; otherwise they too would become a means of murder).

Significance of Suffering. Those who advocate euthanasia usually take the attitude that suffering is meaningless in life and should be eradicated. This attitude is consistent with the position of naturalistic, evolutionary, atheistic humanism. For the atheist, man has but one life, which is here and now. There is no hereafter. It is therefore logical to seek the greatest happiness possible in the present life, and to view suffering as irrational, inhumane, and something to be rid of at all costs. The Christian humanist, on the other hand, sees suffering in a different light. First, he accepts its origin as explained in divine revelation. God originally intended for mankind a happy, pain-free life in Eden. Original man turned away from God, thus meriting the human condition of pain, guilt, and death. We have seen how God in his mercy promised redemption, and that the Second Person of the Trinity became incarnate in Jesus Christ. God the Son chose an intensely painful death as the means of redemption; he thereby sanctified suffering and made it meaningful. Following in his steps, as he admonished his followers to do, one can join one's suffering with Christ's, as atonement for one's own sins and those of others.

To question the goodness of God when one sees dear ones in great pain, or when one personally experiences pain, is a natural human impulse. But this is precisely where Christian faith is operable, in accepting what is not understandable, because it comes from the hand of God, who is Goodness and Love. If there were total understanding of such things, there would be no need of faith.

The Christian is neither a sadist nor a masochist. He does not enjoy the sufferings in others or in himself. He believes that he has a right to alleviate pain whenever possible, but not to the extent of employing an immoral means. The Christian contends that man is but the steward of life, which he has received from God. Man does not have the moral right to murder even in order to alleviate pain. The Christian accepts suffering, offers it in prayer, and believes that in the afterlife God will more than compensate for the trials endured in this life. "Just as man is able to look beyond the darkness of night to a beautiful day, and beyond the dreariness of winter to a glorious spring, so does resignation to suffering enable him to look beyond the material and temporal to things eternal" (McFadden, 1951, p. 138). And, as another has observed, "This is a planned universe. Suffering fits into it, otherside He [Jesus Christ] would have refused it. The cross fits into it, otherwise He would not have embraced it. The crown of thorns fits into it, otherwise He would not have worn it" (Sheen, in McFadden, 1951, p. xi).

SUGGESTED READINGS

1. Grisez, Germain. *Abortion: The Myths, the Realities, and the Arguments.* N.Y.: Corpus Books, 1972. An exhaustive study of the biological, sociological, medical, religious, legal, and ethical aspects of abortion.

2. McFadden, Charles F. *Medical Ethics* (6th ed.). Philadelphia: F. A. Davis, 1956. An analysis of the ethical aspects of various surgical procedures, as well as a moral critique of abortion.

3. Atkinson, G. M. "The Morality of Abortion," *International Philosophical Quarterly* 14 (1974) 347-362. An in-depth examination of the moral and philosophical facets of abortion, and the implications for infanticide and active euthanasia.

4. Whitehead, K. D. *Respectable Killing: The New Abortion Imperative.* New Rochelle: Catholics United for the Faith, 1972. A traditional Catholic perspective on abortion, with an ecumenical appeal.

5. Noebel, David A. *Slaughter of the Innocent.* Tulsa: American's Against Abortion, 1974. A Protestant criticism of the morality of abortion.

6. Marx, Paul. *The Death Peddlers: War on the Unborn.* Collegeville: St. John's Univ. Press, 1971. An analysis of abortion counseling, legal aspects, and the involvement of state and government in the abortion controversy.

7. Horan, D. J., and D. Mall, eds. *Death, Dying, and Euthanasia.* Wash., D.C.: University Publications of America, 1977. Thirty-four contributors comment on ethical, religious, moral, medical, social, and legal aspects of euthanasia.

9

BIOETHICS

"Men ought not to play God before they learn to be men, and after they have learned to be men they will not play God."
—P. Ramsey, *Fabricated Man.*

RELATED to ethical issues concerning respect for human life is an issue that has been introduced by the scientific advances in biology and biochemistry, specifically in biogenetic engineering.

The contemporary age is one of rapid change. Scientific and technological advances of the present day have enabled man to travel to the moon and to replace his own heart, achievements that were fictional but a few years ago. Unfortunately, technological accomplishments have outdistanced the needed reflection on their social, psychological, ethical, and moral implications. Consequently, there is legitimate, widespread concern today about such matters as arms escalation, environmental pollution, depletion of natural resources, and—relevant to the present topic—manipulation of the biological nature and future of mankind. Developments in the science of genetics have unlocked biochemical knowledge that may eventually enable man to change the genetic blueprint of future generations. These technological achievements fall within the scope of biogenetic engineering; and the relevant moral issues compose the subject matter of bioethics. °

For present purposes, biogenetic engineering will be considered to involve the applications of the science of genetics to the detection of prenatal and postnatal genetic disease, the therapy advocated, the research proposed for the control of genetic disease in future generations, and the experimentation on the production of new life-forms. We shall first present these various facets of biogenetic engineering, and then consider the psychological, philosophical, and moral implications.

Genetic Terms

The basic unit of inheritance is the *gene*, a specific length of interlocking double-stranded deoxyribonucleic acid (DNA), which codes for the production of specific proteins, which in turn may control cellular metabolic reactions, order embryonic development, or direct development of body structure, e.g., eyes, ears, and color of hair (Karp, 1976). *Chromosomes* are the microscopically observable structures that contain DNA. Every species of plant or animal contains a specific number of chromosomes; in man the number is forty-six, composed of twenty-three pairs, one of each pair inherited from a respective parent. The chromosomes in a cell can be separated, then arranged according to similar pairs, and given numbers. This procedure is called karotyping, and the resultant "photograph" a *karotype*. An examination of the chromosomes in the cell of an individual can reveal errors in the number of chromosomes. For example, in chromosome pair number 21, sometimes three rather

---

° For a brief discussion of the pastoral aspects of biogenetic counseling, see J. A. Hammes, "Shall We Play God? An Ethical Analysis of Biogenetics," *Homiletic and Pastoral Review* 77 (1977), 59-62.

than two chromosomes are present. In this instance the condition is referred to as "trisomy 21," which is characteristic of Down's Syndrome, or mongolism.

Each human cell contains enough DNA to code for about seven million proteins (L. E. Rosenburg, in Lipkin and Rowley, 1974, p. 3). About ten percent of this DNA is thought to be active, of which only one percent has been chemically or genetically identified, leaving ninety-nine percent a mysterious unknown. Furthermore, this DNA is constantly changing, or mutating, and the number of mutations per germ-cell is estimated to vary from five to ten. The complex picture of human heredity is further complicated by the fact that a human male can produce about eight million genetically distinct sperm during his lifetime; the human female produces from a similar number of possibilities the actual number of consequent eggs (T. C. Schelling, in Lipkin and Rowley, 1974, p. 102).

Genetic Disease and Genetic Pollution

Genetic diseases are those caused by (a) chromosomal abnormalities, (b) single gene defects, and (c) multifactorial interactions between the organism and its environment (Karp, 1976). *Chromosomal abnormalities* may be caused by errors in number, e.g., Down's Syndrome, or in structure, e.g., chromosome fragmentation and improper restructuring. *Single gene* defects are consequent to gene mutation, e.g., Huntington's chorea, Tay-Sachs disease, cystic fibrosis, and sickle-cell anemia. It is estimated that all human beings carry from three to nine mutant genes potentially deleterious under certain circumstances. *Multifactorial* diseases are illustrated by congenital heart disease, diabetes mellitus, epilepsy, cleft lip, club foot, and anencephaly/spina bifida. Genetic factors are also involved in such diseases as arthritis, gout, stomach ulcers, high blood pressure, schizophrenia, and certain forms of cancer (Anderson, 1972). The advances of medical scientific inquiry have enabled mankind to live longer, and also have enabled persons carrying deleterious genes to reach the reproductive age and to pass on their genes to future generations. Those and other factors have led some geneticists to view with alarm what is referred to as the genetic load, or genetic burden, resulting in a so-called pollution of the gene pool (Francoeur, 1972).

Whether future mankind faces a genetic "apocalypse" if we do not take immediate remedial steps has been questioned (Lappe, 1972). Genetic material is self-correcting through compensatory action by non-deleterious genes, such that genetic predictions are not always accurate. Also, to eliminate to a great extent reproduction on the part of deleterious gene carriers would be to eliminate the adaptive value of nature's genetic diversity. Also, the overall gene pattern that may be transmitted by deleterious gene carriers, e.g., schizophrenic parents, may contain desirable features that outweigh the schizoid transmission (Lappe, 1972). Such is certainly the case with such individuals as diabetics. In short, the problem of genetic defects should be put into proper perspective. As Kass has pointed out, "Who uses up more of our irreplaceable natural resources and who produces more pollution—the inmates of an institution for the retarded or the graduates of Harvard College? It is probably as indisputable as it is ignored that the world suffers more from the morally and spiritually defective than from the genetically defective" (Kass, 1972). The modern attitude toward the genetically defective is based on a value judgment, a subject to which we shall return later.

Genetic Screening and Counseling

Genetic screening is the systematic examination of populations for purposes of detecting carriers of hereditary abnormalities capable of producing disease in themselves or their descendants (Karp, 1976). Genetic therapy refers to the methods used to correct genetic disease. Let us first discuss genetic screening.

Diseases that can be genetically screened include phenylketonuria (PKU), Tay-Sachs disease, sickle-cell anemia, coronary heart disease, hemophilia, muscular dystrophy, diabetes mellitus, hypertension, anencephaly/spina bifida, Klinefelter Syndrome, and Turner Syndrome (Karp, 1976). Genetic screening and counseling deal with two kinds of situations, prenatal and postnatal. In the postnatal situation, therapy is directed toward correction of the disease in the patient. In prenatal circumstances, the direction of therapy can likewise be toward correction; but if the disease is not treatable, the alternative often proposed is to kill the patient, namely, the unborn individual. Thus, the actual practices of those involved in prenatal genetic counseling have included recommendation of eugenic abortion, thus raising the moral question involved.

Genetic Therapy

There are three terms in genetics that involve different aspects in the applications of this science (Karp, 1976). *Eugenics* refers to manipulation of genes for supposed improvement of the general health and quality of the human race. We shall discuss this approach under the heading of reproductive engineering. *Euphenics* concerns the genetic health of the individual rather than of the species, and includes pre- and postnatal diagnosis, screening, and therapy. *Euthenics* is therapy directed to the manipulation of the environment, e.g., prostheses and drug therapy in the cure or control of genetic disease (Motulsky, 1972).

Genetic therapy has successfully utilized diet and drug treatment (e.g. in diabetes and epilepsy) and surgery (e.g., in retinoblastoma and polypsis of the colon). Proposed future therapy includes microsurgery aimed at elimination or replacement of faulty genes, and the control of viral disease by introducing tailor-made "interferon" molecules as an override (Anderson, 1972; Roblin, 1972). Artificially introduced corrective genes might also be used to control cancer growth, or to slow normal aging processes. Genetic therapy is sometimes referred to as "negative eugenics," and reproductive engineering as "positive eugenics" (Jones, 1972).

Reproductive Engineering

Reproductive engineering is that field of research which attempts to reproduce the human species by means other than heterosexual intercourse. It includes experimentation in artificial insemination, cryobanking, *in vitro* fertilization, and cloning.

Artificial insemination dates back to 1776. At least ninety-five percent of all cattle in the U.S. are born as the result of artificial insemination (Francoeur, 1972). The artificial insemination of a woman was apparently first recorded in 1799, in England, in an attempt to assist a childless couple to have children. Artificial insemination by husband (AIH) is usually distinguished from artificial insemination by donor (AID). The latter procedure has been advocated in cases of male infertility, or to avoid transmission of known genetic disease; it is urged by some geneticists (e.g., H. J. Muller) for improvement of the human species by using the sperm of supposedly superior men. *Cryobanking*, the frozen cold-storage of semen and eggs, has been proposed for similar uses (Karp, 1976).

In vivo ("in the living") fertilization is that which occurs in the natural manner of sexual intercourse. The egg is fertilized within a female parent. *In vitro* ("in glass") fertilization is the procedure by which a ripened egg is removed from the woman's body and fertilized by sperm in a laboratory setting. Implantation, in the natural course of events, occurs at the blastocyst stage, and therefore, when the zygote has reached this stage it must be implanted in a female recipient to permit further embryonic growth. *In vitro* embryonic experiments have been successfully completed in mice, rats, rabbits, guinea pigs, hamsters, gerbils, cats, squirrel monkeys, and baboons (Brackett, in Lipkin and Rowley, 1974; Karp, 1976; and Kraemer *et al.*, 1976). Experiments with human eggs have been conducted by R. G. Edwards and P. Steptoe (Karp, 1976, p. 172), but none have been successfully implanted and brought to term. One purpose for conducting *in vitro* fertilization experiments is that of helping mothers, who cannot themselves bring an initiated pregnancy to term, by removing and implanting the fertilized egg in a substitute mother. This procedure has also been suggested as a way of avoiding transmission of genetic disease, by implantation of substitute fertilized eggs. Such endeavors have also been defended in the name of pure scientific research. We shall later examine the moral validity of these procedures.

Cloning is the artificial reproduction of the exact genetic copy of a living organism. "Clone" comes from the Greek *klon*, meaning "twig." In the cloning procedure known as nuclear transfer, the nucleus of a mature but unfertilized egg is removed, by microsurgery or by irradiation, and replaced by the nucleus of a specialized body-cell of an adult organism, e.g., an intestinal or skin cell (Karp, 1976; Kass, 1972). This new nucleus brings to the egg cell a complete set of forty-six chromosomes, which would have ordinarily been accomplished in natural processes by the summing of twenty-three chromosomes of a sperm cell with the twenty-three chromosomes of the egg cell. In the cloning procedure, the consequence is an individual genetically identical to the donor of the new nucleus. Cloning can also be accomplished by embryo fission, a procedure in which the embryo at the two-cell stage is divided, such that each cell becomes a separate embryo which can be implanted in a female recipient and brought to term. Embryo fission can be considered the experimental equivalent of twinning. Cloning has been successfully conducted with frogs and mice. On the human levels, the technical problems include the obtaining of mature eggs, their enucleation, and the insertion of the donor nucleus, and implantation of the renucleated egg in an adult female uterus. Reasons advanced for cloning include replicating the healthy, the gifted, and the beautiful; providing children to infertile parents; selecting the sex of a child; providing sources of organ transplants; building superior military forces; and the scientific improvement of the human species (Kass, 1972). Whether such purposes and ends are praiseworthy is subject to debate. And, even if some of these intentions are admirable, the ethical evaluation of the means proposed to achieve them still requires consideration.

Experimenting with New Life-Forms

Biological scientists have succeeded in inserting pieces of DNA from cells of one species into the cells of another species, with the hope of eventually producing a new species of life. The usual host in such experiments is the bacterium *Escherichia coli*, a common inhabitant of the human intestinal tract. The potential dangers, or biohazards, to

man are evident, if the products of such research ever escape into the atmosphere, and ethical debate has consequently ensued (Callahan, 1977; Fields, 1977; *Time* magazine, 1977; Wade, 1976). The benefits of such research
include the production of compounds useful in medicine
and agriculture; the risks involve the unknown consequences in recombining DNA of different species.

This concludes our sketch of biogenetic engineering. Let
us now consider the psychological, ethical, and moral implications.

Psychological Aspects of Biogenetic Engineering

By psychological aspects of biogenetic engineering we
shall mean the human reactions and attitudes involved in
this area of technological development. First, let us consider genetic screening and counseling.

At one time there was no foreknowledge of the genetic
character of the newborn. Parents conceived and looked
forward to having average, normal children. The emotional
impact of the birth of a genetically afflicted child is well
known. The sequence of adjustment on the part of the parents has been compared with that of coping with bereave-
ment (Shore, ch. 15 in Birch and Abrecht, 1975). First,
there is the denial of reality, then depression and resentment, followed by grief, and perhaps irrational guilt. Finally, if these reactions are successfully worked through, there
is acceptance. The afflicted child, if it is intelligent enough,
also eventually needs to work through such feelings. The
development of genetic-screening techniques has added an
additional parental burden—the choice of either bringing a
diagnosed-defective embryo to term, or aborting it in the
womb. Parents who consider eugenic abortion the equivalent of murder may face the additional stress of opposing

the usual counseling directive to resort to abortion. Regardless of the choice, guilt may be engendered.

It is natural for parents to adopt the norms of health and beauty from the society of which they are members. Consequently, they are prone to react negatively to a child who does not fit that norm. The stereotyped concept of what contemporary society considers normal and beautiful is quite explicit; the genetically afflicted child cannot measure up. The parents therefore are not only disappointed, but also feel rejected by that society which has rejected their child. Even members of the medical professions refer to the abnormal newborn as "monsters" or "monstrosities" (Karp, 1976, p. 41). People hide or institutionalize the genetically abnormal, out of embarrassment and shame. Society would, further, disown any moral or financial responsibility to such persons.

But must this attitude be inevitable? Could not society's opinion be changed, such that the genetically afflicted, born and unborn, would be considered intrinsically human, equal in dignity and in nature to those who are "normal" and "beautiful"? From a Christian perspective, they too are destined for eternal life with God—and consequently deserve society's respect, compassion, and care. Why should the genetically deprived, who are not responsible for their condition, be shunned? And why should their families be made to feel rejected? The Christian perspective is certainly humane in its concern for those in that situation. But because contemporary society has largely rejected the Christian frame of reference, the situation prevails.

The psychological aspects of *in vitro* experimentation are of a different nature from those in genetic screening and counseling. The problem, however, is again one of attitude. The fertilized egg, blastocyst, and early embryo are evaluated *behaviorally:* i.e., they do not look like or act like a human being, and therefore it is concluded that they are not human. This same behavioral assessment is applied by contemporary society to the genetically afflicted and also to the very old and the psychotic. For example, the person deprived of cortical function, whether as the result of age or trauma (e.g., an auto accident), is spoken of as a "vegetable," since the individual appears to be functioning only at the vegetative level of existence. This behavioral attitude in the evaluation of what is human and what is not stems directly from the positivistic or mechanistic scientific model, which accepts as admissible evidence only that which is concrete. Because the unseen, intangible, and intrinsic aspects of human nature are ignored, *in vitro* experimentation is considered a legitimate endeavor.

With regard to experimentation in *cloning* a human being, other psychological variables are involved, which derive from pride. Contemporary man believes he can improve human nature. "The next step for evolution is ours. . . . A fairer species will arise—a being newer and finer to expand to the meaning of life" (Sinsheimer *et al.*, 1973, p. 350). "By divine command we are creators. Why, then, should we be shocked today to learn that we can or soon will be able to create the man of the future?" (Francoeur, 1972, p. 429). Such pride is accompanied by the thrust toward limitless freedom, under the assumption that because man has the capability to achieve a technological feat, he must achieve that feat (Fromm, 1968), or that because he has the capacity to control nature, he must control nature (Crotty, 1972; Lappe, 1972; Szebenyi, 1972). It is one easy step further to conclude that there is even a moral obligation to carry out what is technically feasible, and that not to do so constitutes a shirking of moral responsibility.

Ethical and Moral Implications
of Genetic Screening and Counseling

We have seen that genetic screening and counseling involve two kinds of situations, the postnatal and prenatal. Procedures for the *postnatal* patient are directed toward correction of the disease or its effects, with a view also to preventing the transmission of the disease to future generations. Restoring health, or helping a patient cope with personal illness, is obviously good. Indeed, the intentions of genetic screening and counseling are not blameworthy; it is in regard to the means employed that ethical and moral questions arise. For example, should carriers of Tay-Sachs disease, sickle-cell anemia, and diabetes be sterilized? If so, should the procedure be voluntary or compulsory? The *prenatal* counseling situation further involves a second party, the unborn individual. Although the detection of fetal abnormality need not necessarily result in the counseling of eugenic abortion, such is usually the consequence (Serra, in Birch and Abrecht, 1975, p. 112). Reasons given for eugenic abortion include "quantity and quality of human existence" (Morison, in Hilton *et al.*, 1973, p. 209), alleviation of human suffering, the financial cost to the family and society in the care of defectives, the assertion that parents do not have the right to procreate knowingly a defective child (Serra, in Birch and Abrecht, 1975, p. 113; Ramsey, 1970, p. 58), and the claim that the unborn are not human and lack rights, particularly the right to life.

Let us consider some of these reasons advanced for counseling eugenic abortion. The "cost-benefit" rationale balances the emotional and financial "costs" of caring for the defective child, and in some instances the physical or emotional suffering of the child, against any "benefit" the child may have for its family or for society, and in this computation the "benefit" is usually outweighed (Karp, 1976, pp. 81, 121; Birch, in Birch and Abrecht, 1975, p. 14; Morison, in Hilton *et al.*, 1973, p. 208). Instances in which eugenic abortion is advocated range from Down's Syndrome or mongolism (Birch, in Birch and Abrecht, 1975, p. 11), to hemophilia (Karp, 1976, p. 121) and muscular dystrophy (Latimer, in Lipkin and Rowley, 1974, p. 25). The "cost-benefit" approach is also used in an effort to have the government finance abortions of unwanted children, on the grounds that the cost for an abortion operation is less than that of raising unwanted children on welfare. The same argument is used on behalf of active euthanasia, in order to save federal spending for the elderly, terminal patient (Castelli, 1977).

A cost-benefit rationale for eugenic abortion deserves effective rebuttal. Can a quantitative assessment be placed on the value of an unborn member of the human species? In the U.S., we are apparently willing to invest more than $100 billion annually on national defense, yet balk over the comparatively paltry expense of providing medical care for defective children. Similarly, the "benefit" of the defective child, seen in terms of his productive contribution to society, is usually calculated to be zero. No value is attached to the child for simply being, in the Christian perspective, what he actually is—a human being with intrinsic dignity derived from his creation in the image of God, and destined for immortal life. No physical defect or limitation can deprive him of this value. Also, as Kass has observed, the cost-analysis is not accurate, for it does reflect the offset cost of raising the child if he were normal (in Hilton, *et al.*, 1973, p. 193). The "cost" approach is sometimes presented in terms of emotional and physical suffering, on the part of both the parents and the defective child. However, as Murray has pointed out (in Birch and Abrecht, 1975, p. 176), if the prevention of suffering is an acceptable reason for eugenic abortion, then where is the line drawn? Who decides how much suffering is acceptable, and, therefore, who is to live? Should we abort children born to parents below the poverty-income-level? What is perceived to be suffering, as well as whether or not one can cope, is dependent on one's philosophy of suffering. An atheistic, materialistic mentality can, of course, see no meaning or value in suffering.

The "cost-benefit" approach thus sees the defective child as an emotional and financial threat to the family and to society. As with any "enemy," it can therefore be destroyed, in the name of "justice" and "responsibility" (Fletcher, in Hilton *et al.*, 1973, p. 224), and the appropriate, and legal, time to do so is before the infant emerges from the womb.

Eugenic abortion has also been counseled by some geneticists (e.g., Glass) on the grounds that only the child with the capacity for a "normal, adequate hereditary endowment" has the right to be born (in Birch and Abrecht, 1975, p. 57). Thus the condition of *freedom from genetic defects* is posed as the basis for the right to life. Callahan disagrees, asserting that "we will indeed have descended into the pit if we make genetic perfection a condition for the right to exist" (Callahan, in Hamilton, 1972, p. 95). Serra (in Birch and Abrecht, 1975, p. 115) agrees that serious mental or physical impairment does not deprive one of the right to life. Murray (*ibid.*, p. 179) contends that devaluing a child with chronic illness is unethical and immoral, and that eugenic abortion logically leads to infanticide. Kass (in Hilton *et al.*, 1973, p. 191) also rejects the principle that "defectives should not be born," observing that such an attitude can logically be generalized to include those who escaped "the net of detection and abortion" (p. 189). "A child born with Down's Syndrome or hemophilia or muscular dystrophy will be looked upon by the community as one unfit to be alive, . . . as a person who need not have been, and who would not have been, if only someone had gotten to him in time" (p. 188). As to the matter of the "social value" of the defective child, Kass quotes Pearl Buck on the beneficial effect that caring for defective children has had on those who care for them—"lessons of patience, understanding, and mercy, lessons which we all need to receive and to practice with one another, whatever we are" (p. 194). If every human being is required to have a normal, healthy constitution, the implication is that the unhealthy person, particularly the defective individual, cannot live the "fully human" life. Exploring that implication, Kass asks if we should therefore genetically abort blind or deaf children, and the diabetic too. The mongoloid, so commonly the target for eugenic abortion, can live a happy, affectionate life. Lejeune, two days after he rejected the stance of eugenic abortion during a televised debate, received a letter from a 16-year-old mongoloid girl with an I.Q. of 40. The letter said, in poorly written but readable words, "I like you because you love the Mongol" (Hilton *et al.*, 1973, p. 213).

Ramsey (Hilton *et al.*, 1973, p. 152) has pointed out that advocacy of eugenic abortion will inevitably extend to justification for infanticide and eventually even shape society's attitudes toward carriers of genetic disease, who are themselves otherwise normal and in good health. Infanticide has already been openly promulgated by some geneticists. The example of James Watson has already been mentioned (Chapter 8). Kass applies Abraham Lincoln's indictment of slavery to an indictment of the principle that defectives should not be born. Lincoln had observed that once the "right" of slavery was granted to be legitimate, the slave-owner himself was subject to enslavement (*ibid.*, p. 191). Kass contends that the principle "defectives should not be born" would eventually, upon discovery of more precise ways of detecting genetic defects, be applicable to practically everyone.

A position akin to asserting that the defective child has no right to life is the supposition that the child has a right "not to be born," if its life would be one of "extreme suffering and/or the inability to know who and what it is" (Augenstein, 1969, p. 122). This motive for eugenic abortion purports to be one of compassion for the suffering of the afflicted child. The basis for such a "right" not-to-be-born assumes, of course, that one has absolute dominion over human life and can terminate it for reasons of compassion. A similar argument is used to justify active euthanasia, i.e., putting to death a terminally ill patient. The criticism of such arguments is to be directed not at the intention of the agent or the ends of the act (namely, compassion and relief from pain, respectively), but rather at the *means* employed to achieve such purposes. Traditional Christian teaching has always held that a good end or purpose cannot be used to justify evil means. Situational ethicists have attempted to overthrow this principle, but it is defensible on solid philosophical and theological grounds (Hammes, 1975c; Ramsey, 1970). Innocent life may not be destroyed even for the noblest of reasons. This observation implies, of course, that suffering must be borne in resignation if the only means to alleviate it are immoral.

We have seen that eugenic abortion has been counseled for expectant mothers who are carrying genetically defective embryos, and we have criticized this advice. A related problem concerns parents who know they are carriers of a genetic defect and who wish nonetheless to bear children. Do such parents have the right to conceive, when there is every indication that the consequent child will be genetically defective? Reasons given for a negative answer range from compassion for the child to his medical care falling as a financial burden on society (Ramsey, 1970, p. 58; Glass, in Birch and Abrecht, 1975, p. 56). Reasons given by parents who wish to conceive such children range from the willingness and capability of assuming care of the child to the religious viewpoint that the child's eternal afterlife in heaven more than compensates for its comparatively brief life on earth. It would appear that a prudent decision would rest on the circumstances of individual cases. The parental right to procreate is a natural human right, but it need not always be exercised. Even if weighty reasons for not bearing children were agreed upon, the question still remains as to which means might be used to achieve that objective. The popular view favors contraception or eugenic sterilization. The opposing view is that those means are intrinsically immoral, and that voluntary celibacy should rather be the solution (McFadden, 1976, ch. 3, 8).

Whatever the reasons advanced for eugenic abortion, the crux of the moral problem is the nature of unborn life. Is the embryo or fetus human? All considerations of moral and legal rights of the unborn are based on the two alternative answers to this question. Some say the fetus is human but not a "person," and on that grounds deny the fetus the right to life (Fletcher, in Lipkin and Rowley, 1974, p. 96). Others insist that the defective embryo is a "tumor" that can be removed when it causes "misery" to the mother (Stetten, in Hilton *et al.*, 1973, p. 212). Another writer rejects "sacredness of life" as an indefensible reason for eugenic abortion (Edwards, in Birch and Abrecht, 1975,

p. 49); and one observer writes, "I fail to see why the right to life among featherless bipeds is any more sacred than the right, if right there be, to life on the part of mosses, insects, or cancer cells" (Aiken, in Hilton *et al.*, 1973, p. 183). The U.S. Supreme Court has declared that a woman's right to privacy is greater than her unborn child's right to life; this verdict has legalized abortion in general and eugenic abortion in particular.

The biological, philosophical, and religious evidence for the humanity and essential personhood of the unborn child, beginning with the moment of the conception of a new and distinct individual, has already been summarized, and is available in more detail elsewhere. This evidence supports the following scenario: The fertilized egg, or zygote, develops from within as a separate organism, to emerge as an infant after nine months of dependency on the uterine environment. What makes it to be a member of the human species was present from the moment of conception, unseen but nonetheless real. The necessity for a temporal development of this human potential does not render it less human in early stages of growth. The zygote is human potential, not potentially human. It is a member of the human species; there is no other species it could be. If it *were* a species other than human, it would emerge as that species. The arbitrariness of the argument that the fetus may be human, but not yet a person, and that only "persons" have moral or legal rights, is immediately evident. Why not say, if saying will make it so, that personhood begins with brain development, or at the moment of emergence from the womb, or when the child reaches the age of reason, or when he becomes socialized by his culture?

From a religious perspective, both the Old and New Testaments indicate the presence of humanity within the womb (Grisez, 1972). Early Christianity condemned abortion, and this position is still upheld in the teaching of the Roman Catholic Church (Abbott, 1966). Jewish and Protestant traditions generally permit therapeutic abortion, a distinction discussed elsewhere (McFadden, 1976). Both traditional viewpoints condemn eugenic abortion.

Some, while acknowledging the embryo or fetus to be human and to have a right to life, argue that this right must give way to other rights, including the right of parents to be spared the sacrifice and suffering of having a defective child, or the right of society to be spared the financial burden of providing medical care for defective children, or the right of privacy (as endorsed by the Supreme Court), or the right of a woman, for any reason she might have, to destroy the fetal life within her.

The moral question thus becomes, When does the right to life overrule other rights or wishes? It is beyond the scope of this book to discuss the relative weighing of rights; it will only be noted here that the right to life is fundamental, and certainly prior to the derivation of other rights pertaining to the "pursuit of happiness." The weakness, helplessness, and inability of the unborn to exercise their right to life has too often been taken advantage of in the battle over rights.

Ethical and Moral Implications of AIH, AID, and In Vitro Fertilization

Moral objections to AIH (artificial insemination by husband) and AID (artificial insemination by donor) are based on the interpretation of the natural moral law and the meaning of the marital covenant. Traditional Catholic teaching, as well as very traditional Protestant teaching, morally objects to the *means* by which semen is usually obtained for artificial insemination. This means, masturbation, is regarded as intrinsically evil; and acts that are intrinsically evil are never morally permissible, even for the best of intentions or reasons (National Conference of Catholic Bishops, 1971). Furthermore, the concept of marriage as a covenant reflecting Christ's love for his Church is also brought forward to indict artificial insemination, especially AID (McFadden, 1976; Ramsey, 1970, p. 32). From a Christian perspective, AID is an extension of adultery, in the sense that only the husband has the moral right to impregnate his wife. Ramsey contends that the unitive (love) and procreative aspects of marriage are not intended in the divine plan to be separated; AID violates this principle. Traditional Catholic teaching applies this view further in the rejection of contraception (Paul VI, 1968; May, 1976) and sterilization (May, 1977) as immoral.

To those who reject either the natural moral law as a moral norm, or the concept of Christian marriage as presented here, both AIH and AID would be acceptable procedures to follow, for the reasons earlier discussed.

In vitro experimentation, as well as the consequent abortion involved, has been defended in the name of "scientific purposes" and "social benefits" (Birch, in Birch and Abrecht, 1975, p. 48; Brackett, in Lipkin and Rowley, 1974, p. 37). Karp contends that the eggs and embryos resulting from such research belong to the donor, who has a moral right to decide that they may be used for research or for implantation in other women, or that they can "simply be washed down the sink." He adds, "Flushing away a human blastocyst would not be a compunctious act for me, but anyone who is concerned that this microscopic ball of cells might have a soul ought not to engage in ectogenetic work. It seems as simple as that" (Karp, 1976, p. 182). Others, in similar vein, claim that the right of blastocysts in research must be subordinated to the "general good of society" (Edwards, quoted by Jones, in the *Journal of the American Scientific Association*, 1974).

In contrast, there are those who consider *in vitro* experimentation and research to be unethical and immoral. Kass observes that "another human being, the child-to-be, . . . cannot give informed consent to have such risks imposed upon him" (Kass, in Hamilton, 1972, p. 27). He adds, "Morally, it is insufficient that your motives are good, that your ends are unobjectionable, that you do the procedure 'lovingly,' and even that you may be lucky in the result: You will be engaging nonetheless in an unethical experiment upon a human subject" (*ibid.*, p. 30). Ramsey agrees: ". . . the decisive moral verdict must be that we cannot rightfully get to know how to do this without conducting unethical experiments upon the unborn who must be the 'mishaps' (the dead and retarded ones) through whom we learn how" (Ramsey, 1970, p. 113). The moral legitimacy of *in vitro* experimentation also hinges, therefore, on the question of whether fertilized eggs, blastocysts, and embryos are considered intrinsically human, and therefore possess rights, or whether they are not human and can be subjected to research and abortion.

Ethical and Moral Implications of Cloning

The attempt to clone a human being has also been defended in the name of science. Although human cloning is at present but science fiction, the paving of the ethical road is already under way. With regard to manipulation of human genes, one geneticist exclaims, "I think the experiment itself is so eloquent as to be equivalent to being ethical" (Clarke, quoted by Latimer, in Lipkin and Rowley, 1974, p. 25). Another geneticist, Lederberg, has proposed somatic, psycho-sociological, and genetic criteria for the selection of the phenotypes to be perpetuated through cloning. Of the human aberrations that will inevitably result from general genetic experimentation, Lederberg says, "they may be such interesting *objects* for humane observation and experimentation that it may be well worth making very great efforts to keep them alive once they have started to exist" (Ramsey, 1970, p. 86; italics added). Karp is optimistic about the consequences of cloning supermen, and claims we need not fear possible enslavement by them. "Such admirable specimens of humanity could be expected to contain a large measure of decency, and to demonstrate love and respect for their creators. Our fear is based on projection of the manner in which we ourselves might behave in a similar circumstance" (Karp, 1976, p. 213).

There are practical, as well as ethical, doubts about human cloning. First, there is the assumption on the part of some biogeneticists that man can improve on the present plan of genetic diversity achieved in natural reproduction. But the adaptive value of a cloned population in a future, unpredictable environment is highly questionable (Lappe, 1972). The chance diversity of *naturally* procreated genotypes would have a better probability rate of survival. From a theological point of view, the ability of man to improve on God's plan is also questionable (Ramsey, 1970). The adequacy of human wisdom in the control of genetic breeding is also doubtful. Ramsey quotes Donald MacKay's indictment of the present generation's planning of the genetic blueprint of future generations: "In short, to navigate by a landmark tied to your own ship's head is ultimately impossible" (Ramsey, 1970, p. 54). Kass contends our knowledge is much too limited to plan genetic directions, and he concludes that "we can be wise enough to know that we are not wise enough. When we lack sufficient wisdom to do, wisdom consists in not doing" (Kass, 1972, p. 62).

Finally, the assumption that moral and character traits are genetically transmissible can be challenged. Muller, quoted by Ramsey, supposes that such traits as "creativity, wisdom, brotherliness, loving-kindness, perceptivity, expressivity, joy of life, fortitude, vigor [and] longevity" are genetic in nature (Ramsey, 1970, p. 52). But do traits such as loving-kindness, wisdom, fortitude, and brotherliness have a genetic basis? Intelligence may be related to genetic brain-structure, but the correlation of intelligence with the virtue of wisdom is zero. Traditional Christian belief includes God's creation of a spiritual, immortal human soul not reducible to physiological, biophysical, or chemical terms. Geneticists who assume a monistic, materialistic, mechanistic model of man naturally conclude that all human traits are functions (results, products) of genetic determination. The mechanistic model of man has been critiqued elsewhere (Hammes, 1971). The Christian perspective views moral and character traits as functions of the spiritual essence of man, together with the human response to God's grace and the gifts of the Holy Spirit. These have no genetic, molecular formulas.

From an ethical and moral perspective, the objections advanced against AID and *in vitro* fertilization apply also to human cloning. The primary objection is that cloning experimentation will inevitably involve mishaps and consequent abortion. Even if the mishaps are permitted to survive, does one in the first place have the ethical right to create them? A further objection is that cloning can be considered a violation of the marriage covenant and the "abolition of man's embodied personhood," as Ramsey has observed (Ramsey, 1970, p. 88). Kass adds the question of whether or not we have the moral right to determine specifically the genotypes of future generations. Also, these individuals may feel they have been created in a dehumanized and unethical manner (Kass, in Hamilton, 1972, pp. 45ff). Barbour, among others, agrees: "There is a certain presumptuousness and arrogance in manipulating the lives of others. . . . We could lose all sense of humility and limitation as well as respect for the dignity of man" (Barbour, 1970, p. 92).

The Alternatives of Unlimited and Limited Freedom

What, then, are the ethical alternatives in the face of biogenetic engineering? The fact that what man *can* do, he eventually *will* do, is the reason some observers predict abusive use of biogenetic procedures (Kass, 1972; Lappe, 1972; Ramm, 1972). A general characteristic of technological thinking is what could be termed the "technological imperative," or the "can do—must do" mentality (Francoeur, 1972; Szebenyi, 1972; Fromm, 1968). Lappe suggests the further motive of Western man's intolerance of chance, such that he has the compulsion to control chance and reduce uncertainty wherever he finds it (Lappe, 1972).

There is a short step from the "can do—must do" mentality to the "can do—right to do" mentality. We can perform *in vitro* experiments and we are on the verge of being able to clone a human being; therefore we have the right to do these things. The fallacy in that reasoning soon is evident when we consider that there are many things one can do, e.g., lie, steal, murder, but that any such capability does not confer any "right." The insistence on rights as exclusively a function of capabilities can be based only on atheistic humanism, which claims for man limitless freedom. Such humanism, centered on man alone, contends that he is free to create his own rights and determine his own responsibilities.

Within the Christian community, too, there are some who take a similar view. Several liberal Christian observers grant man almost limitless freedom. Barbour writes: "Man's dominion over nature now includes dominion over himself as part of nature. . . . Creation is not complete. We

are participants in creativity, helping to shape the future"
(Barbour, 1970, p. 89). Rahner states, "Man is essentially a
freedom-event. As established by God, and in his very nature, he is unfinished" (Rahner, 1968). Francoeur contends
that man is "by nature a creator, like his Creator. . . . By
divine command we are creators. Why, then, should we be
shocked today to learn that we can or soon will be able to
create the man of the future? Why should we be horrified
and denounce the scientist or physician for daring to 'play
God'?" (Francoeur, 1972, p. 429).

As should be evident, this book sides with those who support the traditional Christian viewpoint, contending there
are some things that man may be technically capable of
doing but should not do, because to do them is to assume
divine prerogatives to which he has no rightful moral claim.
Ramsey, for example, believes that man has no right to play
God; and, as we have seen, he and Kass assert that man cannot engage in genetic experimentation on human beings
without violating absolute ethical principles concerning the
use of immoral means, or without destruction of the marriage covenant. Ramsey is convinced also that human procreative capacities, as well as the genotypes transmitted to
future generations, are held in stewardship, by divine purpose, and that we do not have an absolute right over their
use (Ramsey, 1970). The traditional Christian, in summary,
maintains that human freedom is bound by absolute moral
principles, contained in the commandments, as well as in
such principles as "A good end cannot justify immoral
means."

Alternative Views as to What Constitutes Human Life.
The question of whether or not human freedom is limited
pertains also to the alternative views on the moral legitimacy of *in vitro* experimentation. The question of whether the
unborn individual is human, in its embryonic or earlier

form, also enters here. If intrinsic humanity (and therefore personhood) is present from the moment of conception, then this new life cannot be capriciously manipulated. The casual, and at times callous, disposal of fertilized eggs, blastocysts, and embryos is, in this view, grievously immoral. The defense of unborn human life from the moment of its inception seems to be voiced most strongly today by the Catholic Church (Abbott, 1966, "The Church Today," art. 127), joined by those various pro-life movements seeking to overthrow constitutionally the Supreme Court's abortion decision of 1973. The morality of eugenic abortion, as well as abortion for other reasons, also depends directly on how unborn life is regarded.

Alternative Views as to the Morality of Suffering

Pain and suffering are part of the human condition. If such experiences are considered to be but the agonies of evolution, then the desire to be totally free of them is understandable. From the Christian perspective, however, suffering has *personal* significance, being seen as a consequence of an original rebellion of man against God, who in his compassion restored man to divine friendship through the sacrificial death of Jesus Christ. When personal suffering is joined with Jesus' passion and death, its significance is magnified. Suffering in resignation to the divine will takes on inestimable value. This latter view does not embrace masochism; it rather understands suffering in the light of divine revelation, rather than cursing it as the result of a blind, atheistic, evolutionary force.

In the Christian perspective, it is good and right to correct and remove suffering whenever possible, but not to the extent of using immoral means. Furthermore, the moral responsibility to aid in alleviating suffering is to be carried out in a spirit of respect and compassion. On the basis of the observations already made, it is clear that the traditional Christian would not apply a "cost-benefit" approach to the genetically afflicted individual, and neither would he endorse eugenic abortion as a solution. Serra, for one, rejects the concept that society has any right to reduce the number of seriously handicapped persons, and their expensive care, by condemning them to death. As he points out, the care of such persons is implied by society's duty to protect human life (Birch and Abrecht, 1975, p. 117). Doxiades has argued, in the case of handicapped children, that they are not different children, that they could be anybody's children, and that all members of society therefore share responsibility for their care (*ibid.*, p. 189).

From the Christian perspective, therefore, there is an obligation to assist the genetically afflicted child, and to give financial and emotional support to his family, in the compassionate spirit of Christ himself. The value and dignity of a defective child should be seen in terms of a life, once conceived, that is destined for an immortal existence and for eternal happiness with God. Contrast this perspective with one that establishes the value of human life on the basis of financial liability, or inconvenience, or simply "unwantedness." Nevertheless, whereas procreation is a natural, inalienable, human right, it does not follow that mankind must produce all the human offspring possible. Parents who are carriers of a serious genetic disease have a good reason not to procreate. Overpopulation could be another reason not to procreate. Good and worthy as such objectives may be, however, from the traditional Christian perspective they should not be achieved by immoral means.

Who Is to Decide?

The moral and ethical alternatives are clear. But it is not so clear who is to decide which principles will guide the thrust of biogenetic engineering. The possibilities include ethicists, lawyers, the courts (Ramm, 1974), parents, a scientific elite, a government commission (Barbour, 1970; Anderson, 1972; Augenstein, 1969), and groups that "represent" society as a whole (Crotty, 1972; Francoeur, 1972; Kindig, Sidel, and Green, in Hilton, *et al.*, 1973; Cooke, in Lipkin and Rowley, 1974). The late H. J. Muller favored a scientific elite. In responding to critics, he stated, "Can these critics . . . really believe that the persons of unusual moral courage, progressive spirit, and eagerness to serve mankind, who will pioneer in germinal choice, and likewise those who in a more enlightened age will follow in the path thus laid down, will fail to recognize the fundamental human values?" (Ramsey, 1970, p. 52). Muller's very optimistic trust in geneticists is not shared by all. As we have seen, genetics is a field of study in which there is rather widespread disregard for the value of unborn human life, with little attention being given to the morality of the means to be used to achieve genetic objectives.

Scientific expertise and technological skill in no way guarantee ethical restraint or even good judgment. As one ethicist noted, "Medical experimentation under the Nazis was technically admirable, and Hiroshima and Nagasaki are monuments to technical skill and perfection. Yet what took place in these cases was ethically abhorrent" (Crotty, 1972). Lerner, cited by Birch (in Birch and Abrecht, 1975, p. 7), has observed that genetic engineers lack the requisite wisdom to make decisions that involve moral issues, a view shared by Edwards (*ibid.*, p. 47). Kindig and Sidel warn, "Professionals may seek certain policies not because they are best for the population they serve, but because they consciously or unconsciously seek to perpetuate and strengthen their own power base and their own satisfaction" (Hilton *et al.*, 1973, p. 373). Aner (Birch and Abrecht,

1975, p. 68) caustically criticizes those scientists who say they must "play God" when they have not even been asked to assume that role. He is further suspicious of "elites," contending they are good for many things, but not for deciding the worth of "elites" as such. Green warns against the possible withholding of scientific information from the public by those assuming an elitist role: "With respect to some technologies, there has been a calculated policy of not fully informing the public as to potential adverse consequences for fear that the public would become 'unduly alarmed.' Indeed, I suspect that there are some scientists who would discourage public discussion and debate about potentially frightening aspects of the possible use of genetic knowledge because of their concern that such debate might lead to curtailment of their obviously beneficial research" (Hilton *et al.*, 1973, p. 391). Green also observes: "The issues involved in the genetic area may be different, but the mechanisms for public policy decision-making are, or at least should be, exactly the same as they are with respect to any other kind of public policy issue. The fact that science or medicine happens to be the subject, rather than economic policy or social policy, does not alter the basic mechanisms through which public policy decisions are made" (*ibid.*, p. 385).

It is the consensus of several commentators that the American public should be intimately involved in genetic policy decision-making. Kindig and Sidel quote Thomas Jefferson: "I know no safe depository of the ultimate powers of the society but the people themselves; and if we think them not enlightened enough to exercise this control with a wholesome discretion, the remedy is not to take it from them, but to inform their discretion" (Hilton *et al.*, 1973, p. 378). The last phrase in this statement holds the key to correct moral choices. The members of a society need to be fully informed about ethical alternatives and the seriousness of their implications for that society, present and future. It is here that the Christian can play an important role, and indeed is morally obligated to speak out.

It seems clear that the basic issue involved in eugenics (and in all ethical problems, for that matter) is related to the "absolutism-relativism" controversy. If there are no absolute moral and ethical principles, everywhere and for all times morally directing and limiting human endeavor, then man can do as he pleases; there is no "should" to consider. But when man does as he pleases, he always leaves a trail of moral corruption. A popular moral consensus *based on absolute moral values* would be effective in arriving at appropriate ethical decisions in, and safeguards regarding the uses of, biogenetic engineering.

SUGGESTED READINGS

1. *The Hastings Center Report.* Published by the Institute of Society, Ethics, and the Life Sciences (Hastings-on-Hudson, N.Y.). A bimonthly publication covering such issues as the ethics of biomedical research, use of human participants, abortion, euthanasia, and biogenetic research.

2. McFadden, Charles J. *The Dignity of Life: Moral Values in a Changing Society.* Huntington, Ind.: Our Sunday Visitor, 1976. An analysis of the ethical aspects of medical surgery, biogenetic engineering, abortion, and euthanasia.

3. Ramsey, Paul. *Fabricated Man: The Ethics of Genetic Control.* New Haven: Yale Univ. Press, 1970. A discussion and evaluation of the moral and religious implications of genetic control, with particular attention given to cloning.

4. Hamilton, Michael, ed. *The New Genetics and the Future of Man.* Grand Rapids: Eerdmans, 1972. Contributed articles by twelve authors on new beginnings in life, genetic therapy, pollution, and health.

5. *Theological Studies* 33 (September 1972): contributed articles on genetic developments, genetic control, and the ethical and moral implications.

6. *Journal of the American Scientific Affiliation* 26 (December 1972): an issue concerned with the ethical aspects of biogenetic engineering and related topics.

7. Hilton, B., D. Callahan, M. Harris, P. Condliffe, and B. Berkley, eds. *Ethical Issues in Human Genetics: Genetic Counseling and the Use of Genetic Knowledge.* N.Y.: Plenum Press, 1973. Thirty contributors present the multiple aspects, legalities, and social implications of biogenetics.

8. Birch, C., and P. Abrecht, eds. *Genetics and the Quality of Life.* Elmsford, N.Y.: Pergamon Press, 1975. Chapters by eighteen authors cover ethical and political issues in the field of genetics.

10

ON RELATIVISM AND ARATIONALITY

"The Christian is the real radical of our generation, for he stands against the monolithic, modern concept of truth as relative. . . ."
— F. Schaeffer, *The God Who Is There.*

W HY are relativism and arationality so highly valued in contemporary society? The emergence of these phenomena, together with a Christian appraisal of them, is the subject of this chapter.°

Relativism Today

Relativism runs rampart in our contemporary age. In many respects, it functions as a religion (Hammes 1976b). This perspective, insisting that all things change, and that there are no values, myths, or realities of eternal validity, is found in many areas of modern thought. In science, there are those who idolize the "scientific method," which yields only probable knowledge. In philosophy, many have given up the reasoned search for absolutes, turning instead to focus on the "relativity" of human language. In ethics, as we have seen, the situationists reject absolute moral precepts in favor of changing, circumstantial considerations (Hammes, 1975a). In theology, "process" theologians have

---

°This chapter includes material previously published (Hammes, 1973c, 1975-76, and 1976b).

rejected the notion of the Absolute God in favor of an evolving God. Even in the realm of ordinary, everyday behavior, relativism is evident in the widespread hedonistic pursuit of ever-changing goals and values (Hammes, 1973c).

Relativism, being essentially the rejection of absolute reality, takes away every basis of meaningfulness, particularly the spiritual Absolute, or God. But man still has a need for God. (This need cannot logically be used as the basis for "projecting" a God to fulfill it; I do not wish to be understood as implying that man needs God, therefore God exists.) Man has a need for God because this yearning has been instilled in human nature. It is so strong that the relativists, after rejecting God, have set up their own gods to fulfill their continuing need for some absolute. The First Commandment has been replaced by the command to love oneself, to the point where man becomes the measure of all things. Consequently, "modern" people today tend to worship various dimensions of human nature: the intellect (atheistic, naturalistic humanism), human will and freedom (situational ethics), the senses (scientific positivism), or emotions and feelings (counterculture humanism). Many people try to pay homage to the spiritual dimension of life by involvement in transcendental meditation, or by dabbling in oriental mysticism with emphasis on some impersonal deity such as Brahma, or through a vacuous, contentless repetition of a magical "mantra."

The Root of Relativism. The basic root of all forms of relativism is human pride, not in the sense of boastfulness (although this element may be present) but in the sense of asserting the self-sufficiency of man (thus rejecting God) or in the sense of defying God by pitting personal freedom against his will. Relativism is *made possible* by the intelligence and freedom given to man by his Creator. More precisely, it is made possible through the perversion of the absolute, which occurs whenever man, created in the Divine Image, worships the image rather than the One of whom man is only a reflection. It was pride that led to man's original rebellion against God. It was pride also that led in human history to the enthronement of reason over faith, to the homage paid to modern science and to the rise of technic reason, to the de-mythologization urged in radical theology, and to the throwing off of moral restraints by today's hedonistic culture.

The Contemporary Need for the Absolute

Relativism is related to contemporary alienation. We discussed earlier the human condition of alienation and the fourfold estrangement of man, divorced from himself, his fellow man, nature, and God. Relativism offers no solution for this alienation; neither can it explain evil, guilt, suffering, and death. Indeed, it actually intensifies the threat and anguish of these basic human experiences. A direct consequence of relativism is a sense of meaninglessness. Purposeless existence has been called *the* neurosis of our times (Frankl, 1966).

Every person needs a fundamental reason for existing, a self-significance, and an appreciation of who he or she *is*, apart from any other consideration. Unless a person discovers the ultimate meaning of human existence, and unless he becomes aware of the inner core of his personality, nothing else can be truly meaningful. Life will be a macabre deception, a playing of roles, a game of delusions and diversions.

Alice von Hildebrand (1971) quotes Kierkegaard as saying that if man has no God, neither has he a self. It is only through an awareness of God, the Absolute, that man can be aware of himself; only in that way can he appreciate the fact that he has been made in God's image. When one has that awareness of God, all other things fall into place and are seen in true perspective. Human origin, purpose, and destiny are then comprehensible; the ultimate meaning of one's personal existence is grasped. It was said earlier that relativism stemmed from a prideful rejection of God. The recognition of God, on the other hand, leads to the opposite attitude, that of humility. More important, it leads to faith. It has always been recognized that humility and faith are both inversely related to pride; the greater those virtues are, the less will be human pride.

In his search for the meaningfulness of things, man needs an eternal, unchanging, absolute point of reference. The human need to be aware of God and to perceive him in relation to human existence will never be satisfied by a relativistic *Weltanschauung*. As St. Augustine summed it, the human heart remains restless until it rests in God. As another writer has expressed it, man needs "a God who is, with an Incarnation that is earthly and historical, with a salvation that is at cross purposes with human nature, with a Resurrection that blasts apart the finality of death. . . ." And one's faith in such a God "is able to provide an alternative to the sifting, settling dust of death and through a new birth open the way to new life" (Guinness, 1973, p. 392).

Arationality in Modern Society

Arationality is coming to be valued by contemporary society as superior to rationality in the hierarchy of human functions, and even superior to the spiritual dimension. "Arationality" as used here refers to the *affective-intuitionistic-feeling* aspect of human experience. In historical terms, the emphasis on arationality has figured prominently in the revolt against technology, the dethroning of reason, the stress on personalism, the emphasis on religious emotionalism, and the emergence of contemporary hedonism. Also, society today increasingly invokes the affective-feeling experience as a guide to moral behavior; and arationality has thus become an important factor in determining the rightness and wrongness of moral conduct (Hammes, 1975-76). "If it feels good, it's all right, so do it" expresses a common attitude. There are many reasons why arationality has come to be so highly favored in our culture.

Reasons for Arationality. Philosophically considered, many people today seem to have lost all sense of objectivity, to the extent that their rational processes have become subjectivistic, relativistic, and reducible, at best, to impulse or to ad hoc opinions. Stripped of its credibility, reason has been easily dethroned by affectivity. In *religion*, the notion of a Christianity that appeals to rational argument and validation has given way to a faith based on emotionalism, such as that displayed by some present-day Pentecostal or Charismatic groups, or in some aspects of the so-called Jesus Movement.

The increased interest in the affective dimension of human experience has been attributed to the rise of technology, which has resulted in the dehumanization and depersonalization of man. According to this *alienation hypothesis*, the resulting need for warmth and community has led to the proliferation of so-called encounter and growth groups (Back, 1972). The conflict between rationality and arationality has been described as one between rationality and irrationality (Frankel, 1973), the cerebral and the emotional, the conscious and the intuitive, the empirical and the rhapsodic (Roszak, 1969), and the Apollonians and the Dionysians (Holton, 1974). The explanation I favor is based on human needs and *cultural suppression* of those needs.

When approached in that way, arationality can be seen as the result of overemphasizing rationality (with accompanying suppression of emotionality). Man has the innate need to fulfill himself in all aspects of his being—sensory, emotional, intellectual, and spiritual. "Emotional" as used here includes aesthetic experience, passion, sensualism, and arationality. By "intellectual" is meant reason or rationality. "Spiritual" includes a religious orientation and all that constitutes the ultimate meaning which all men seek. According to our hypothesis, whatever aspect of human nature is most suppressed, repressed, stifled, ignored, or neglected in one age will be most likely to manifest itself in a cultural rebellion in the age to follow. Let us apply this hypothesis to that period of human civilization extending roughly from the Middle Ages to the present time.

The Age of the Id

During the period we call the Middle Ages, the prevalent themes were divine revelation and a God-centered universe. It was an age of faith, with a focus on eternity; permanence and the absolute stability of religion were assumed. Man's awareness was spiritual, and his "posture" may be described as that of kneeling. Borrowing a term from Freudian psychology, we could call this period of history the Age of the Superego. The historical changes that occurred during the Renaissance and the Reformation included the dominance of reason over faith and of philosophy over theology. Speaking now only of Western culture, we may say that man's perception of the universe changed from God-centered to man-centered. Rising from his knees, as it were, man stood erect; but at the same time he soon dropped his vision from an eternal horizon to a temporal, earthly one. His consciousness of the divine became overshadowed by the awareness of his mental prowess. The new age was an age of reason, rationalism, individualism; it was fertile ground, therefore, for the growth of atheistic humanism. This period can be characterized as the Age of the Ego. The next few hundred years brought the industrial revolution and the development of technology. As man effectively mastered his environment, philosophic reason gave way to technic reason. Fascinated by his scientific capability, man became convinced that because something could be done, it should and must be done. Also, as more time became available for leisure, his posture changed from that of standing to sitting.

However, uncontrolled technology led to another rebellion. Contemporary existentialism and humanism, in addition to accelerative changes in culture and life-style, contributed to a revolt against technological evils. The revolt expressed itself most strongly among youths who blamed technology for the present dehumanization of man. With simplicity as their motto, they have adopted childhood's pleasures as a way of expressing their rebellion, thus preparing for the rise of their most prominent spokesman, Charles Reich (1970). Reich's primary theme has been the sensual worship of the uninhibited self. He has encouraged affective hedonism, pursuit of pleasure, and escape from the barrenness of technic culture into sensuality—particularly sexual and hallucinogenic. Bodily awareness was sought; intellectual awareness was ignored. Emphasis on the present has overbalanced remembrance of the past or any planning for the future (for there may be no future). Having finally assumed the prone posture, seeking only passion, feeling, and sensualism, man lies now in the Age of the Id.

Pleasure and Feeling as Moral Directives

Not only is arationality the hallmark of the present day; it has come to be valued as a moral directive or moral norm.

Let us consider the validity of using the affective-feeling in-tuitionistic dimension of human nature as a moral compass.

Hedonism as a way of life is not new. Aristippus of Cyrene (435-355 B.C.) and his followers equated pleasure with happiness; they therefore considered feeling the only valid criterion of truth (Sahakian, 1968a). Later, Epicurus (341-270 B.C.) contended the morally right action to be that which produces the most pleasure. In early nineteenth-century philosophy, Jeremy Bentham claimed pleasure to be the criterion of right conduct, a point of view labeled by his critics a "pig philosophy" (Sahakian, 1968b).

Now, the term "feeling" has been variously defined by lexicographers as sensation, emotion, affection, sentiment, passion, and unreasoned opinion and belief. The extension of the meaning of the word from the aesthetic realms to the moral realm is questionable. In some instances, it is true, one's "feelings" accurately recognize certain behavior as morally evil. Most people "feel" a revulsion against sadism and condemn it. But in other situations, feeling may affirm as morally good what is actually otherwise. Acts of fornica-tion and adultery are accompanied by good "feelings" in the participants; but the traditional Christian perspective regards such acts as morally evil. Emotional factors or feel-ings are also used to justify active euthanasia (mercy-killing) and direct abortion, both of which are rejected by the Christian tradition as morally evil. Again, feeling (as an affective experience) is the primary motive underlying drug abuse.

Compassion is a wonderful human trait, and pleasure another God-given gift; but do affective factors such as these qualify as moral norms? Love, as we have seen, is the basis of the Gospel message. But is the *emotional* aspect of love its essence, and is that aspect intended to be a moral directive? Traditional Christianity considers valid discrimination of evil and immorality to be based on a spiritual and intellectual (rational) judgment, rather than upon an affective-feeling (arational) reaction. Moral good and moral evil lie in the preservation or violation, respectively, of the proper relationship between human acts and God's laws governing those acts. Morality is therefore based on an objective norm, recognized and implemented in rational (reasonable) rather than in arational (affective-feeling) ways. Acts of fornication and adultery are seen as transgressions of God's commandments. The affective or "feeling" aspect of sexual intercourse is the same pleasurable experience for married spouses, adulterers, and fornicators, and the emotional aspect of love may be the same in each case. The distinctions among the moral aspects of these situations rest not on whether love is present but on a rational decision as to whether they conform to God's law. No such moral distinctions can be made on the basis of "feelings," which can be cited either to support or condemn such behavior. The use of feeling as a moral norm is but another variety of relativism. For, who is to say, when "feelings" of one person contradict those of another, e.g., the murderer or rapist versus his victim, which feelings are morally good and which are not? If feeling is used as the guide to moral behavior, the inevitable result is moral chaos.

In our earlier discussion of the impediments to conscience, we saw that arationality does play a role in moral behavior, but not as a norm. Rather, arationality affects the degree of culpability involved. Emotions and feelings, e.g., love, hate, and fear, can attenuate (lessen) the degree of moral guilt. Even so, they do not dictate the moral norm, nor do they mitigate its obligatory, binding character.

The Appropriate Hierarchy of Human Dimensions

The advocates of the affective-intuitionistic-feeling emphasis are sincere in their efforts to oppose the depersonalization and dehumanization of man in a computerized, mechanistic age. Indeed, the counterculture is an understandable revolt against such depersonalization (Roszak, 1969). The revolt against "technic" reason has unfortunately led also to the demeaning of reason altogether, in the sense that rationality has been placed below affectivity in relative importance.

The Christian does not demean the affective-feeling dimension of man, but rather, in the realm of moral (value) judgment, places it in proper perspective. The Christian acknowledges that affective-feeling experiences are the source of great pleasure and joy, and especially so when they accord to God's purposes. But the Christian, being a realist, recognizes that man, in the "human condition," lacks the internal harmony once enjoyed by original man, and that arationality can lead one astray when used as a criterion of moral judgment. The fact that affective-sensual motives can tempt man to sin is a common theme in the New Testament, which recommends resistance to the cravings of the flesh (Gal 5.16-24, Col 3.5-10) and the practice of penance and self-denial in the shouldering of one's daily cross (Matt 16.24, Mark 8.34, Luke 9.23).

The traditional Christian, therefore, does not consider what "feels good" to be necessarily morally good behavior. Perhaps original man's "feelings" were consonant with rational judgment; but man in the present human condition lacks such internal harmony that he may have once had (Hammes, 1975b). It is therefore the intelligent, rational analysis of moral behavior, rather than an affective-feeling experience, that reveals moral goodness or evil. The Ten Commandments forbid much behavior that "feels" good. These laws were given to man as a check against the power of feelings to lead one to immoral behavior. Such precepts, according to the Christian perspective, *inform* one's conscience and enable one to *form* correct moral judgments. This is *not* to say, however, that rationality alone is an adequate moral norm. Impaired human judgment, a consequence of man's original fall, is in need of more trustworthy moral guidance. For the Christian in general, objective norms are provided by the Scriptures. (And, for the Catholic, moral guidance is given by the Apostles' successors as well.)

Philosophers in the traditional Christian position have always regarded the rational dimension of human nature (intellect and will) as superior to the sentient dimension (sense perception, emotions, and feelings). While man shares sentient activity with sub-human life, it is primarily the rational dimension that distinguishes man from, and makes him essentially superior to, all other life-forms on earth (Adler, 1968; Hammes, 1971). It is only appropriate, therefore, that the essentially human quality of rationality (reason) be seen as superior to arationality (feeling) as a norm for behavior that is itself uniquely human, namely, moral behavior. One is led to conclude, therefore, that the skepticism, estrangement, and emptiness experienced so widely by contemporary man are the results of the present cultural emphasis on arationality and sensualism, together with the neglect of spiritual and intellectual aspects of human nature.

Future Alternatives

The question arises, will this condition continue? There are at least three possibilities for the future. The first is a continuance of the drug orientation, leading eventually to a vegetative society, a final negation of human dignity, the lowest depth to which man could descend. A society that is based on the assumption that life is painful will look for a way to escape from life, and thus enter the Age of Nirvana (translatable as "blown-out").

A second possibility is a return to the reign of reason, if the storm-tossed ship of technology could recover its stability and a controlled course. Even so, it would still chance shipwreck on the shoals of accelerative change and "future shock" (Toffler, 1970).

A third possibility is an emergence of the spiritual aspect of human nature. Such diverse interests as the social concern for minority rights, the revived philosophic turn to Eastern mysticism, and growing interest in religion bespeak an attempt to give due prominence to the human spirit.

What is the significance of these alternative predictions for a Christian? First, from a Christian perspective, man has been turned upside down. The Christian hierarchy of spirit, mind, senses, and emotions must be restored, and the challenge to the Christian is to set things aright. Made in the image and likeness of God (Gen 1.26), man is seen in the traditional Christian perspective with the spiritual dimension at the top of the hierarchy of human functioning, with rationality next, and arationality last. In Freudian terms, the spiritually illumined Superego should guide the Ego, and both should control the Id. Second, the Christian should help society recover a sense of the absolute, which is both reasonable and necessary for personal and social stability. Third, convinced that God has communicated himself to man in the Word Incarnate, Jesus Christ, the Christian must witness this good news. To a world victimized by relativism, skepticism, alienation, and despair, the Christian must bring the Light of the World and the Way of salvation (John 1.46, 14.6). Fourth, in recognizing the validity of man's need to actualize in some degree of fullness his human potential (spiritual, intellectual, sensory, and emotional), the Christian must give evidence that such can be achieved through the Christian perspective (Hammes, 1971). Fifth, he should welcome and cooperate with all attempts to restore the sense of dignity to human life. In his striving toward these objectives, the Christian can indeed exert a positive influence in a world bent on its own destruction.

SUGGESTED READINGS

1. Back, Kurt W. *Beyond Words: The Story of Sensitivity Training and the Encounter Movement.* Baltimore: Penguin Books, 1973. A review of the historical background of the encounter movement, with critical evaluation of its positive and negative aspects.

2. Toffler, Alvin. *Future Shock.* N.Y.: Random House, 1970. An examination of transience, and the effect of accelerative change on the limits of human adaptability. Strategies for survival are also discussed.

3. Frankel, Charles. "The Nature and Sources of Irrationalism." *Science* 180 (1973), 927-931. A presentation and critical evaluation of irrationalism in contemporary society.

11

ON SEXUALITY AND LOVE

"God loved the world so much that he gave his only son" — John 3.16.
"God is love" — 1 John 4.8.

IN THIS chapter we shall compare Christian and contemporary views on the values of sexuality and love.

Sexuality

The Christian has a unique concept of sexuality, in sharp contrast to the sexual permissiveness condoned in contemporary society (National Conference of Catholic Bishops, 1975). Sexuality, created by God as an integral part of human nature, is a wonderful gift to be used according to the divine purpose. Sex is ugly only when abused. Sexual attraction draws man and woman together so that their physical union may result in procreation. Secondarily, sex provides a pleasurable means of expressing mutual love. In the Old Testament, God gave mankind two prohibitions concerning sexual behavior: "You shall not commit adultery," and "You shall not covet your neighbor's wife" (Ex 20.14, 17). In the New Testament, Jesus Christ further refined the prohibition against adultery: "You have learned how it was said: You must not commit adultery. But I say this to you: if a man looks at a woman lustfully, he has already committed adultery with her in his heart" (Matt 5.27-28). After giving admonitions on other kinds of immoral behavior, Jesus concludes, "You must therefore be perfect just as your heavenly Father is perfect" (Matt 5.48).

Paul repeatedly exhorts the early Christian communities to avoid all forms of immorality. "You know perfectly well that people who do wrong will not inherit the kingdom of God: people of immoral lives, idolaters, adulterers, catamites, sodomites, thieves, usurers, drunkards, slanderers and swindlers will never inherit the kingdom of God" (1 Cor 6.9-11). "Keep away from fornication. All the other sins are committed outside the body; but to fornicate is to sin against your own body. Your body, you know, is the temple of the Holy Spirit, who is in you since you received him from God. You are not your own property; you have been bought and paid for. That is why you should use your body for the glory of God" (1 Cor 6.18-20). "When self-indulgence is at work the results are obvious: fornication, gross indecency and sexual irresponsibility; idolatry and sorcery; feuds and wrangling, jealousy, bad temper and quarrels; disagreements, factions, envy; drunkenness, orgies, and similar things" (Gal 5.19-21). "Among you there must be not even a mention of fornication or impurity in any of its forms, or promiscuity . . . or salacious talks and jokes. . . . Nobody who actually indulges in fornication or impurity or promiscuity . . . can inherit anything of the kingdom of God" (Eph 5.3-6). Finally, "What God wants is for you all to be holy. He wants you to keep away from fornication, and each one of you to know how to use the body that belongs to him in a way that is holy and honorable, not giving way to selfish lust like the pagans who do not know God" (1 Thess 4.3-5).

Homosexuality

The traditional Christian perspective on the nature of love is the basis also for its position on homosexuality. In the Old Testament, the sinfulness of the people of Sodom was punished by God's destruction of that city (Gen 19.4-26), whose name became synonymous with sodomy. In Leviticus, the death penalty is prescribed for homosexuality. In the New Testament, it is condemned as immoral and paganistic (Romans 1.26-27, 1 Cor 6.9-10). The early Christians regarded homosexuality as a form of perversion and condemned it. The *Didache* (*Teaching of the Twelve Apostles*), a second-century Christian document, describes the "way of life" and the "way of death" (Glimm, 1947). The way of death encompasses the various violations of the Ten Commandments, including the practice of homosexuality. Furthermore, the traditional Christian concept of the natural law condemns all use of sexual expression outside of the marital union of man and woman.

As we have seen, the Christian distinguishes between the *objective* and *subjective* aspects of morality. The judgment of immorality is based on objective grounds, independent of subjective opinion. It is this distinction that also allows compassion on the sinner without approval of his sin. In regard to homosexuality, the Christian can condemn homosexual acts as immoral, and yet not judge, nor should he judge, the conscience of the homosexual. The responsibleness or guilt of the homosexual is known to God alone. The subjective-objective distinction is also the ground for denying the wish of the homosexual that not only he, but also his tendencies, be morally approved. The Christian cannot accept sin, no matter what its guise. He is rather bound to accept the sinner, and to do what he can to convert the sinner (Kelly, 1976).

Homosexuals often say they cannot help their sexual orientation. From a psychological point of view, there are conflicting theories as to whether their behavior is genetically innate, or whether it has been learned and is consequently subject to reform. Regardless of the factors involved, there is no evidence to support any contention that the homosexual drive is stronger than that of the heterosexual. If heterosexual activity can be voluntarily controlled and, in the case of the celibate, completely abstained from, then it should be possible for the homosexual to do the same. The problem is one of insight and motivation. The Christian believes that the grace and strength of God are available to the homosexual, as they are to everyone seeking to live a good moral life (Cavanagh and Harvey, 1977; National Conference of Catholic Bishops, 1973).

Love*

Love, as everyone knows, is what makes the world go round. Those who have experienced love contend it to be the ground of meaning, whether human or divine. Let us consider some of the reflections on love offered by humanistic writers in the area of psychology. Then we shall contrast these observations with the Christian perspective.

Humanistic Concepts of Love. Maslow (1962) defines authentic love as "B-love," which is the love for the being of another person, involving admiration, wonder, and awe. "B-love" is unselfish love, an unneeding love. Frankl (1966) defines love as the experience of another person in all his uniqueness and singularity. Loving is a coming to relationship with another as a spiritual being. For Rollo May

---

*Some of these observations will appear in a forthcoming article, "Love in Christian and Non-Christian Perspectives," in the journal *Faith and Reason.*

(1969), love is paradoxical in that it opens one to grief, sorrow, and disappointment, as well as to joy, fulfillment, and intensity of consciousness. To love is to give up the center of oneself, and love carries with it the threat of self-annihilation. Fromm also emphasizes the giving of oneself in love (Fromm, 1956). It is the person who gives rather than the person who receives who is rich. Additionally, authentic love includes care, responsibility, respect, and knowledge. From his evolutionary point of view, Fromm sees love as overcoming the estrangement resulting from man's original separation from nature. To practice love successfully is an art requiring the overcoming of one's narcissism, as well as having an attitude of faith in the loved one, and the courage to become vulnerable. Fromm correctly observes that any theory of love begins with a theory of man and of human nature.

These writers go on to describe various kinds of love. Frankl speaks of three dimensions of the human person—the somatic, the mental, and the spiritual. Corresponding to these dimensions are three attitudes of love—the sexual, the erotic, and authentic love. May offers a fourfold classification of love—sex (lust, libido), eros (the drive to create or procreate), philia (friendship, brotherly love), and agape or caritas (love devoted to the welfare of others). Fromm describes brotherly love, motherly love, erotic love, self-love, and love of God. Fromm is careful to point out, however, that by "God" he means an entity that man himself has created.

In their discussion of the deterioration of love in Western society, these writers deplore the reduction of love to sex. May speaks of a "new puritanism" that promotes a state of alienation from the body and the use of the body as a machine. He contrasts the old with the new puritanism by observing that the Victorian individual tried to have love without falling into sex, whereas the modern person attempts to have sex without falling into love. May criticizes the "playboy" philosophy of sex, drawing support from Harvey Cox's *The Secular City* (1965). Fromm agrees that love and sexuality have unfortunately become divided. He and Frankl both also reject the playboy concept of love and sex.

In addition to the perversion of reducing love to sex, these authors point out other abuses of authentic love. For example, Maslow contrasts "B-love" with "D-love," or deficiency love. Deficiency love is selfish, self-gratifying, and a needing love, in the sense of a crippling dependence on the loved person. Fromm treats at length what he considers to be various forms of neurotic love. These include a person's overattachment to mother or father; a masochistic relation to the loved one; any form of idolatrous love; any substitution of another love as compensation for an appropriate love, e.g., a wife's transferring her unrequited need for her husband's love to her children; domineering love; and lastly, any reforming type of love, wherein the loved one cannot be accepted as he or she is but, in the eyes of the lover, needs improvement as a requisite for a love relationship.

These observations of non-Christian writers on the nature of authentic human love are noble indeed. Christian love, however, goes beyond such considerations, and, even more important, can be validated apart from mere human opinion of what genuine love should be. Let us now examine that perspective.

Christian Concept of Love. How is the Christian response of love to be different? Christian love is measured in relation to the Divine Love that invites it. "God so loved the world that he gave his only Son" (John 3.16). "As the Father has loved me, so have I loved you" (John 15.9). "There is no greater love than this: to lay down one's life for one's friends" (John 15.13). Paul says God emptied himself of divinity, so to speak, in becoming man, and went further to express his love by dying for mankind on the cross (Phil 2.6-8).

The Christian, therefore, is expected to love in the manner in which God has loved him—completely, totally, and unconditionally. It is to be a lifelong commitment, to God and to fellow man, and of such depth as to require death— the death of selfishness and egocentricity. "The way we came to understand love was that he laid down his life for us; we too must lay down our lives for our brothers" (1 John 3.16). "I give you a new commandment: Love one another. Such as my love has been for you, so must your love be for each other. This is how all will know you for my disciples: your love for one another" (John 13.34-35). As God has emptied himself to become man, the Christian is to empty himself to become God-like. He is to destroy the old man and gain a new flesh, a new spirit (Ez 11.19; Gal 5.16-17). He is to be born again (John 3.3-5). He is to be a temple of God, a bearer of love (1 Cor 6.19).

Jesus was asked what one must do to gain eternal life. Jesus replied that one should love God with one's whole heart, whole soul, and whole mind, and second to that, one must love one's neighbor as oneself (Matt 22.36-40; Mark 12.28-31; Luke 10.25-28). Thus we can see how the two-fold commandment to love God and to love neighbor are related. We are to love God in response to his love for us; we are to love our fellow man because God loves him as well. Jesus thus gives divine sanction to the so-called Golden Rule (Matt 7.12; Luke 6.31). Also, we are to love our neighbor to the extent that Christ loved him, so as to give our lives in service of others.

Life through Death. Christian love paradoxically involves life through death. We have previously discussed the doctrine of the Cross, a "stumbling block to the Jews, and an absurdity to Gentiles" (1 Cor 1.23). Jesus said that unless the seed dies, it cannot bring forth fruit (John 12.24). Jesus also stated that he who would save his life would lose it, but he who loses his life for Jesus' sake will find it (Matt 16.25, 10.39; Mark 8.35; Luke 9.24; John 12.25)—contrast this teaching with the contemporary stress on self-actualization through self-indulgence. The Christian is to die to self, and in that way, paradoxically, fulfill and actualize himself. This death is necessary in order to eliminate selfishness, egocentricity, and pride, all of which are tendencies of fallen human nature. Through prayer and self-denial, particularly in the service of others, the Christian can reach the pinnacle of human perfection.

The Content of Christian Love. The reason for Christian love, and the degree of love invited and expected, therefore marks Christian love apart from all other interpretations of love, as advocated by other religions or by atheistic humanism. Furthermore, Christian love is given specific direction. Jesus said he had come not to destroy the law, but to fulfill it (Matt 5.17). Therefore, he did not abolish the Ten Commandments, but rather affirmed them, and went further to summarize them in the twofold commandment to love God and neighbor. Christians were to show the proof of their love by following the directions given in the commandments. "This love involves our walking according to the commandments" (2 John 6). "The love of God consists in this: that we keep his commandments—and his commandments are not burdensome" (1 John 5.3). We have seen that the first commandment, love of God, has been subsumed under the second commandment, love of neighbor, by radical Christian thinkers (e.g., situational ethicists). We have also seen the moral confusion that results when the love of God, and his revealed absolute moral law, are subordinated to love of neighbor.

To Love One's Enemies. Another important aspect of Christian love is that it is to embrace not only one's friends, but one's enemies as well. Jesus instructed his followers to love their enemies, to do good to them, and to pray for them (Matt 5.44, Luke 6.27-28). Furthermore, Christian love embraces not only behavior but also thought. Jesus stated, "You have heard the commandment, 'You shall not commit adultery.' What I say to you is this: anyone who looks lustfully at a woman has already committed adultery with her in his thoughts" (Matt 5.27-28). Again, "What emerges from within a man, that and nothing else is what makes him impure. Wicked designs come from the deep recesses of the heart: acts of fornication, theft, murder, adulterous conduct, greed, maliciousness, deceit, sensuality, envy, blasphemy, arrogance, an obtuse spirit. All these evils come from within and render a man impure" (Mark 7.20-23).

Along the same vein, John tells us, "Anyone who hates his brother is a murderer, and you know eternal life abides in no murderer's heart" (1 John 3.15). Thus did Jesus probe the depths of a person's heart, and pronounce judgment on one's innermost thoughts in relating them to love and the commandments.

The Christian Love of Self. Thus far we have spoken of the Christian's response in loving God and neighbor. There is also Christian teaching on love of self. Again, it is based on the Christian view of man's relationship to God. Paul says, "Are you not aware that you are the temple of God, and that the Spirit of God dwells in you?" (1 Cor 3.16). "Do you not see that your bodies are members of Christ?" (1 Cor 6.15). "But whoever is joined to the Lord becomes one spirit with him. Shun lewd conduct. Every other sin a man commits is outside his body, but the fornicator sins against his own body" (1 Cor 6.17-18). These words are at odds with the contemporary view that there is no moral harm in sexual permissiveness. Paul continues, "You must know that your body is a temple of the Holy Spirit, who is within —the spirit you have received from God. You are not your own. You have been purchased, and at a price. So glorify God in your body" (1 Cor 6.19-20). Paul reiterates his exhortation in another letter (1 Thess 4.1-7), in which he stresses God's call to holiness. Christians see this as a magnificent concept on which to base self-love—we are temples of God, of the Holy Spirit, ransomed from sin and death by the price of Jesus' redemptive love. Human dignity, therefore, resides not in what we do, in terms of success, or achievement, or failure, but rather in who we are. The aged, the senile, the psychotic, the retarded—these too are deserving of love because they are temples of God.

The Practice of Christian Love

To express *Christian* love, whether of God, of others, or of oneself, is not easy. It would be impossible without God's help. However, the Christian is expected to cooperate, primarily through prayer and self-denial, with God's help. Jesus taught men the Our Father, in which God is praised, his will accepted, his providence sought, and his protection requested, as a loving father's concern for his children. Jesus also advocated almsgiving, fasting, and penance, to be done in secret and not in order to be seen and praised by others (Matt 6.1-4, 16-18; Luke 13.3-5). Part of Christian love is to forgive one's enemies, to forgive them times without number (Matt 18.21-22; Luke 17.4): and it is as one forgives others that one will be forgiven (Matt 6.12; Luke 11.4). In these ways is Christian love expressed.

In his first letter to the Corinthians, Paul beautifully summarizes the nature of Christian love. After speaking of the various gifts of the Holy Spirit, Paul states that the highest is that of love: "If I have all the eloquence of men or angels, but speak without love, I am simply a gong booming or a cymbal clashing. If I have the gift of prophecy, understanding all the mysteries there are, and knowing everything, and if I have faith in all its fullness, to move mountains, but without love, then I am nothing at all. If I give away all I possess, piece by piece, and if I even let them take my body to burn it, but am without love, it will do me no good whatever.

"Love is always patient and kind; it is never jealous; love is never boastful or conceited; it is never rude or selfish; it does not take offense, and is not resentful. Love takes no pleasure in other people's sins but delights in the truth; it is always ready to excuse, to trust, to hope, and to endure whatever comes.

"Love does not come to an end. But if there are gifts of prophecy, the time will come when they must fail; or the gift of languages, it will not continue forever; and knowledge—for this, too, the time will come when it must fail. . . . There are three things that last: faith, hope, and love; and the greatest of these is love" (1 Cor 13).

SUGGESTED READINGS

1. May, Rollo. *Love and Will*. N.Y.: Norton, 1969. An examination of the relationship of love to will, sex, death, and the daimonic.

2. Frankl, Viktor. *The Doctor and the Soul*. N.Y.: Alfred A. Knopf, 1966. A treatise on the meaning of life, death, suffering, work, and love.

3. Lewis, C. S. *Mere Christianity*. N.Y.: Macmillan, 1960. A Protestant perspective on the moral law, sex, love, and Christian virtue.

4. Sheen, Fulton. *Peace of Soul*. Garden City: Doubleday, 1954. A Catholic perspective on anxiety, guilt, sex, and love.

5. Christenson, Larry. *The Christian Family*. Minnesota: Bethany Fellowship, 1970. A conservative Protestant treatise on love in the family.

6. Fromm, Erich. *The Art of Loving*. N.Y.: Harper & Row, 1956. An analysis of the various kinds of appropriate and inappropriate love relationships.

7. Cavanagh, J. R., and J. F. Harvey. *Counseling the Homosexual*. Huntington, Ind.: Our Sunday Visitor, 1977. A discussion of the legal, religious, social, medical, psychological, and historical aspects of homosexuality and lesbianism.

12

ON DRUGS, OCCULTISM, MYSTICISM, AND DEATH

"For it is not against human enemies that we have to struggle, but against Sovereignties and the Powers who originate the darkness in this world."

— Ephesians 6.12.

THE only reason that the topics mentioned in the title to this chapter are grouped together is that of convenience. Drugs, occultism, and mysticism are held in high regard by the contemporary counterculture. We shall present an appraisal of these phenomena, followed by a Christian perspective on the meaning of death.

Drugs

Hallmarks of the counterculture are rock music and drugs (Reich, 1970). "To blow one's mind" on either or both is the ultimate experience. Leary, a past guru of the beat generation and famous for the expression "Turn on, tune in, and drop out," describes LSD as "the sacrament that will put you in touch with the ancient two million year old wisdom inside you" (Roszak, 1969, p. 167). Others disagree. Guinness (1973), quoting Coleridge, refers to the drug experience as the "counterfeit infinity." He traces the history of the use of psychedelic drugs, including marijuana, mescaline, and LSD. The term "psychedelic" was apparently coined in 1957 by Humphrey Osmond to describe their mind-expanding qualities.

The biblical passages cited previously in regard to immorality are a good basis for the Christian attitude toward drugs. The so-called hard, or addictive, drugs would obviously be rejected. With regard to psychedelics, is the oceanic experience described by some users actually a religious or spiritual experience? Though undoubtedly pleasurable, if the "trip" is a "good" one, the psychedelic experience is also reported to be vague and impersonal, as though one were caught up in some vast, mysterious, overwhelming reality (Guinness, 1973). For those who have not experienced God, the psychedelic experience would likely be a substitute for a true supernatural experience. Those who have experienced the true reality of God have no need of the psychedelic experience.

Practical objections to the use of psychedelic drugs include physiological and psychological dependence, as well as their use as a flight or escape from reality and from problems that should be faced rather than avoided (Blum, 1969). However, the Christian can further question the use of psychedelic drugs in terms of whether they abuse one's body. Does one have the right to tamper with awareness and consciousness in this manner? It would seem that the mental confusion, or even euphoria, that is induced by such drugs is inappropriate for the Christian. Inhibition of rational control invariably leads to irrationality, the arousal of concupiscence, and the passion of sin.

The Occult

Guinness (1973) has presented an analysis of the rise of interest in the occult. He attributes its popularity to several factors, such as the death of rationalism, the loss of the supernatural in liberal theology, the influence of Eastern religions, the identity crisis and loss of a personal center, and the fascination for psychic and parapsychological phenomena. Guinness also discusses three areas of the occult: superstition (astrology), spiritism (seances), and Satanism. The interest in Satanism can be in a light vein, e.g., rock-group names, or in dramatic sensationalism, e.g., La Vey's satanic church, or be of a deeper, more sinister nature, in which Satan is acknowledged as an existing spirit, to be worshiped as a god. Let us consider closely this last aspect of Satanism.

Radical Christian thinkers and biblical de-mythologizers have adopted the attitude of rejecting the existence of angels in general, and devils or demons in particular. The traditional Judeo-Christian tradition accepts the existence of such spiritual creatures, who in their nature are superior to humans (Heb 2.7). The Old Testament is replete with references to angels, the messengers of God who did his bidding, and who often related his wishes to mankind. In the New Testament, the Book of Revelation constantly refers to angelic activities.

From the Scriptures we know the names of four angels, sometimes referred to as archangels because of their high rank and prominence. Two are mentioned in Revelation, in connection with the existence of Satan, as well as with the fall of man. "And now war broke out in heaven, when Michael with his angels attacked the dragon. The dragon fought back with his angels, but they were defeated and driven out of heaven. The great dragon, the primeval serpent, known as the devil or Satan, who had deceived all the world, was hurled down to the earth and his angels were hurled down with him" (Rev 12.7-10). Also, "Then I saw an angel come down from heaven with the key of the Abyss in his hand and an enormous chain. He overpowered the dragon, that primeval serpent which is the devil and Satan, and chained him up for a thousand years" (Rev 20.1-2). Two other archangels known by name are Raphael and Gabriel. God sent Raphael in disguise to aid Tobit, Tobiah, and Sarah in their tribulations. Eventually, Raphael identified himself. "I am Raphael, one of the seven angels who enter and serve before the Glory of the Lord" (Tb 12.15). We are introduced to Gabriel in the New Testament. Gabriel was sent by God to tell Mary she had been chosen to be the mother of Jesus, the Savior of the world. "In the sixth month the angel Gabriel was sent by God to a town in Galilee called Nazareth, to a virgin betrothed to a man named Joseph, of the House of David; and the virgin's name was Mary" (Luke 1.26-27).

Jesus himself spoke of the angels. In reference to the end of the world, he said, "The Son of man will send his angels . . ." (Matt 13.14). In speaking of hell, he referred to the "eternal fire prepared for the devil and his angels" (Matt 25.41). Indeed, Jesus was tempted by Satan, but repudiated him (Matt 4.1-11; Mark 1.12-13; Luke 4.1-13). We have also seen in an earlier part of this book how Jesus demonstrated his divinity by driving out devils who possessed men. Jesus spoke too of the good angels, the so-called guardian angels (Matt 18.10), and the angels whom he could call upon for help. When Peter struck with the sword to prevent the arrest of Jesus, Jesus declared, "Put your sword back. . . . Or do you think I cannot appeal to my Father who would promptly send more than twelve legions of angels to my defense?" (Matt 26.52-53). Earlier, in the Garden of Gethsemane, Jesus was comforted in his agony by an angel (Luke 22.43). At the end of the gospel story, we once again encounter angels, this time upon the occasion of the resurrection of Jesus (Matt 28.2-7; John 20.11-12).

Thus, in the traditional Christian perspective, angels are quite real, especially that haunting, threatening personality of Satan. Paul reminds us, "For it is not against human enemies that we have to struggle, but against Sovereignties and the Powers who originate the darkness in this world, the spiritual army of evil in the heavens" (Eph 6.12). And Peter warns, "Be calm and vigilant, because your enemy the devil is prowling round like a roaring lion, looking for someone to devour" (1 Pet 5.8). The Christian, therefore, sees a real danger in courting the company of Satan and the demons of antiquity. To seek actively those associated with evil, whether devils or men, is to invite a liaison that one will later bitterly regret. To probe the world of the occult is the first step toward such disaster.

Mysticism

Mysticism is to be distinguished from involvement in the occult. The mystic attempts to experience union with God; the occultist seeks the prince of darkness. Mysticism is represented in all of the world's living religions. However, the purpose and content of the meditative methodologies greatly differ. The nature of the god, or gods, of oriental and Eastern mysticism, e.g., Hinduism and Buddhism, is largely pantheistic and impersonal. Meditation is directed toward higher states of consciousness in an attempt to escape the boundaries of the human condition. In contrast, Judeo-Christian mysticism is directed toward closer union with a personal God. The Christian mystic goes further to define this union as an identity with Jesus Christ, the Son of God and Second Person of the Triune God. The personal God of Christian mysticism forms the content of Christian meditation, much unlike the impersonal contemplation followed by the oriental mystic.

Popular today is a form of meditation called "transcendental meditation" (Holden, 1975), which apparently is an effective means of escaping the hectic pace of modern life.

This practice, though founded on Hinduistic philosophy and religion, is basically an auto-suggestive relaxation technique, and is actually not a form of mysticism.

The traditional Christian would not object to various kinds of prayer, meditation, and contemplation as long as they do not involve superstition or idolatry. We have previously established the validity of the Christian claim of possessing the fullness of divine revelation, specifically in Jesus Christ, God's incarnate communication of himself. As the Alpha and the Omega (Rev 1.8, 21.6, and 22.13), Jesus is the means by which persons come to know the Father and to possess the Holy Spirit (John 14.7-17). If good men of other than Christian persuasion arrive at holy and mystical insights, the Christian contends it is because Christ is gently leading them on to a fuller revelation in himself.

The Meaning of Death

In earlier chapters we have described the alienation and estrangement that is part of the human condition. The fact of death is probably the greatest challenge to one's philosophy and theology of meaning. If we were to classify various perspectives on death, they would likely fall into one of two basic points of views—atheism, which rejects God and human immortality, and theism, which affirms these realities. Now, the meaning of death is intimately related to the meaning of life, for if death is meaningless, so is life. The atheist contends that there is no God, and that man is the chance product of blind, impersonal, evolutionary forces. The atheist goes further to say that death is the final termination of each human being's existence, and that no one survives death.

If this perspective were to be true, then it would logically follow that human life is futile. Indeed, if death were final, then other characteristics of the human condition, those of suffering, pain, guilt, and evil, would also be without significance or meaning. It is not surprising, therefore, that the prominent atheistic, existentialistic philosopher Jean Paul Sartre finally concluded, "It is absurd that we are born; it is absurd that we die" (Williams, 1965, p. 73).

In contrast to atheism, there is the theistic position. What, then, is the Christian meaning of death?

Christian Attitude toward Death

The redemptive death of Christ, together with his resurrection, gives meaning not only to human suffering but also to human death. On the natural level, death is the ultimate threat to existence, and the transition from *being* to *non-being* contains elements of anxiety and dread. In a study of the changes in attitude occurring in those who know they are going to die, Kübler-Ross (1975a, b) observed five sequential stages: denial and isolation (refusal to accept death); anger and resentment; bargaining (with God); depression; and finally, in a great majority of cases, acceptance and hope. These natural reactions, on the part of a self-aware, intelligent being, fighting against the threat of nonexistence, are to be expected. The primary instinct of all living creatures is self-preservation, which is destroyed by death. Although the Christian experiences such anxiety and fear on the natural level, it is on the supernatural level that he finds solace, strength, understanding, and the true meaning of death. For the Christian, death is not a termination, but rather a transition; not an end, but a beginning. Death is a threshold, through which one passes not to nothingness but to a different life, a life to which one has been supernaturally destined, even before the fall of mankind's first parents brought death into the world. They, too, though not subject to our kind of death, were eventually to live a life beyond that of Eden.

Human grief, as well as anxiety, accompanies death. We are told that Jesus himself wept before the tomb of Lazarus, his friend (John 11.35). It was also on this occasion, before raising Lazarus from the dead, that Jesus exclaimed, to his generation and to the world, "I am the resurrection and the life: whoever believes in me, though he should die, will come to life; and whoever is alive and believes in me will never die" (John 11.25-26). So in the midst of tears, the Christian is sustained by the reality of the resurrection of Christ, which has also been promised to man. The night before he died, Jesus told his disciples, "Do not let your hearts be troubled. Trust in God still, and trust in me. There are many rooms in my Father's house; if there were not, I should have told you. I am going now to prepare a place for you, and after I have gone and prepared you a place, I shall return to take you with me; so that where I am, you may be too" (John 14.1-3). St. John tells us, echoing Isaiah, "He will wipe away all tears from their eyes; there will be no more death, and no more mourning and sadness" (Rev 21.4). St. Paul's words are similarly resassuring: "We want you to be quite certain, brothers, about those who have died, to make sure that you do not grieve about them, like the other people who have no hope. We believe that Jesus died and rose again, and that it will be the same for those who have died in Jesus: God will bring them with him. . . . So we shall stay with the Lord forever. With such thoughts as these you should comfort one another" (1 Thess 5.14-18).

Atheistic and relativistic philosophies and models of man are inadequate to cope with the finality of death, which can only be seen as a meaningless end to an absurd existence. Only a belief-system that transcends the temporality and finiteness of man and the material cosmos can give meaning to death (Becker, 1973). This need, however, is not the Christian basis for the belief in ultimate and Absolute reality. Rather, the Christian bases his belief in human resurrection and immortality on the promise and revelation of an existent God who communicated himself to the world as its Creator and its Savior. In his illumined faith, the Christian, having lived his life for love of God and neighbor and having already been dying to self in the implementation of this commitment, can anticipate with great joy the new and eternal life that awaits beyond the threshold of death.

SUGGESTED READINGS

1. Guinness, Os. *The Dust of Death*. Downers Grove: InterVarsity Press, 1973. See ch. 6, "The East, No Exit" (mysticism); ch. 7, "The Counterfeit Infinity" (drugs); and ch. 8, "Encircling Eyes" (occultism).

2. Kübler-Ross, Elizabeth. *On Death and Dying*. N.Y.: Macmillan, 1975. A synthesis of experiences with dying patients and the psychological stages of their confrontation with death.

3. Blum, Richard H., and Associates. *Society and Drugs* (vol. I); *Students and Drugs* (vol. II). San Francisco: Jossey-Bass, 1969. Volume I gives a history of drug usage; volume II analyzes drug abuse in high schools and colleges.

4. Sheen, Fulton. *Peace of Soul*. Garden City: Doubleday, 1954. See ch. 11, "Fear of Death."

13

BUILDING A VALUE-SYSTEM

"Value judgments are inescapable demands of life. . . . For however unconscious and undeliberate the choice, every man finds himself inextricably entangled in a web of values on which his very life depends."
— W. G. Cole, *The Restless Quest of Modern Man*.

IN THIS chapter, we shall consider various facets of building a system of values, as well as the role of the Christian in helping others to discover authentic values.

Value Definitions

The noun "value" is derived from the Latin verb *valere*, "to be strong" or "to be worth." Contemporary dictionaries define it as the quality or fact of being worthwhile, excellent, useful, or desirable. As a transitive verb, *to value* generally means "to rate highly, to hold in high esteem, to regard as important or significant."

Since the experience of what is considered worthwhile is personal, a diversity of value-definitions is to be expected. Rescher (1969) cites various authors who interpret value in terms of perception, motivation, and social standards. Values can also be based on human needs, an approach that will be followed in this chapter.

Since values involve a relationship between a person and some other entity, one can see that values have a dual characteristic. The personal experience or perception or recognition that an object is of value or is desirable can be designated the *subjective* aspect of a value. The object itself can be designated the *objective* aspect of a value. The subjective aspect is therefore the person's value preference; the objective aspect is that which fulfills this preference. This dual characteristic of value is related to its validity as well. An individual may be correct or incorrect about the factual value of an object. For example, food is properly seen to be a health-value, but a young child may mistakenly judge paint to be a nourishing liquid. Therefore, a value may be characterized as having *subjective validity* when it is perceived to be of worth, and having *objective validity* when it is indeed so. The capability of distinguishing true values from false values on objective grounds is, of course, important to forming one's personal value-system.

Criteria for a Good System of Values

We have observed the confusion in values that is characteristic of today's pluralistic and relativistic society. Are there ways of forming a personal value-system that will help one to acquire personal stability and a sense of direction? Let us consider some criteria basic to a healthy system of values.

First, a good value-system should be *internally consistent*. That is, one should not hold to values that are contradictory (e.g., the Christian who contends he loves his neighbor and yet sees no necessity to help the poor). Also, one must guard against a defense mechanism known as logic-tight compartmentalization, by which contradictory values are unconsciously kept separate to avoid the guilt that would follow on the conscious awareness of their incompatibility.

Second, values should be *objectively valid,* i.e., grounded in a reality apart from human opinion. To be objective is to see things as they are, not as we would like them to be. For example, alcohol can be perceived by the alcoholic to have positive value, whereas objectively, for him, it is of negative value, for it tends to destroy him. Again, we have seen the hedonist's error of placing a high value on pleasure, and using pleasure as justification for immoral behavior that, from a Christian perspective, is objectively evil and of negative value.

Third, one's values should be *flexible,* in the sense that one should be prepared to adjust to a world of change. However, such flexibility, as we have seen, would not extend to values in the area of absolute reality, which is changeless.

Fourth, one's deepest values should provide *stability* amidst the vicissitudes of daily living, enabling one, as it were, to weather the storm of life.

Fifth, values should invite *commitment,* in the sense of providing directional goals worthy of dedicated effort. The uncommitted person, as Keniston (1960) has observed, usually succumbs to a meaningless existence.

Sixth, values should not be acquired and internalized without *conscious examination* of the premises and implications they contain. We have discussed, in connection with situational ethics, the contemporary acceptance of the position that immoral means can be justified by good intention or purpose. Such an ethical premise denies absolute principles and values, and leads to moral relativism and a breakdown in morality.

Seventh, personal values should span the entire spectrum of human nature and lead to *personal fulfillment,* or self-actualization. Human values fulfill human needs, and are based on human needs. The hierarchy of human needs, from lowest to highest, includes those dimensions of human nature known as sensory, affective (emotional), cognitive, conative, and spiritual (Table 6). Needs within each of these human dimensions can be classified as *innate* (or primary), and *acquired* (or secondary). For example, an innate primary *sensory* need is hunger, satisfied by food. Food therefore has innate, primary value. A specific food, e.g., ice cream, has acquired or secondary value. A primary *affective* need is illustrated by the need for emotional expression, which consequently is a primary value. Secondary acquired values that satisfy affective needs may be derived from art, music, and drama. *Cognitive* need, as used here, refers to the innate drive to know and to understand, which is satisfied by educational experiences, formal and informal. *Conative* need is the need to express freedom-in-choice behavior. Human freedom is a primary, innate need and has throughout human history been considered a primary value. Secondary conative values lie in the specific alternatives freely chosen.

The highest human values are those deriving from the *spiritual* nature of man. One such value is the innate, primary yearning for ultimate and absolute meaning. Other spiritual values, basic to human nature, are the need for total commitment to some reality higher than oneself, as well as the social needs (e.g., the needs for friendship and love). Specific spiritual values include one's adopted worldview or philosophy of life in the commitment to ideological goals, and in the individuals whom one loves in particular.

Eighth, one's value system should respond to the basic questions of life: *Who am I? Why am I here? Where am I going?* The first of these questions refers to self-identity, the second to the purpose of human existence, and the third

Table 6. A Value Classification Based on Human Needs.

Human Dimension	Examples of Innate (Primary) Values	Examples of Acquired (Secondary) Values
Affective (Emotional)	Need or drive: *Emotional experience* Value: *Pleasure, joy*	Art, music, drama, sports
Cognitive	Need or drive: *Curiosity* Value: *Knowledge in general*	Educational experiences
Conative	Need or drive: *Choice behavior* Value: *Freedom of choice*	Preferred alternatives, freely chosen
Spiritual	Need or drive: *Attainment of ultimate meaning and absolute values; need for total commitment to something or someone greater than oneself; authentic love of God and fellow man* Value: *Spiritual peace; peace of mind*	Specific world-view or value-system; commitment to certain principles: love of specific persons

to human destiny, individually and historically. The reader is familiar by now with the answers that the author would give to these questions: Man is made in the divine image, and from this image derives his human worth and dignity. Human purpose consists of authentically loving God and neighbor. Present human destiny lies in the establishment of God's kingdom of peace, justice, and love on earth, and man's ultimate future is an immortal life with God in his heavenly Kingdom.

Ninth, a value system should encompass the human condition, providing strength and support in times of pain, suffering, evil, guilt, and death. Whereas the atheistic mentality perceives the human condition as meaningless and a curse of inadequate evolutionary development, the Christian, on the basis of divine revelation, knows how evil and death came into human experience, of how both were conquered by him who redeemed mankind, and who through his own death gave meaning to suffering, and who through his resurrection validated the hope for immortal life.

These, then, are some of the criteria for developing a healthy system of values. Some will be acceptable to all; some will be accepted only by those who have experienced "absolute meaning." The questions posed by these criteria are worthy of consideration, even by those who do not accept the Christian synthesis. Perhaps they will lead the inquiring mind to an appreciation of the necessity of divine revelation for the fulfillment of mankind's quest for ultimate meaning and ultimate values.

On Counseling Values

In a confused world looking for direction, the Christian will be presented with opportunities for communicating his values to others. It is primarily in giving witness, in the *way* in which he lives, that the Christian conveys his beliefs about human origin, purpose, and destiny. Mahatma Gandhi, the great Indian social and religious leader, once remarked that if he had ever met a Christian, he would become one. There is some truth in this observation. If those who claimed to be the followers of Christ really lived out their convictions, it would not be long before the whole world would be led to believe. But why should anyone become a follower of Christ when he sees Christians acting and behaving no differently than the rest of men? Surely, if Christians really possess the fullest of divine revelation, the gifts of the Holy Spirit, and God himself in the Eucharist—then these wonderful prerogatives should inspire them to transcend selfishness and sinfulness and be a light to the world. But it is because of this lack of appreciation that Christians fall short of their spiritual calling, and hence fail to lead others to Christ.

Fortunately, there will always be a remnant faithful to Christ. In the context of the present topic, how then is the faithful Christian to give counsel to others, especially when his advice is sought in value-formation?

Peterson (1970) has discussed in general the problem of value-neutral counseling. He points out that in the counseling process it is impossible to remain value-neutral, because consciously or unconsciously, verbally or nonverbally, the counselor will inevitably communicate his own values to the client. Peterson cites other prominent therapists and counselors who have arrived at the same conclusion. Lowe (1965) discusses the problem in terms of the various possible value-orientations that the counselor can hold, presenting the alternatives of naturalism, culturalism, humanism, and theism. We have earlier examined such models in relation to the meaning of man. Lowe concludes that whatever value-orientation is taken, the counselor should be aware of his position and how it affects the counseling relationship. Regardless of one's frame of reference, a general ethical principle upon which all counselors agree is that one's values should never be imposed on another. The inevitability of value communication need not violate this principle, however. The counselor can avoid coercion by making his values clear to the client, by providing the client with alternatives, and by enabling the client, through therapy or counseling, to arrive at his own value-decisions.

The communication of values from counselor to client also applies to problems involving moral principles. Even if the counselor assumes indifferentism on an ethical or moral issue, the client will detect a value posture. It would be better for the counselor to speak out clearly on such issues, feeling free to express his own moral convictions in an explicit manner. The Christian counselor should likewise assume the same freedom; for his perspective, like any other, can be presented in such a way as not to be imposing or coercive. The principle to remember is that the client's dignity lies in his freedom to choose; the counselor but offers alternatives among which to choose. The Christian counselor should remember also that *he* has responded freely to the invitation of Christ, and that such freedom is also a prerogative of the individual he counsels. The latter's freedom, however, is not abused when the Christian explicitly imparts the rationale of his belief and the validity of his moral values, whenever such advice and help are sought. Indeed, the good news of Christ is intended to be for all people of all times, of all ages. Even so, no one can be coerced to be a Christian, for the Christian faith is a gift from God and can be given by God alone. The Christian, in giving witness by word and, more important, by deed, merely prepares the ground to receive the seed of faith. Whether it bears fruit is a personal matter between God and that individual (Matt 13.18-23; Mark 4.13-20; Luke 8.11-15).

The Christian Example

We have stressed the importance of Christian witness; for the only way in which others will be attracted to Christ is through those who follow him faithfully. Jesus cautioned his disciples on this matter: "You are the salt of the earth. But if salt becomes tasteless, what can make it salty again? It is good for nothing, and can only be thrown out to be trampled underfoot by men. You are the light of the world. A city built on a hill-top cannot be hidden. No one lights a lamp to put it under a tub; they put it on a lampstand where it shines for everyone in the house. In the same way your light must shine in the sight of men, so that, seeing your good works, they may give praise to your Father in heaven" (Matt 5.13-16). What a magnificent calling to Christians—to be the light of the world! In faithful witness to Christ, Christians can indeed lead men out of the darkness of the contemporary age to him who is the Way, the Truth, and the Life (John 14.16).

SUGGESTED READINGS

1. Barclay, James R. *Foundations of Counseling Strategies.* N.Y.: John Wiley, 1971. Cultural and philosophical foundations of counseling, including a survey and critique of intentionality, phenomenology, existentialism, and behaviorism.

2. Peterson, James A. *Counseling and Values: A Philosophical Examination.* Scranton: International Textbook

Company, 1970. A discussion of the value-crisis in modern society, goals in counseling, and the problems involved in counseling values.

3. Aden, L. "Pastoral Counseling as a Christian Perspective," in P. Homans, ed., *The Dialogue between Theology and Psychology*. Univ. of Chicago Press, 1968. A presentation of the Christian answer to the problem of finitude, alienation, and guilt.

4. Nunokawa, Walter D. *Human Values and Abnormal Behavior*. Glenview: Scott, Foresman, 1969. Articles on value-orientations, and the place of values in counseling and psychotherapy.

5. Rescher, Nicholas. *Introduction to Value Theory*. Englewood Cliffs: Prentice-Hall, 1969. A study of the various definitions of values, the dimensions of values, and axiology, the theory of values.

6. Baier, Kurt, and Nicholas Rescher, eds. *Values and the Future*. N.Y.: Free Press, 1969. Contributed commentaries on value-change, value-commitment, and technology.

APPENDICES

APPENDICES

APPENDIX A

Atheistic and Christian Perspectives
on the Human Condition°

Myth, according to its etymology, is taken from the Greek *mythos,* interpreted as fable, tale, talk, or speech; of uncertain origin. Myth can be taken as a veiled explanation of an objective reality, or as existing only in the imagination. Whether considered to be objectively valid or only subjectively imagined, myths have provided guidance for human ideologies throughout the ages. In modern time, myth has supposedly become exposed and banished by science, but critics maintain that science in this regard has but set itself up as another "myth" in directing the aspirations of mankind.

There are those who claim that the supposed demise of clearly delineated myth contributes to contemporary estrangement and alienation. Keniston (1960) describes the disintegration of "positive Utopian myth" and the rise of "negative counter-Utopian myth," the latter exemplified by Orwell's *1984* and Skinner's *Walden Two.* Phenix (1964) has detailed the contemporary attacks in all areas that formerly provided guidance in the development of ideology. Campbell (1968) believes that no longer can one grand

°The contents of this appendix were previously published, in substantially this form, in the *Journal of Psychology and Theology* 3 (1975), 36-41.

mythology guide mankind, but rather the individual must tailor a personal mythology to meet his own needs. Pluralism and relativism are the hallmarks of contemporary thought.

There are some historical events, which, from a traditional Christian point of view, are not classified as myths. For example, the traditional Christian does not consider the story of Adam and Eve, or the resurrection of Jesus Christ, as myths. To him these are events that not only have historical validity but are of vital importance in the question of man's origin and destiny. Let us contrast the humanistic and Christian interpretations of the story of Adam and Eve, together with their implications for the human condition and a psychological model of man.

The Story of Adam and Eve

The primeval story of the creation of man is related in Genesis, the first book of the Scriptures. God established a garden of delight (Eden, Paradise) for the first human beings he created. He permitted them to partake of all its fruits but that of one tree, the tree of knowledge of good and evil. The serpent tempted Eve by telling her that the reason God forbade that particular fruit was that it would give her and Adam powers equivalent to God's. Eve succumbed to this temptation and so did Adam. They were consequently banished by God from the garden (Genesis 1-3). The concept of the "fall of man" is found in all theistic theologies of antiquity. The common theme is that God created man with intelligence and freedom, but man abused his freedom by turning away from God, and he was subsequently punished. The resultant alienation of man from God is the root of the present "human condition," one of suffering, guilt, and death.

The Christian Interpretation

Traditional Christianity holds to the following interpretation of the creation of man. First, Adam and Eve were created from the motive of God's love, and therefore created in God's image (Genesis 1.27). This "image" was reflected in man's self-awareness, intelligence, and freedom. Early Christianity, and traditional Catholicism, held that man also enjoyed certain gifts, not essential to his nature, but additional prerogatives, termed supernatural and preternatural gifts: *justice* referred to a special life of love and friendship with God, called the state of sanctifying grace; *integrity* referred to complete self-control; and *immortality* meant freedom from death. It was also believed that original man was free from pain and suffering (Abbott, 1969).

Freedom, however, requires alternatives among which a free subject may choose. God, in making man in his image, gave him the freedom to love or to refuse to love his Creator. Man chose to turn away from God, to reject Divine Love, in favor of self-love. Man wanted to be God and therefore defied God. The creature demanded status equal to that of his Creator. This abuse of his gift of human freedom, referred to as the first or "original sin," led to man's punishment. He lost the gifts of justice, integrity, and immortality. He became alienated and estranged from God, from himself, and from his fellow man. He became subject to concupiscence, pain, suffering, guilt, and death. Man retained, however, those capabilities which were natural to his being, the qualities of self-awareness, intelligence, and free will.

God, however, had compassion on man. In the same breath of pronouncing punishment, God promised redemption. A future son of woman was to crush the head of Satan (Genesis 3.14-15). This future redeemer was to be Jesus

Christ, the Word made flesh (John 1.14, 3.16). God would become man, to redeem man, to restore him to the state of justice or sanctifying grace, to reconcile him once more with Divine Love, and thus to enable man to accomplish his original destiny of immortal life with God.

Lutheran and Calvinist (Reformed) traditions added little to the description of man's pre-fallen state, and were more pessimistic in the interpretation of man's condition after the Fall. Traditional Lutheranism, for example, held that man retained free will in the natural order of everyday choice, but in his utter depravity lacked free will in the God-relationship, could do nothing to restore that friendship, and even after justification could not merit grace through good works. Man is justified by faith, and any good works flow in recognition of such justification rather than contributing to it (Luther, 1855). The Reformed tradition teaches a similar doctrine on the depravity of man, going further to stress the utter nothingness of man in confrontation with the Divine (Calvin, 1953; The Heidelberg Catechism, 1962; Niesel, 1956). Barth has commented on the contrasts between earlier and later Christian interpretations of man after the Fall: "This does not mean, as we have seen, that he has ceased to be a man. He has not lost—even in part—the good nature which was created by God, to acquire instead another and evil nature. In the many conflicts on this point it has often been stated how far this loss or alteration can go and cannot go—the loss or alteration being made as great as possible on the Augustinian-Reformed side and as little as possible on the Roman Catholic-Neo-Protestant side" (Barth, 1961, p. 492). Nonetheless, Barth too preserved the radical otherness between God and man (Barth, 1967).

Such is the traditional interpretation of the Fall of man. However, in contemporary Christian theology, Barbour states, "Adam is interpreted by most Protestant writers not as a historic individual but as a symbol of Everyman's journey from innocence to responsibility, sin, and guilt" (Barbour, 1966, p. 379). He further cites Langdon Gilkey and Rudolph Bultmann as supporting such dymythologization of Scripture. Some contemporary Catholic writers, while supporting the existence of original man and his initial turning away from God, contend that the condition of prefallen man never occurred, but was rather offered to man, who rejected it, a sinful repudiation resulting in the human condition (Schoonenberg, 1965).

Despite these differences among traditional and contemporary Christian writers, there are fundamental points of agreement, including these: (a) God exists, (b) man turned away from God, with (c) the consequent human condition of suffering, guilt, and death.

The Atheistic-Humanistic Interpretation

The interpretation by contemporary atheistic humanism of the story of Adam and Eve differs radically from the Christian view. Erich Fromm, for example, pictures Eden as a place where "there is no choice, no freedom, no thinking either" (Fromm, 1969a, ch. 2). He then goes on to describe man's disobedience against God's command as an act of freedom and the beginning of reason. However, this new freedom from the "sweet bondage of paradise" left man alone, powerless, and afraid. And once paradise was lost, man cannot return to it. He must resolve his problem by "only one possible, productive solution for the relationship of individualized man with the world: his active solidarity with man and his spontaneous activity, love and work, which unite him again with the world, not by primary ties but as a free and independent individual" (Fromm, 1969a, ch. 2).

Rollo May also sees the disobedience of Adam and Eve in a favorable light. He draws parallels in the conflicts of Adam with God, Prometheus with Zeus, Oedipus with his father, and Orestes with matriarchal powers (May, 1953, ch. 6). The common theme is that self-awareness, maturity, freedom, and responsibility emerge only through the reaction against authority. May's authority-figures are portrayed as jealous, vindictive rulers who feel threatened by man's efforts to free himself from a crippling, authoritarian bondage. May also interprets Adam and Eve's partaking of the "tree of knowledge" as the dawn of the experience of "moral consciousness" (May 1967, p. 219). He cites Hegel as describing the myth of Adam as a "fall upward."

Critique

First of all, contemporary humanism sees the story of Adam and Eve as a myth rather than as an actual event. As such, the event may be interpreted in many ways. There is one common difficulty, however, in the interpretation favored by such writers as Fromm and May. Man in the garden is pictured *without* freedom, self-awareness, or moral consciousness. Then, by rebellion against God, these admirable qualities are suddenly acquired. The question is, from where? Where did these qualities come from, if not originally created in man by God? Man could not have given himself what he did not have. For man to freely disobey, he must first have the capability to do so.

A step-by-step comparison of the Christian perspective with the contemporary humanistic view is given in the Table. It should be noted that while the contemporary humanistic interpretation begins and ends on a negative note, the Christian view begins and ends with a positive note.

Interpretations of the Adam and Eve Story

Traditional Christian Interpretation	Atheistic-Humanistic Interpretation
1. God is real, and so were "Adam" and "Eve" (original mankind).	1. "God," and the first humans, "Adam" and "Eve," are myths with no counterpart in reality.
2. Man, created in God's image, was given *freedom*, self-awareness, and intellect. (Positive condition)	2. Man was created in bondage and slavery to "God." No thinking; no self-awareness, no choice, no freedom; a robot. (Negative condition)
3. Man freely chose to abuse his freedom by deliberately disobeying or turning away from God. (Negative condition)	3. Man rebelled against slavery, disobeyed "God," asserted his independence of "God." Seen as first human act, beginning of reason, emergence of self-awareness. (Positive condition)
4. By turning away from God, man lost God's gifts of *justice, integrity*, and *immortality*. (Negative condition)	4. Man finds himself free from bondage, but now alone, powerless, afraid, separated from nature (Eden), aware of guilt and death. (Negative condition)
5. At time of rebellion, God promised Redemption in Christ, who provides divine grace to help man return to God. (Positive condition)	5. Man must now use his new freedom to rebuild community relation with nature, by productive work and love. (Positive condition)
6. Present "human condition" is solved by supernatural grace. (Positive condition)	6. Present "human condition" will be solved by future evolutionary trend. (Positive or negative, contingent on future)
7. Future of individual person is resurrection after death and immortality, life with God forever. (Positive condition)	7. Future of individual person is death and termination of existence. (Negative condition)

The Human Condition

In his discussion of the "human situation," Fromm (1969a, ch. 2; 1968, ch. 3) couches the Adam and Eve story in atheistic evolutionary terms. Eden represents the point of evolution where prehuman man is still basically animal, rooted in nature. When man becomes aware of himself, that is, human, he begins to transcend nature and experience the anxiety and alienation resulting from the severance of nature's ties. Fromm states, "Cast into this world at an accidental time and place, he is forced out of it, again accidentally" (Fromm, 1968, ch. 3). The term "accidental" refers to the blind evolutionary development of the organism, man, and his final termination, death. The discrepancy between man's striving for life and the opposing fact of death is called by Fromm the most fundamental "existential dichotomy" (1969b, ch. 3) of which man is aware but for which he has no explanation, and over which he has no control. Indeed, Fromm maintains that man attempts to negate the fact of death by fashioning such ideologies as the Christian concept of immortality (1969b, ch. 3).

Contemporary atheistic humanism views suffering, pain, guilt, and death as fate that should be fought against with courage (Kurtz, 1969). But, if this is a natural fate decreed by evolution, why does man fight against it, or at least see it as unreasonable? Man must either be suffering from a delusion in his conviction that these experiences are unreasonable, or else be correct in his observation. If he is correct in his observation, it follows that the *present* state of affairs was not the originally intended condition of man. This last realization is compatible with the Christian interpretation of the fall of man. (And, on the other hand, even if one prefers to believe that man's conviction that the unreasonableness of his present condition is a delusion, one must still explain the origin of the delusion, that is, how did man arrive at the realization, even though delusionary, that his present condition should not have been?)

Christian Conclusions on the Human Condition

In closing, the Christian point of view on the human condition may be presented as follows:

(1) Pain, suffering, evil, and death (hallmarks of the human condition) are "non-rational," that is, "unreasonable," or against the natural human propensity toward survival, health, goodness, and happiness.

(2) Explanations on the level of reason, or philosophy, including evolution and atheistic humanism, are therefore bound to fail, precisely because the facts to be explained are "unreasonable," or beyond natural analysis.

(3) The Christian alternative to explain the "human condition" is based on divine revelation, as recorded in the Scriptures. Hence,

    (a) Suffering, evil, and death were never intended by God (and absent in the Garden of Paradise);

    (b) These occurred through man's rebellion, such that the "human condition" became one of ignorance, sin, suffering, and death;

    (c) Whether one accepts the Christian interpretation or the contemporary atheistic-humanistic explanation of the fall of man and the present human condition depends ultimately on whether or not one believes in the existence of God and in divine revelation as recorded in the Scriptures;

    (d) The human condition has been remedied, though not removed, by the Incarnate Word and Redemption. Man is consoled by the promise of eternal happiness after death, and lifetime on earth is but a moment when compared to this ultimate eternal existence;

(e) Faith in divine revelation is a gift of God, accessible to all (Hammes, 1971, ch. 15);

(f) While in this life on earth, man is to know, serve, and love God, joyously accepting the cross of life in the strength of divine grace, giving of himself in the service of his fellow man. In summary, Christians are to put on Christ (Gal 3.27), in bringing peace, love, and wisdom to all they encounter (Hammes, 1971, ch. 16).

Implications for Psychology

The interpretations of the Adam and Eve story have both theoretical and practical implications for psychology. Theoretically speaking, with regard to a psychological model of man, is he to be considered a child of evolution or a child of God? Is he created in the image of God or is he animal alone? Is he ordained to final termination in death, or to a glorified individual immortality? Practically speaking, the interpretations of the Adam and Eve story bear on the deepest existential problems encountered in counseling and psychotherapy. Carl Jung once declared that the basic problem of almost all of his patients over thirty-five years of age was finding a religious outlook on life (Jung, 1969). Viktor Frankl's logotherapy is wholly based on the search for life's meaning (Frankl, 1963). Our age is characterized by anxiety, meaninglessness, and a search for enduring values — problems relating basically to the human condition. Whether or not one can give satisfactory and authentic answers to today's questions on the meaning of guilt, suffering, and death rests ultimately on one's interpretation of the Fall of man.

APPENDIX B

Beyond Freedom and Dignity:

Behavioral Fixated Delusion?[*]

B. F. Skinner's most recent and widely read book, *Beyond Freedom and Dignity* (1971), has once again sounded the war drums of behavioral science against the traditional concept of autonomous man. Skinner contends that the literatures of freedom and dignity are leading us to destruction, and must be dispensed with in favor of a behavioral technology. Furthermore, they are supposedly based on false premises, whereas his behavioristic model is the one to be accepted, particularly since it is supported by behavioral data and Skinner's interpretation of that data. The present paper is an attempt to respond both to Skinner's theoretical position and to the charges he levels against traditionalism.

One cannot fault Skinner's experimental data, which stand on their own merit. It is his theoretical formulations, based on this data, that can seriously be questioned, and, in this writer's opinion, adequately refuted. There have been excellent critiques of Skinner in the past (Chomsky, 1959; Koestler, 1964, 1967; Krutch, 1953; Malcolm, 1964; Matson, 1964). The present paper offers a complementary eval-

[*]The contents of this appendix were previously published, in substantially this form, as an article in the *Journal of Psychology and Theology* 1 (1973), 8-14.

uation in terms of logical fallacies and gratuitous assumptions.

Argumentum ad Hominem

In *Beyond Freedom and Dignity* (1971), Skinner unfortunately resorts to *argumentum ad hominem* in describing his opponents. The following quotes are taken from Skinner (1971), p. 200:

"What is being abolished is autonomous man—the inner man, the homunculus, the possessing demon, the man defended by the literatures of freedom and dignity." Note the abuse of contemporary vitalism and natural dualism, which certainly does not propose any "homunculus," a vestige of primitive animism and exaggerated dualism. To continue: "His abolition has been long overdue. Autonomous man is a device used to explain what we cannot explain in other ways. He has been constructed from our ignorance, and as our understanding increases, the very stuff of which he is composed vanishes." This is a caricature of traditionalism. Skinner's charges of "ignorance" are patently false.

"Science does not dehumanize man, it de-homunculizes him, and it must do so if it is to prevent the abolition of the human species." Thus Skinner's charge that the literatures of freedom and dignity are leading to man's destruction, and science must save man. To the contrary, it is man's freedom to abuse freedom that leads to self-destruction. The literatures of freedom and dignity do not advocate such self-destruction; indeed, they exhort man to act rationally, not irrationally.

Rejection of Intervening Variables
and the Level of Inference

Consider the following three statements in Skinner's fundamental work, *Science and Human Behavior* (1953): "The events appealed to in early mentalistic explanations of behavior have remained beyond the reach of observation" (p. 30). "Since mental or psychic events are asserted to lack the dimensions of physical science, we have an additional reason for rejecting them" (pp. 30-31). And, "The objection to inner states is not that they do not exist, but that they are irrelevant in a functional analysis" (p. 35).

Several comments are in order. First, Skinner is inconsistent in his reasons for rejecting intervening variables, first giving their *non-quantitative* insusceptibility to physical measurement as one reason, then rejecting this reason in favor of the *irrelevancy* of such variables for a functional analysis. However, both reasons can be criticized. While it is granted that intervening variables are irrelevant to a functional S-R analysis, why should the functional approach be the only one admissible to the study of behavior and its sources? Secondly, Skinner is correct in observing that intervening variables are not quantifiably measurable, but is that a legitimate reason for rejecting them from study? The reality of intervening variables can be arrived at by the method of immediate inference (Hammes, 1971). Skinner, however, has defined observation as valid only in terms of "S" and "R." Therefore, the existence of intervening variables arrived at by reflection and inference is ruled out by an arbitrary definition of what constitutes "observation." (It should be clear that by the term "intervening variable" I am referring to actually existing variables within the organism, lying beyond external observation but legitimately inferred.)

Rejection of Man's Inner Nature

In reference to consciousness, another aspect of the traditionalist inner man, Skinner has commented, "The scientist humbly admits that he is describing only half the universe, and he defers to another world—a world of mind or consciousness—for which another mode of inquiry is assumed to be required. Such a point of view is by no means inevitable, but it is part of the cultural heritage from which science has emerged. It obviously stands in the way of a unified account of nature. The contribution which a science of behavior can make in suggesting an alternative point of view is perhaps one of its most important achievements" (Skinner, 1953, p. 258). Skinner consistently sees the opposition's mode of inquiry to be an *assumption*, because he does not accept the validity of the method of inference. Also, by contending this method to be "cultural," Skinner can more easily reject it. His charge that the opposition's point of view stands in the way of a unified science is purely conjectural. And the last part of the above passage is a statement of Skinner's mission.

Skinner spends the rest of that chapter "reducing" private events to observable responses. However, he does concede (p. 279) that "one is still free, of course, to assume that there are events of a non-physical nature accessible only to the experiencing organism and therefore wholly private." Note again the use of the term "assumed," since Skinner rejects evidence that would make this a conclusion rather than an assumption. Skinner impugns the concept of inner causality (formal causality) in man: "The function of the inner man is to provide an explanation which will not be explained in turn. . . . He is a center from which behavior emanates. He initiates, originates, and creates, and in doing so he remains, as he was for the Greeks, divine. We say that he is autonomous—and, so far as a science of behavior is concerned, that means miraculous. The position is, of course, vulnerable. Autonomous man serves to explain only the things we are not yet able to explain in other ways. His existence depends upon our ignorance, and he naturally loses status as we come to know more about behavior" (Skinner, 1971, p. 14). Skinner thus reveals his faith that all behavior is or will be ultimately explainable in terms of efficient causality alone, further defined exclusively in terms of environmental causes. He thereby reduces final and formal causality to efficient causality. However, the evidence for final and formal causes indicates these factors to be just as real as Skinner's efficient (environmental) causes (Hammes, 1971).

Dignity of Man as a Function of Environment

Skinner rejects the traditional concept of human dignity as being within the person. "What we may call the literature of dignity is concerned with preserving due credit. It may oppose advances in technology, including a technology of behavior, because they destroy chances to be admired and a basic analysis because it offers an alternative explanation of behavior for which the individual himself has previously been given credit. The literature thus stands in the way of further human achievement" (Skinner, 1971, p. 58). Skinner is wrong in attributing the motive of "preserving due credit" to those supporting the dignity of man. This is another example of setting up a "straw man" to reject. The dignity-of-man supporters do so on the basis of human nature, not from any jealous desire to guard credit or "to be admired." The literature of dignity does not "stand in the way of human achievement" but rather *accounts* for human achievement. The achievement of man is a function of his unique nature and inherent dignity.

Skinner has also stated, "We recognize a person's dignity or worth when we give him credit for what he has done" (Skinner, 1971, p. 58). True, but personal dignity or worth is not contingent on behavior. (At least in the Christian perspective, the mongoloid, the psychotic, the so-called "neurological vegetable" resulting from brain damage—all possess dignity and worth because man is created in the Divine Image (Genesis 1.26-27). Thus the Christian "recognizes" human dignity in what is intrinsically present and inferred, rather than only in terms of behavior, the manifestations of such worth.

Environmental Determinism

There are at least ten varieties of determinism, each of which is subject to logical criticism (Hammes, 1971). Skinner's position falls into the category of *environmental determinism*. "The hypothesis that man is not free is essential to the application of scientific method to the study of human behavior. The free inner man who is held responsible for the behavior of the external biological organism is only a prescientific substitute for the kinds of causes which are discovered in the course of a scientific analysis. . . . He is the product of a culture which generates self-control or cultural design as a mode of behavior. *The environment determines the individual even when he alters the environment*" (Skinner, 1953, pp. 447-448, emphasis added).

However, neither determinism nor freedom can be proved or disproved by Skinner's scientific method, since an S-R analysis indicates only *what* happened, and reveals nothing about whether or not such behavior was free *or* determined.

Skinner, by assuming a functional analysis or S-R explanation to be the only acceptable method of studying man, rejects the basis for freedom, which rests on an analysis of internal variables existing within man. However, it is not the purpose of this paper to present the evidence for freedom, but rather to show that Skinner's environmental determinism does not necessarily follow from his S-R data; nor indeed is determinism a necessary adoption for a viable behavioral science. Skinner says, "We must assume that behavior is lawful and determined" (1953, p. 6). Must we? Might not freedom be one of the "laws" of human nature? Even so, *on the behavioral level* it is impossible to prove *or* disprove freedom *or* determinism. Knowing *what* a person does gives no evidence supportive of freedom *or* coercion.

Also, it would appear that Skinner's interest in manipulable and presumably determined behavior has led him to ignore those human aspects which are not susceptible to manipulation and control. He summarily dismisses these aspects as of no interest to him, and he further presumes they are of no interest or relevance to any science of behavior (Evans, 1968, p. 23).

Again, the traditionalist does *not* claim man is free *not* to seek good (positive reinforcement), since it is basic human nature to seek good and avoid evil, or pain. Human freedom lies in the choice among means to attain goals of positive reinforcement. Even the basic goals men seek are modifiable by free choice. Thus man is *not* free *not* to seek happiness, but he *is* free in (a) deciding upon the various kinds of happiness he may pursue, and (b) deciding the various means in attaining same.

Skinner does not even confront the traditionalists' evidence for free choice. He merely *assumes* it to be false, by refusing to admit intervening, innate variables within man; and it is *within* man that such evidence for free choice exists.

Skinner attributes a determining role to the reinforcement given by government and religion. However, while it is admissible that reinforcement influences behavior, it does not follow that reinforcement *determines* behavior. Reinforcement provides the motive for choice, but this motive (final cause) need not be coercive.

Blaming Traditionalism for World Situation

In the last chapter of *Beyond Freedom and Dignity* ("What Is Man?"), Skinner unleashes a concluding attack on traditionalism and freedom. He describes traditionalists as suffering "wounded vanity" at the hands of behavioral scientists, as reacting with aggressive tendencies for having their free model of man usurped, or perhaps indulging in "wistful" nostalgia for the times when the inherent dignity of man and the importance of spiritual values were recognized. All of this is easily recognizable as *argumentum ad hominem*. Skinner avoids confronting the rational basis for the traditional model; and by misrepresenting the traditionalists' motives to be but emotional, he easily dismisses them.

In summary, Skinner blames the world mess on the literatures of freedom and dignity. Therefore, the presumably false premises (autonomy, freedom) underlying the traditional view should be abolished as delusionary, to be replaced with Skinner's controlled social contingencies of reinforcement. The traditionalist would reply to these charges: (1) the world is a mess because of the capacity of man to abuse his freedom (a remarkable characteristic of human freedom); (2) Skinner's assumption of determinism is not warranted by his S-R level of functional analysis (but, then, neither can freedom be proved solely by behavioral observation); (3) human freedom is capable of being proved (Hammes, 1971); (4) man cannot dispense with human freedom, he can only abuse or not abuse it; and (5) Skinner's solution to the world situation is itself based on the false assumption and delusion of environmental determinism.

Evolution as a Determining Cause

After rejecting traditional "mentalistic" interpretations of human behavior, Skinner relates his environmental determinism to evolution. First, he observes, "There is a much more important reason why we have been slow in discarding mentalistic explanations: it has been hard to find alternatives" (Skinner, 1971, p. 16). This is simply not so. The autonomous model of man is founded on positive evidence and a positive method, not on ignorance or difficulty in explanation. We have seen that Skinner is prone to present the opposition in "straw man" images that he can easily repudiate.

Skinner continues: "For thousands of years in the history of human thought the process of natural selection went unseen in spite of its extraordinary importance. When it was eventually discovered, it became, of course, the key to revolutionary theory" (p. 217). "The environment not only prods or lashes, it selects. Its role is similar to that in natural selection, though in a very different time scale . . ." (p. 18). Thus Skinner postulates the environment as efficient cause, a natural consequence of the assumption of S-R determinism. Also, Skinner, in speaking of evolutionary "selection," becomes vulnerable to the criticism of introducing *purpose,* or final causality. Some evolutionists personify natural selection, while at the same time rejecting purpose. Though *consciously* rejecting purpose, they *unconsciously* recognize it in the use of the term "selection."

"The man that man has made is the product of the culture that man has devised. He has emerged from two quite different processes of evolution: the biological evolution responsible for the human species, and the cultural evolution carried out by that species. Both of these processes of evolution may now accelerate because they are both subject to intentional design" (p. 208). Recall, however, that Skinner's "intentional design" does not originate in the inner man, but in the "selective environment."

Skinner's interpretation of evolution is shared by atheistic naturalism, which has a large following among psychologists and other scientists today. This position has been critiqued elsewhere (Hammes, 1971; American Scientific Affiliation, 1971).

Controller, Controlled, and Culture

In his earlier work *Science and Human Behavior* (1953), Skinner discussed the concepts fundamental to the expansion of this topic in the later work, *Beyond Freedom and Dignity* (1971). "The ultimate strength of a controller depends on the strength of those whom he controls" (Skinner, 1953, p. 443); and, "The first step in the countercontrol of a powerful agency is to strengthen the controllee" (p. 447). It would seem that these two statements negate each other. For how can the controllee be strengthened if the controller, being what he is, decides to prevent it? Skinner further states, "If the governing agency cannot be made to understand the value of the individual to the agency itself, the individual himself must be made to understand his own value" (p. 447). The sentiment is admirable, but again, the controller could conceivably prevent, by manipulating contingencies of reinforcement, any such insight on the part of the controlled. Who is going to bell the cat? And how? Although Skinner insists on a reciprocal relationship between controller and controlled, where does the control start? If in the controller, then he could decide to retain control and not reciprocate. If in the controlled, they would become the controller, and in turn could reach the same decision.

Obligation, Ought, and Values

Skinner believes that science can be a source of values. "It is commonly argued that there are two kinds of knowledge, one of fact and the other of values, and that science is necessarily confined to the first. . . . It is not true that statements containing 'should' or 'ought' have no place in scientific discourse" (1953, p. 428). He then takes the statement "You ought to take an umbrella" and interprets it as an exhortatory statement based on reinforcing grounds; that is, if you do not take an umbrella, you will get wet. Skinner recognizes this example of "ought" as not entailing any obligation. But then Skinner goes further to consider the "ought" of ethics: "You ought to love your neighbor" is convertible to two other statements, "The approval of your fellow men is positively reinforcing to you," and, "loving your fellow men is approved by the group of which you are a member" (p. 429). Now, the latter two statements are correct in describing *one* kind of reinforcement that follows the implementation of this precept. However, it does not necessarily follow that this reinforcement is the controlling and determining motive. A deeper motive is that human beings are made in the image of God; and because of this they can, and ought to, love one another (Mark 13.30-31). Even so, we are not determined to do so, but can freely do otherwise. Again, Skinner omits the *sense* of obligation and responsibility involved in the moral "ought," which is rooted in conscience as an intellectual function (Hammes, 1971; Knight, 1969).

Lastly, it can be observed that to derive *ought*-conclusions from *is*-statements is to commit the "naturalistic fallacy" in ethics (Adler, 1965; Sahakian, 1968). Skinner believes that the study of reinforcement will yield value judgments of what is good or bad and, consequently, the "ought" of human behavior. However, this statement is ethically questionable. For example, marital intercourse, adulterous intercourse, and fornication are all positively reinforcing, yet the Christian "ought" (the Commandments) to support one and condemn the others (Exodus 20.14; Matthew 5.27-28; Ephesians 5.5). The traditional Christian does not use "feeling" as the sole criterion of good and bad, of what ought or ought not be done (Galatians 5.16-24; Romans 7.14-23). Furthermore, all *evil* behavior is done under the guise of *good*. Rape, theft, and murder are all acts done for reasons of personal positive reinforcement. Skinner's ethical position is subject to the criticisms leveled against all forms of relativistic, naturalistic ethics.

Compatability of Both Traditional and Skinnerian Views with Data on the Behavioral Level

Perhaps the most telling criticism of Skinner is that behavioral data, gathered on a level on which he insists we must stay in formulating a model of human nature, supports his critics as much as it supports him. That is, the behavioral level fails to discriminate Skinner from traditionalism; behavioral data is equally compatible with both perspectives, both models of man. Behavioral data does not prove or disprove either point of view.

Skinner shows some degree of insight into this fact. He states, "Neither view can be proved, but it is in the nature of scientific inquiry that the evidence should shift to the second" (1971, p. 101). In this concession statement, Skinner is guilty of logical error. Since he has previously defined "scientific inquiry" in terms of a functional S-R paradigm, he nows "proposes" that such inquiry will resolve the problem in favor of his position. It should be obvious that a methodology stemming from a theoretical position under question cannot be used to validate that position.

Since the behavioral data is compatible with both perspectives, how then can one decide upon the validity of traditionalism and the "literatures of freedom and dignity" versus Skinner's position of environmental determinism? The resolution is beyond the behavioral level, in a reflective analysis on the level of immediate inference (Hammes, 1971). This procedure naturally has hazards, as does any exercise of reason, but attendant dangers do not invalidate the proper use of rational analysis. One can, of course, remain on the behavioral level, but it should be remembered that this is but one option, not necessarily the most desirable, and that it logically involves the acknowledgment that alternatives other than Skinner's are equally consistent with the behavioral data.

In conclusion, it may be said that Skinner, in his dogmatic condemnation of traditionalism, is guilty of the contradiction inherent in all relativistic positions claiming to yield absolute certitude. To make absolute statements about the validity of one's own position and the invalidity of the opposition is a prerogative that cannot be logically claimed by any relativist, Skinnerian or otherwise.

BIBLIOGRAPHY

Abbott, W. M., ed., *The Documents of Vatican II* (N.Y.: Herder, 1966).

Abbott, W. M., et al., *The Bible Reader: An Interfaith Interpretation* (N.Y.: Bruce, 1969).

Aden, L., "Pastoral Counseling as a Christian Perspective," in P. Homans, ed., *The Dialogue between Theology and Psychology* (Univ. of Chicago Press, 1968).

Adler, M. J., *The Conditions of Philosophy* (N.Y.: Dell, 1965).

Adler, M. J., *The Difference of Man and the Difference It Makes* (N.Y.: World, 1968).

Alexander, A. F., *College Apologetics* (Chicago: Regnery, 1954).

Allers, R., *Existentialism and Psychiatry* (Springfield: Charles C. Thomas, 1961).

American Scientific Affiliation, "Creation and/or Evolution," *Journal of the American Scientific Affiliation* 23 (1971), 121-160.

Anderson, W. F., "Genetic Therapy," in M. Hamilton, ed., *The New Genetics and the Future of Man* (Grand Rapids: Eerdmans, 1972).

Anton, J. P., "Human Excellence," in P. Kurtz, ed., *Moral Problems in Contemporary Society* (Englewood Cliffs: Prentice-Hall, 1969).

Armerding, H. T., ed., *Christianity and the World of Thought* (Chicago: Moody, 1968).

Atkinson, G. M., "The Morality of Abortion," *International Philosophical Quarterly* 14 (1974), 347-362.

273

Augenstein, L., *Come, Let Us Play God* (N.Y.: Harper & Row, 1969).

Back, K., *Beyond Words: The Story of Sensitivity Training and the Encounter Movement* (Baltimore: Penguin, 1973).

Baier, K., "Meaning and Morals," in P. Kurtz, ed., *Moral Problems in Contemporary Society* (Englewood Cliffs: Prentice-Hall, 1969).

Baier, K., and N. Rescher, eds., *Values and the Future* (N.Y.: Free Press, 1969).

Barbour, I. G., *Issues in Science and Religion* (N.Y.: Prentice-Hall, 1966).

Barbour, I. G., *Science and Secularity* (N.Y.: Harper & Row, 1970).

Barclay, J., *Foundations of Conseling Strategies* (N.Y.: Wiley, 1971).

Barnette, H. H., *The New Theology and Morality* (Philadelphia: Westminster, 1967).

Barrett, W., *What Is Existentialism?* (N.Y.: Grove, 1964).

Barth, K., *Church Dogmatics*, vol. 4 (Edinburgh: T. Clark, 1961), pt. 1, "The Doctrine of Reconciliation."

Barth, K., *The Faith of the Church* (London: Fontana, 1967).

Bertalanffy, L. von, *General Systems Theory: Essays on Its Foundation and Development* (N.Y.: Braziller, 1968).

Billings, E., J. Billings, and M. Catarinich, *Atlas of the Ovulation Method: The Safe Period Based on the Mucus System* (Collegeville, Minn.: Human Life Center, St. John's Univ., 1973).

Birch, C., and P. Abrecht, eds., *Genetics and the Quality of Life* (Elmsford, N.Y.: Pergamon, 1975).

Bittle, C. N., *Reality and the Mind: Epistemology* (Milwaukee: Bruce, 1936).

Bittle, C. N., *The Whole Man: Psychology* (Milwaukee: Bruce, 1945).

Bittle, C. N., *Man and Morals: Ethics* (Milwaukee: Bruce, 1950).

Blackham, H. J., ed., *Reality, Man, and Existence: Essential Works of Existentialism* (N.Y.: Bantam, 1965).

Blum, R. H., and Associates, *Society and Drugs* and *Students and Drugs* (San Francisco: Jossey-Bass, 1969), 2 vols.

Borzaga, R., *Contemporary Philosophy* (Milwaukee: Bruce, 1966).

Bourke, V. J., *Ethics: A Textbook in Moral Philosophy* (N.Y.: Macmillan, 1966).

Bourke, V. J., *History of Ethics*, vol. 2, *Modern and Contemporary Ethics* (Garden City: Doubleday, 1970).

Boylan, M. E., *This Tremendous Lover* (Westminster: Newman, 1954).

Bridgman, P., *The Way Things Are* (N.Y.: Viking, 1961).

Bruce, F. F., *The New Testament Documents: Are They Reliable?* (Downers Grove: InterVarsity, 1974a).

Bruce, F. F., *Jesus & Christian Origins outside the New Testament* (Grand Rapids: Eerdmans, 1974b).

Bube, R., *The Encounter between Christianity and Science* (Grand Rapids: Eerdmans, 1968).

Bugental, J. F. T., *Challenges of Humanistic Psychology* (N.Y.: McGraw-Hill, 1967).

Buhler, C., and F. Massarik, *The Course of Human Life* (N.Y.: Springer, 1968).

Burghardt, W. J., *Towards Reconciliation* (Washington, D.C.: U.S. Catholic Conference, 1974).

Byrne, E. F., and E. A. Maziarz, *Human Being and Being Human* (N.Y.: Appleton, 1969).

Callahan, D., "New Beginnings in Life: A Philosopher's

Response," in M. Hamilton, ed., *The New Genetics and the Future of Man* (Grand Rapids: Eerdmans, 1972).

Callahan, D., "Recombinant DNA: Science and the Public," *Hastings Center Report* 7 (1977), 20-23.

Calvin, J., *Institutes of the Christian Religion,* tr. H. Beveridge (London: J. Clarke, 1953).

Campbell, J., *The Hero with a Thousand Faces* (Princeton Univ. Press, 1968).

Castelli, J., "There Are Some in Media and Congress Who See Abortion as Money-Saver for Public," *Our Sunday Visitor* (24 July 1977).

Cavanagh, J., and J. Harvey, *Counseling the Homosexual* (Huntington, Ind.: Our Sunday Visitor, 1977).

Cell, E., ed., *Religion and Contemporary Western Culture* (Nashville, Abingdon, 1967).

Christenson, L., *The Christian Family* (Minneapolis: Bethany Fellowship, 1970).

Chomsky, N., review of B. F. Skinner's *Verbal Behavior,* in *Language* 35 (1959), 26-58.

Cole, W. G., *The Restless Quest of Modern Man* (N.Y.: Oxford Univ. Press, 1966).

Collins, J., *The Existentialists* (N.Y.: Regnery, 1952).

Connell, F. J., *Outlines of Moral Theology* (Milwaukee: Bruce, 1958).

Cox, H., *The Secular City* (N.Y.: Macmillan, 1966).

Crotty, N., "The Technological Imperative: Reflections on Reflections," *Theological Studies* 33 (1972), 440-449.

Cunningham, R. L., ed., *Situationism and the New Morality* (N.Y.: Appleton, 1970).

Darling, H. W., *Man in Triumph: An Integration of Psychology and Christian Faith* (Grand Rapids: Zondervan, 1969).

Donceel, J. F., "Immediate Animation and Delayed Hominization," *Theological Studies* 31 (1970), 76-105.

Durand, G., *The Facts of Death* (Glendale: Committee of Ten Million, 1973).

Duska, R., and M. Whelan, *Moral Development: A Guide to Piaget and Kohlberg* (N.Y.: Paulist, 1975).

Ellul, J., *The Technological Society* (N.Y.: Vintage, 1964).

Evans, R. I., *B. F. Skinner: The Man and His Ideas* (N.Y.: Dutton, 1968).

Fabro, C., *God in Exile: Modern Atheism* (N.Y.: Newman, 1968).

Feigl, H., "Ethics, Religion, and Scientific Humanism," in P. Kurtz, ed., *Moral Problems in Contemporary Society* (Englewood Cliffs: Prentice-Hall, 1969).

Fields, C., "High-Risk Genetics Study Gets NIH Guidelines," *The Chronicle of Higher Education* 12 (1976), 6.

Fletcher, J., "Love Is the Only Measure," in R. L. Cunningham, ed., *Situationism and the New Morality* (N.Y.: Appleton, 1970).

Francoeur, R. T., "We Can—We Must: Reflections on the Technological Imperative," *Theological Studies* 33 (1972), 428-439.

Frankel, C., "The Nature and Sources of Irrationalism," *Science* 181 (1973), 927-931.

Frankl, V. E., *Man's Search for Meaning* (N.Y.: Washington Square, 1963).

Frankl, V. E., *The Doctor and the Soul* (N.Y.: Knopf, 1966).

Frankl, V. E., *Psychotherapy and Existentialism* (N.Y.: Washington Square, 1967).

Frankl, V. E., *The Will to Meaning* (N.Y.: New American Library, 1969).

Frankl, V. E., "The Feeling of Meaninglessness: A Challenge to Psychotherapy," *American Journal of Psychoanalysis* 32 (1972), 85-89.

Fremantle, A., ed., *A Treasury of Early Christianity* (N.Y.: Viking, 1953).

Fried, C., "Reich and the Romantics," in P. Noble, ed., *The Con III Controversy: The Critics Look at the Greening of America* (N.Y.: Pocket Books, 1971).

Fromm, E., *The Sane Society* (Greenwich: Fawcett, 1955).

Fromm, E., *The Art of Loving* (N.Y.: Harper & Row, 1956).

Fromm, E., *The Revolution of Hope* (N.Y.: Bantam, 1968).

Fromm, E., *Escape from Freedom* (N.Y.: Avon, 1969a).

Fromm, E., *Man for Himself* (N.Y.: Fawcett, 1969b).

Gaer, J., *What the Great Religions Believe* (N.Y.: New American Library, 1963).

Gallagher, K. T., *The Philosophy of Knowledge* (N.Y.: Sheed & Ward, 1964).

Giorgi, A., *Psychology as a Human Science: A Phenomenolocally Based Approach* (N.Y.: Harper & Row, 1970).

Gleason, R. W., *Situational Morality* (Albany: Magi, 1967).

Glimm, F., J. Marique, and G. Walsh, *The Fathers of the Church: The Apostolic Fathers* (N.Y.: Cima, 1947).

Goodier, A., *The Passion and Death of Our Lord Jesus Christ* (N.Y.: Kenedy, 1944).

Gray, W., F. J. Duhl, and N. D. Rizzo, eds., *General Systems Theory and Psychiatry* (Boston: Little Brown, 1969).

Grisez, G., "Toward a Consistent Natural-Law Ethics of Killing," *American Journal of Jurisprudence* 15 (1970), 64-96.

Grisez, G., *Abortion: The Myths, the Realities, and the Arguments* (N.Y.: Corpus, 1972).

Guinness, O., *The Dust of Death* (Downers Grove: Inter-Varsity, 1973).

Hall, C. S., and G. Lindzey, *Theories of Personality*, 2d ed. (N.Y.: Wiley, 1970).

Hammes, J. A., *Humanistic Psychology: A Christian Interpretation* (N.Y.: Grune & Stratton, 1971).

Hammes, J. A., "Beyond Freedom and Dignity: Behavioral

Fixated Delusion?" *Journal of Psychology and Theology* 1 (1973a), 8-14.

Hammes, J. A., "Humanistic Psychology, Therapy, Religion, and Values," in R. H. Cox, ed., *Religious Systems and Psychotherapy* (Springfield: Charles C. Thomas, 1973b).

Hammes, J. A., "The Christian in the Age of the Id," *Journal of Psychology and Theology* 1 (1973c), 34-37.

Hammes, J. A., "A Christian Response to Atheistic and Scientific Humanism," *Journal of Psychology and Theology* 3 (1975a), 104-108.

Hammes, J. A., "Atheistic and Christian Perspectives on the Human Condition," *Journal of Psychology and Theology* 3 (1975b), 36-41.

Hammes, J. A., "Situational Ethics: Tower of Wisdom or Tower of Babel," *Homiletic and Pastoral Review* 75 (1975c), 6-23.

Hammes, J. A., "Arationality as a Contemporary Behavioral Norm," *Faith & Reason* 1 (1975-76), 38-43.

Hammes, J. A., review of R. Duska and M. Whelan's "Moral Development: A Guide to Piaget and Kohlberg," in *Christian Scholar's Review* 6 (1976), 237-238.

Hammes, J. A., "Today's Substitute Gods—Pride and Perversion of the Absolute," *Friar* 46 (1976b), 23-25.

Harrington, M., "The Defoliation of Charles Reich," in P. Nobile, ed., *The Con III Controversy: The Critics Look at the Greening of America* (N.Y.: Pocket Books, 1971).

Healy, E. F., *Medical Ethics* (Chicago: Loyola Univ. Press, 1956).

Harvey, J. F., "Law and Personalism," *Communio* 2 (1975), 54-72.

Heidelberg Catechism (Philadelphia: United Church Press, 1962).

Helleger, A. E., "Fetal Development," *Theological Studies*

31 (1970), 3-9.

Hildebrand, Alice von, *Introduction to a Philosophy of Religion* (Chicago: Franciscan Herald, 1971).

Hildebrand, D. von, *True Morality and Its Counterfeits* (N.Y.: David McKay, 1955).

Hilton, B., et al., eds., *Ethical Issues in Human Genetics: Genetic Counseling and the Use of Genetic Knowledge* (N.Y.: Plenum, 1973).

Hitt, W. D., "Two Models of Man," *American Psychology* 24 (1969), 651-658.

Holden, C., "Maharishi International University: 'Science of Creative Intelligence,' " *Science* 187 (1975), 1176-1180.

Holton, G., "On Being Caught between Dionysians and Apollonians," *Daedalus* 103 (1974), 65-81.

Howell, F. C., *Early Man* (N.Y.: Time, Inc., 1965).

Horan, D. J., and D. Mall, *Death, Dying, and Euthanasia* (Washington D.C.: University Publications of America, 1977).

Humanist, The, 33 (1973), No. 5 (Sept.-Oct.).

Hume, R. E., *The World's Living Religions* (N.Y.: Scribner's, 1959).

Jones, D. G., "Making New Men: A Theology of Modified Man," *Journal of the American Scientific Affiliation* 26 (1974), 144-154.

Josephson, E., and M. Josephson, *Man Alone: Alienation in Modern Society* (N.Y.: Dell, 1962).

Jung, C., *Psychology and Religion: West and East*, vol. 2 of *The Collected Works of C. G. Jung*, ed. H. Read, M. Fordham, and G. Adler, 2d ed. (Princeton Univ. Press, 1969).

Karp, L. E., *Genetic Engineering: Threat or Promise?* (Chicago: Nelson-Hall, 1976).

Kass, L. R., "New Beginnings in Life," in M. Hamilton, ed., *The New Genetics and the Future of Man* (Grand Rapids: Eerdmans, 1972).

Kaufman, W., *From Shakespeare to Existentialism* (Garden City: Doubleday, 1960).

Kaufman, W., "The Inevitability of Alienation," in R. Schacht, *Alienation* (N.Y.: Doubleday, 1970).

Kelly, G. A., "A Second Look at the Gay Activist Movement," *Homiletic & Pastoral Review* 76 (1976), 10-19.

Kemp, C. G., *Intangibles in Counseling* (N.Y.: Houghton Mifflin, 1967).

Keniston, K., *The Uncommitted: Alienated Youth in American Society* (N.Y.: Dell, 1960).

Kippley, J. F., *Covenant, Christ, and Contraception* (N.Y.: Alba, 1970).

Knight, J., *Conscience and Guilt* (N.Y.: Appleton, 1969).

Koestler, A., *The Ghost in the Machine* (N.Y.: Macmillan, 1967).

Koestler, A., *The Act of Creation* (N.Y.: Macmillan, 1964).

Kohlberg, L., "Moral Development," in *International Encyclopedia of Social Science* (N.Y.: Macmillan Free Press, 1968).

Kopkind, A., "The Greening of America: Beyond the Valley of the Heads," in P. Nobile, ed., *The Con III Controversy: The Critics Look at the Greening of America* (N.Y.: Pocket Books, 1971).

Kovach, F. J., "A Critical Evaluation of Fletcher's *Situation Ethics*," *American Journal of Jurisprudence* 15 (1970), 99-115.

Kraemer, D., G. Moore, and M. Kramen, "Baboon Infants Produced by Embryo Transfer," *Science* 192 (1976), 1246-47.

Krutch, J. W., *The Measure of Man* (N.Y.: Grosset & Dunlap, 1953).

Kübler-Ross, E., *On Death and Dying* (N.Y.: Macmillan, 1975a).

Kübler-Ross, E., *Questions and Answers about Death and Dying* (N.Y.: Macmillan, 1975b).

Kurtz, P., ed., *Moral Problems in Contemporary Society: Essays in Humanistic Ethics* (Englewood Cliffs: Prentice-Hall, 1969).

Lamont, C., "The Crisis Called Death," in P. Kurtz, ed., *Moral Problems in Contemporary Society* (Englewood Cliffs: Prentice-Hall, 1969).

Lappe, M., "Moral Obligations and the Fallacies of Genetic Control," *Theological Studies* 33 (1972), 411-427.

Leslie, R. C., *Jesus and Logotherapy* (Nashville: Abingdon, 1965).

Lewis, C. S., *Mere Christianity* (N.Y.: Macmillan, 1960).

Lewis, J., *The Religions of the World Made Simple* (Garden City: Doubleday, 1968).

Lipkin, M., and P. Rowley, eds., *Genetic Responsibility: On Choosing Our Children's Genes* (N.Y.: Plenum, 1974).

Lowe, C. M., "Value Orientations—An Ethical Dilemma," in W. D. Nunokawa, ed., *Human Values and Abnormal Behavior* (Glenview: Scott, Foresman, 1965).

Luther, M., *Luther's Smaller and Larger Catechisms, together with the Unaltered Augsburg Confession*, tr. from the German (Newmarket: Soloman D. Henkel, 1855).

Lutzer, E. W., *The Morality Gap: An Evangelical Response to Situation Ethics* (Chicago: Moody Press, 1972).

Lyons, J., *Psychology and the Measure of Man: A Phenomenological Approach* (Glencoe: Free Press, 1963).

Malcolm, N., "Behaviorism as a Philosophy of Psychology," in W. T. Wann, ed., *Behaviorism and Phenomenology* (Univ. of Chicago Press, 1964).

Maslow, A. H., *Toward a Psychology of Being* (Princeton: van Nostrand, 1962).

Maslow, A. H., *Religions, Values, and Peak-Experiences* (Ohio State Univ. Press, 1964).

Marx, P., *The Death Peddlers: War on the Unborn* (Collegeville: St. John's University Press, 1971).

Matson, F. W., *The Broken Image: Man, Science, and Society* (N.Y.: Braziller, 1964).

May, R., *Man's Search for Himself* (N.Y.: Norton, 1953).

May, R., ed., *Existential Psychology* (N.Y.: Random House, 1961).

May, R., *Psychology and the Human Dilemma* (Princeton: van Nostrand, 1967).

May, R., *Love and Will* (N.Y.: Norton, 1969).

May, R., *Power and Innocence* (N.Y.: Norton, 1972).

May, R., E. Angel, and H. F. Ellenberger, eds., *Existence* (N.Y.: Simon & Shuster, 1967).

May, W. E., *Becoming Human: An Invitation to Christian Ethics* (Dayton: Pflaum, 1975).

May, W. E., "Sex, Love, and Procreation," *Homiletic & Pastoral Review* 76 (1976) 10-29.

May, W. E., "Sterilization: Catholic Teaching and Catholic Practice," *Homiletic and Pastoral Review* 77 (1977), 9-22.

McCracken, S., "The Fuzzing of America," in P. Nobile, ed., *The Con III Controversy: The Critics Look at the Greening of America* (N.Y.: Pocket Books, 1971).

McFadden, C. J., *Medical Ethics*, 2d ed. (Philadelphia: F. A. Davis, 1951).

McFadden, C. J., *Medical Ethics*, 6th ed. (Philadelphia: F. A. Davis, 1967).

McFadden, C. J., *The Dignity of Life: Moral Values in a Changing Society* (Huntington, Ind.: Our Sunday Visitor, 1976).

Menninger, K., *Whatever Became of Sin?* (N.Y.: Hawthorne, 1973).

Misiak, H., and V. Sexton, *History of Psychology* (N.Y.: Grune & Stratton, 1966).

Monden, L., *Sin, Liberty, and Law* (N.Y.: Sheed & Ward, 1965).

Montgomery, J. W., *Where Is History Going?* (Grand Rapids: Zondervan, 1969).

Morgan, J. T., "The Wonder of Myself: Ethical-Theological Aspects of Direct Abortion," *Theological Studies* 31 (1970), 125-148.

Motulski, A. G., "Genetic Therapy: A Clinical Geneticist's Reply," in M. Hamilton, ed., *The New Genetics and the Future of Man* (Grand Rapids: Eerdmans, 1972).

Mumford, L., *The Myth of the Machine: I. Technics and Human Development* (N.Y.: Harcourt, Brace & Jovanovich, 1966).

National Council of Catholic Bishops, *Ethical and Religious Directives for Catholic Health Facilities* (Washington, D.C.: U.S. Catholic Conference, 1971).

National Conference of Catholic Bishops, *Principles to Guide Confessors in Questions of Homosexuality* (Washington, D.C.: U.S. Catholic Conference, 1973).

National Conference of Catholic Bishops, *Declaration on Certain Questions Concerning Sexual Ethics* (Washington, D.C.: U.S. Catholic Conference, 1975).

Neisel, W., *The Theology of Calvin* (Philadelphia: Westminster, 1956).

Nielsen, K., "Ethics without Religion," in P. Kurtz, ed., *Moral Problems in Contemporary Society* (Englewood Cliffs: Prentice-Hall, 1969).

Noebel, D. A., *Slaughter of the Innocent* (Tulsa: Americans Against Abortion, 1974).

Nunokawa, W. D., ed., *Human Values and Abnormal Behavior* (N.Y.: Scott, Foresman, 1965).

O'Donnell, T. J., *Morals in Medicine* (Westminster: Newman, 1956).

Paul VI, Pope, *Humanae vitae* (On the Regulation of Birth; Washington, D.C.: U.S. Catholic Conference, 1968).

Peterson, J.A., *Counseling and Values* (Scranton: International Textbook, 1970).

Phenix, P. H., *Realms of Meaning: A Philosophy of the Curriculum* (N.Y.: McGraw-Hill, 1964).

Rahner, K., "Experiment: Man," *Theology Digest* (1968), pp. 57-69.

Ramm, B., "An Ethical Evaluation of Biogenetic Engineering," *Journal of the American Scientific Affiliation* 26 (1974), 137-143.

Ramsey, P., *Fabricated Man: The Ethics of Genetic Control* (Yale Univ. Press, 1970).

Raughley, R. C., ed., *New Frontiers of Christianity* (N.Y.: Association Press, 1962).

Reich, C., *The Greening of America* (N.Y.: Random House, 1970).

Rescher, N., *Introduction to Values Theory* (Englewood Cliffs: Prentice-Hall, 1969).

Roblin, R., "Some Recent Developments in Genetics," *Theological Studies* 33 (1972), 401-410.

Rogers, C., "Persons or Science?" in F. T. Severin, ed., *Humanistic Viewpoints in Psychology* (N.Y.: McGraw-Hill, 1965a).

Rogers, C., "The Place of the Person in the New World of the Behavioral Sciences," in F. T. Severin, ed., *Humanistic Viewpoints in Psychology* (N.Y.: McGraw-Hill, 1965b).

Rogers, C., *Freedom to Learn* (Columbus: Charles E. Merrill, 1969).

Roszak, T., *The Making of a Counter Culture* (Garden City: Doubleday, 1969).

Roszak, T., "The Monster and the Titan: Science, Knowledge, and *gnosis*," *Daedalus* 103 (1974), 17-32.

Royce, J. E., *Man and Meaning* (N.Y.: McGraw-Hill, 1969).

Royce, J. R., *The Encapsulated Man: An Interdisciplinary Essay on the Search for Meaning* (Princeton: van Nostrand, 1964).

Royce, J. R., "Metaphoric Knowledge and Humanistic Psychology," in J. F. T. Bugental, ed., *Challenges of Humanistic Psychology* (N.Y.: McGraw-Hill, 1967).

Ruitenbeek, H. M., ed., *Psychoanalysis and Existential Philosophy* (N.Y.: Dutton, 1962).

Sacred Congregation for the Doctrine of the Faith, "Declaration on Abortion," *The Pope Speaks* 19 (1975), 250-262.

Sahakian, W. S., *Psychology of Personality: Readings in Theory* (Chicago: Rand McNally, 1965).

Sahakian, W. S., *History of Philosophy* (N.Y.: Barnes & Noble, 1968a).

Sahakian, W. S., *Systems of Ethics and Value Theory* (Totawa: Littlefield, Adams, 1968b).

Schacht, R., *Alienation* (Garden City: Doubleday, 1970).

Schaeffer, F., *The God Who Is There* (Downers Grove: InterVarsity, 1968).

Schilling, S. P., *God in an Age of Atheism* (Nashville: Abingdon 1969).

Schoeps, H. J., *The Religions of Mankind* (Garden City: Doubleday, 1968).

Schoonenberg, P., *Man and Sin* (Univ. of Notre Dame Press, 1965).

Schrader, G. A., ed., *Existential Philosophers: Kierkegaard to Merleau-Ponty* (N.Y.: McGraw-Hill, 1967).

Severin, F. T., ed., *Humanistic Viewpoints in Psychology* (N.Y.: McGraw-Hill, 1965).

Severin, F. T., ed., *Discovering Man in Psychology: A Humanistic Psychology* (N.Y.: McGraw-Hill, 1973).

Sheen, F. J., *Peace of Soul* (Garden City: Doubleday, 1954).

Shehan, L., "Humanae vitae: 1968-1973," *Homiletic and Pastoral Review* 74 (1973), 14-54.

Skinner, B. F., *Science and Human Behavior* (N.Y.: Macmillan, 1953).

Skinner, B. F., *Beyond Freedom and Dignity* (N.Y.: Knopf, 1971).

Snow, C. P., *The Two Cultures and the Scientific Revolution* (Cambridge Univ. Press, 1961).

Starr, R., "Consciousness III: A Trail to Nowhere," in P. Nobile, ed., *The Con III Controversy: The Critics Look at the Greening of America* (N.Y.: Pocket Books, 1971).

Strasser, S., "Phenomenologies and Psychologies," in N. Lawrence and D. O'Connor, eds., *Readings in Existential Phenomenology* (Englewood Cliffs: Prentice-Hall, 1967).

Sutich, A. J., and M. A. Vich, eds., *Readings in Humanistic Psychology* (N.Y.: Free Press, 1969).

Sutter, H. H., letter to the editor, *Science* 168 (1970), 777.

Szebenyi, A., "Reflections of a Biologist," *Theological Studies* 33 (1972, 450-456.

Tillich, P., *The Courage to Be* (Yale Univ. Press, 1952).

Time Magazine (28 May, 1973), p. 104.

Time Magazine, "Tinkering with Life" (18 April, 1977), pp. 32-34, 39-40, 45.

Toffler, A., *Future Shock* (N.Y.: Random House, 1970).

Trilling, L., *Mind in the Modern World* (N.Y.: Viking, 1972).

Tweedie, D. F., *Logotherapy and the Christian Faith: An Evaluation of Frankl's Existential Approach to Psychotherapy* (Grand Rapids: Baker, 1961).

Ungersma, A. J., *The Search for Meaning: A New Approach in Psychotherapy and Pastoral Counseling* (Philadelphia: Westminster, 1961).

Van Kaam, A., *Existential Foundations of Psychology* (N.Y.: Doubleday, 1966).

Wade, N., "Recombinant DNA: A Critic Questions the Right of Free Inquiry," *Science* 194 (1976), 303-306.

Wallace, W. A., *The Elements of Philosophy: A Compendium for Philosophers and Theologians* (New York: Alba House, 1977).

Wann, T. W., ed., *Behaviorism and Phenomenology: Contrasting Bases for Modern Psychology* (Univ. of Chicago Press, 1964).

Wertham, F., *A Sign for Cain* (N.Y.: Macmillan, 1966).

Whitehead, K. D., *Respectable Killing: The New Abortion Imperative* (New Rochelle: Catholics United for the Faith, 1972).

Williams, J. R., *Contemporary Existentialism and Christian Faith* (Englewood Cliffs: Prentice-Hall, 1965).

World Almanac and Book of Facts, The (N.Y.: Newspaper Enterprise Assoc., 1977).

Wu, J. C. H., "Natural Law—Thomistic Analysis," *New Catholic Encyclopedia* (N.Y.: McGraw-Hill, 1967), 10:256-259.

Wyatt, F., "Psychology and the Humanities: A Case of No-Relationship," in J. F. T. Bugental, ed., *Challenges of Humanistic Psychology* (N.Y.: McGraw-Hill, 1967).

INDEX

Names and themes from Scripture are not indexed.